EMPOWERMENT IN
SOCIAL WORK PRACTICE
A SOURCEBOOK

About the Authors

Lorraine Gutiérrez, Ph.D., A.C.S.W., is an associate professor of social work and psychology at the University of Michigan in Ann Arbor, where she teaches courses on multicultural community practice and cochairs the Community Organization Concentration. Her research, practice, and teaching have centered on multicultural practice, women of color, and empowerment.

Ruth J. Parsons, M.S.W., Ph.D., is a professor of social work at the Graduate School of Social Work, University of Denver. She has practiced social work for more than 20 years with a variety of client groups, including families, children, adults with severe and persistent mental illness, and the elderly. Her research and teaching interests focus on empowerment practice and research with oppressed populations.

Enid Opal Cox, D.S.W., is a professor of social work and director of the Institute of Gerontology at the University of Denver. She is coauthor of *Empowerment-Oriented Practice with the Elderly* with Dr. Ruth Parsons and has research, practice, teaching, and publishing experience related to elderly care issues, care-giver issues, issues of older workers, and issues of ethnic minority elders. She also has teaching and research interests in social welfare policy, history of social welfare, and indirect practice interventions with a special emphasis on empowerment-oriented approaches.

EMPOWERMENT IN SOCIAL WORK PRACTICE

A SOURCEBOOK

Lorraine M. Gutiérrez

School of Social Work
University of Michigan

Ruth J. Parsons

Graduate School of Social Work
University of Denver

Enid Opal Cox

Graduate School of Social Work
University of Denver

BROOKS/COLE PUBLISHING COMPANY

I(T)P® An International Thomson Publishing Company

Pacific Grove • Albany • Belmont • Bonn • Boston • Cincinnati • Detroit • Johannesburg • London
Madrid • Melbourne • Mexico City • New York • Paris • Singapore • Tokyo • Toronto • Washington

Sponsoring Editor: *Lisa I. Gebo*
Marketing Team: *Jean Thompson,*
    Christine Davis, and Deanne Brown
Editorial Assistant: *Shelley Bouhaja*
Production Coordinator: *Jamie Sue Brooks*
Production: *Greg Hubit Bookworks*
Manuscript Editor: *Molly D. Roth*

Permissions Editor: *Cathleen C. Morrison*
Interior and Cover Design: *John Edeen*
Typesetting: *Susan Rogin*
Cover Printing: *Phoenix Color Corp.*
Printing and Binding: *Maple-Vail Book*
    Manufacturing Group

For more information, contact:

BROOKS/COLE PUBLISHING COMPANY
511 Forest Lodge Road
Pacific Grove, CA 93950
USA

International Thomson Publishing Europe
Berkshire House 168–173
High Holborn
London WC1V 7AA
England

Thomas Nelson Australia
102 Dodds Street
South Melbourne, 3205
Victoria, Australia

Nelson Canada
1120 Birchmount Road
Scarborough, Ontario
Canada M1K 5G4

International Thomson Editores
Seneca 53
Col. Polanco
11560 México, D. F., México

International Thomson Publishing GmbH
Königswinterer Strasse 418
53227 Bonn
Germany

International Thomson Publishing Asia
221 Henderson Road
#05–10 Henderson Building
Singapore 0315

International Thomson Publishing Japan
Hirakawacho Kyowa Building, 3F
2-2-1 Hirakawacho
Chiyoda-ku, Tokyo 102
Japan

Printed in the United States of America

10   9   8   7   6   5   4   3   2   1

Library of Congress Cataloging-in-Publication Data
Empowerment in social work practice : a sourcebook / [edited by]
   Lorraine M. Gutiérrez, Ruth J. Parsons, Enid Opal Cox.
      p. cm.
   Includes bibliographical references and index.
   ISBN 0–534–34846–7
   1. Social service—United States.   I. Gutiérrez, Lorraine M.
   (Lorraine Margot)   II. Parsons, Ruth J.   III. Cox, Enid Opal
   HV91.E56 1998
   361.3'2—dc21   97–13208
                                                    CIP

To all human service workers—
past, present, and future—
working in partnership with communities
to create a more equitable world.

About the Contributors

Graydon Andrus, M.S.W., has worked for seven years with the Health Care for the Homeless project in Seattle. His work has been divided between two shelter-based sites: one for men over fifty years old and the other serving adults of any age. Though his primary work is with people experiencing mental illness, he has had the opportunity to work with a broad spectrum of the homeless population.

Yolanda Burwell, Ph.D., is an associate professor of social work in the School of Social Work at East Carolina University in Greenville, North Carolina. She has extensive training experience in cross-cultural and empowerment practice issues. Additionally, she is a social welfare historian. She unearths the "lost" voices and unrecognized community-building activities among early African Americans in North Carolina.

Kathryn A. DeLois, M.S.W., Ph.D., is an assistant professor of social work at the University of New England Graduate School of Social Work in Portland, Maine, where she teaches courses on social work research and practice. She has extensive practice experience working in the areas of substance abuse and gender issues. Her research interests include feminist research methods, lesbian identity, and empowerment.

Linnea GlenMaye, Ph.D., is an assistant professor of social work in the School of Social Work at the University of Las Vegas, Nevada, where she teaches courses in the field practicum and human behavior in the social environment. Her research interests include sexual assault, feminist theory, and infusing content on women into the social work curriculum. She is involved in lesbian and gay community organization efforts in Las Vegas.

Vanessa G. Hodges, Ph.D., is an associate professor of social work at the University of North Carolina at Chapel Hill where she chairs the Families and Children Concentration. Her teaching and research interests include family-centered practice, home-based practice with high-risk children and families, strengths-based social work practice, cultural competence in service delivery, developmental research, and evaluation research. Dr. Hodges's practice experience includes family reunification following residential treatment, community integration of developmentally disabled adults, and parent education and training.

Barbara H. R. Joseph, D.S.W., is a teacher, administrator, consultant, trainer, social worker, therapist, writer, lecturer, organizer, and activist with 30 years of experience working with public and private health, education, and welfare agencies. She is associate professor of American studies at SUNY/Old Westbury in New York State. Dr. Joseph speaks and consults widely on issues of "racesexism," empowerment, policy analysis, program evaluation, and community and leadership development with special attention to women and communities of color.

Susan Manning, Ph.D., is an associate professor of social work at the Graduate School of Social Work, University of Denver. Her teaching, research, and publication interests have integrated mental health, ethics, and qualitative methods of discovery. Studies in mental health have focused on the experience of people with severe and persistent mental illness, specifically in relationship to their sense of empowerment. Her work in ethics includes ethical decision making, professional ethics, ethics of managed care, informed consent in practice and research, and the development of ethical guidelines in the community. She has extensive practice experience in the mental health field in clinical and administrative roles. An experienced trainer in these issues, she has presented her work at national and international conferences.

Margo Okazawa-Rey, Ed.D., is a professor of social work at San Francisco State University School of Social Work. Through education, political organizing, and activist scholarship, she works in community and academic settings addressing the issue of racism and other forms of oppression. She is particularly interested in problems affecting peoples of color, especially women of color. Her current research/activist project is examining the effects of violence against women by the U.S. military and the experiences of mixed-race children, offspring of GIs, in Asia.

Debra M. Ortega, M.S.W., is currently a Ph.D. candidate in social work at the University of Washington in Seattle and adjunct faculty member at both Case Western Reserve University and Portland State University. She has extensive practice experience as a home-based family therapist. Her teaching and research interests include ethnocultural mental health, gender, and ethnics.

Stuart Rees, Ph.D., is professor of social work at the University of Sydney in Australia. He has practice experience as a probation officer in England and in Canada and has been a community worker in the United States, Scotland, and Holland. He is currently the director of the Centre of Peace and Conflict Studies. His research interests include empowerment with particular reference to disability; the retention of universal services such as Medicare; the interdependence of policy and practice; and evaluating welfare, legal, and health services. He is the author of *Achieving Power,* a book on the concept and practice of empowerment in social work and social welfare.

Richard Renz-Beaulaurier, Ph.D., is an assistant professor of social work at the School of Social Work at Florida International University. He teaches courses in administration, planning, community organizing, and research. He is currently conducting research on social work practice in health organizations that focuses on work with disabled people. He has published papers on empowering people with disabilities in health and rehabilitation settings. He has also been a presenter at several national social work conferences on this and other topics.

Susan M. Ruhlin, M.S.W., has worked with homeless families since 1988 as an employment case manager and as a shelter counselor and case manager. She presently works at the Fremont Family Shelter/Bethlehem House in Seattle, Washington. She has been involved in social services work since 1981.

Sung Sil Lee Sohng, Ph.D., is an assistant professor of social work at the University of Washington, School of Social Work. Her teaching and research interests lie in participatory action research, cultural diversity and social justice, ethnographic interviewing, and grassroots organizing.

Contents

Part One
An Introduction to Empowerment Practice 1

Lorraine M. Gutiérrez, Ph.D.
University of Michigan, Ann Arbor
Ruth J. Parsons, Ph.D.
University of Denver, Denver, Colorado
Enid Opal Cox, D.S.W.
University of Denver, Denver, Colorado

Part Two
EMPOWERMENT IN PRACTICE: POPULATIONS   25

Chapter 4

EMPOWERMENT PRACTICE WITH
LESBIANS AND GAYS   65

Kathryn A. DeLois, Ph.D.
  University of New England, Portland, Maine

Chapter 5

EMPOWERING PEOPLE WITH DISABILITIES:
THE ROLE OF CHOICE   73

Richard Renz-Beaulaurier, Ph.D.
  Florida International University, North Miami

Part Three
EMPOWERMENT IN PRACTICE:
FOCUSING ON FIELDS   85

Chapter 8

EMPOWERMENT OF YOUTH   130

Stuart Rees, Ph.D.
   University of Sydney, New South Wales, Australia

Chapter 9

Vanessa G. Hodges, Ph.D.
  University of North Carolina, Chapel Hill
Yolanda Burwell, Ph.D.
  East Carolina University, Greenville, North Carolina
Debra Ortega, M.S.W.
  University of Washington, Seattle

Part Four

SPECIAL ISSUES IN
EMPOWERMENT PRACTICE

Chapter 10

Enid Opal Cox, D.S.W.
  University of Denver, Denver, Colorado
Barbara Hunter Randal Joseph, D.S.W.
  SUNY/Old Westbury, New York

Chapter 11
RESEARCH AS AN EMPOWERMENT STRATEGY   187

Sung Sil Lee Sohng, Ph.D.
University of Washington, Seattle

Chapter 12
EVALUATION OF EMPOWERMENT PRACTICE   204

Ruth J. Parsons, Ph.D.
University of Denver, Denver, Colorado

Chapter 13
CREATING OPPORTUNITIES FOR
EMPOWERMENT-ORIENTED PROGRAMS   220

Lorraine M. Gutiérrez, Ph.D.
   University of Michigan, Ann Arbor
Ruth J. Parsons, Ph.D.
   University of Denver, Denver, Colorado
Enid Opal Cox, D.S.W.
   University of Denver, Denver, Colorado

PREFACE:
THE EMPOWERMENT MODEL
FOR PRACTICE

The concept of empowerment has gained currency within the past two decades. The literature in fields as diverse as nursing, education, social work, and management have proposed that one can use empowerment methods to increase consumer choice, contain costs, and reengage individuals in the lives of their organizations or communities. This broad application of empowerment has led some to question its meaning or to propose that social workers discontinue its use.

This lack of specificity and broad application of the idea of empowerment provided the motivation for developing this book. As practitioners, teachers, and researchers working from an empowerment perspective, we believe that the concept has not only meaning, but also a particular relevance in these times of growing inequality, diminishing resources, and increased intergroup conflict. As a philosophy, approach, or method of practice, empowerment provides one way to rethink social work practice.

Because of current and emerging social trends, empowerment should be of particular concern to social workers today and into the future. We view empowerment as a means to achieve needed social change, personally and politically, in ways that meet human needs. Given the growing inequality and intolerance in society that directly affect the communities social workers serve, such workers need to take a deeper look at empowerment theory and practice as a tool for individual and social transformation. Determining how social workers can gain a new consciousness, marshal their skills, and practice to advance social justice is a helpful path to pursue.

To provide tools for social workers who wish to engage in empowerment practice, we offer specific examples of how empowerment can be and has been conducted in the field. The literature on empowerment has emphasized the importance of developing and implementing methods specific to populations, issues, and contexts. Therefore, we asked our contributors to demonstrate how one can use empowerment practice in the various situations, groups, and problems addressed by social workers. Each chapter would present a unique perspective on empowerment in order to clarify how one could implement this perspective in different contexts. In this way, we could demonstrate both the unity and the diversity of empowerment practice as it exists in the field.

In its most basic form, empowerment practice values multicultural perspectives and recognizes that these different perspectives can strengthen social work theory and practice. Therefore, we have asked a diverse group of people to contribute to this book, which includes the perspectives of academics, practitioners, men, women, gays and lesbians, European Americans, and people of color. The contributors were to provide in their given chapter some background on their population or issues, their particular perspective on empowerment, and ways in which this perspective can be and has been translated into practice. Within this general framework, contributors wrote in their own style, interest, and especially voice. Despite a common framework, then, this book offers diverse perspectives in these authors' descriptions of different practice frameworks, fields of practice, levels of analysis, and approaches.

Chapter 1 provides a framework for understanding the perspectives that follow. We focus on the widest view of empowerment and its implications for social work practice, describing the empowerment perspective, its assumptions, and its relationship to other forms of practice. Specific examples illustrate different dimensions or levels of empowerment.

The following section focuses on the implications of empowerment practice with specific populations often encountered by social workers: women, people of color, people with disabilities, and gays, lesbians, and bisexuals. Although one could add other oppressed groups, such as those with insufficient income, to this list, these groups were selected in part because the Council on Social Work Education has mandated their inclusion in social work curricula and because much of empowerment practice has already developed in relation to these groups. Ways in which the authors focus on these specific groups, however, suggest ways in which empowerment practice can be tailored to the needs and issues of other population groups.

In the third section of the book, the analytical lens sharpens to focus on empowerment practice in specific domains of practice: mental health, housing and homelessness, youth, and families. These domains were selected because they represent issues or levels of practice frequently encountered by social workers. In these chapters, practitioners and scholars articulate why empowerment is particularly relevant to their population or service domain and how this practice has been and can be conducted. They therefore help show how empowerment practice can be developed to work toward individual, family, and community change.

The final four chapters look at ways in which social work administration and research methods can contribute to empowerment practice. The focus here is twofold: How can one conduct research and administration practice from an empowerment perspective, and how can these methods support the empowerment of clients, workers, and communities? These chapters mainly provide a holistic vision of how empowerment methods can influence, through social work practice, the creation of socially just institutions.

As a whole, this book provides information on the depth and breadth of empowerment practice and its use in different settings, with different populations, and in different levels of practice. Taking the long view, one can see similarities among the methods in various chapters and group them as participatory, educational, or capacity building in nature. Another similarity is the focus on working within a group context for providing services, building support systems, or engaging in social change. This closer look also reveals significant differences in application. For example, the use of cultural and religious practices with African-American grandparents differs qualitatively from the use of action research methods with homeless youth. However, in each example, the principle of tailoring one's methods to fit the community through dialogue reflects empowerment practice in general.

We hope this book will serve as a resource for faculty, students, practitioners, and researchers interested in understanding what empowerment practice is and how it can be conducted. Through dialogue with our contributors and the communities they represent, we have gained in knowledge and understanding of this concept.

Acknowledgments

This book has been a complex and enormous undertaking spanning more than three years and continents! So many individuals and institutions have contributed to this volume that it would be impossible to recognize them all. Specifically, we would first like to acknowledge the contributions of our students, whose questions regarding the applications of empowerment in the "real world" motivated us to take on this project. Their probing and often challenging questions led us into dialogue regarding the usefulness of a book such as this one.

The institutions in which we work have also supported our work on this volume. The universities of Denver, Washington and Michigan provided support in the form of time, staff, and helpful colleagues. We would like to acknowledge in particular the support of Nancy Hooyman at the University of Washington, who provided funds for the national conference on empowerment practice that brought us together. Edith Lewis at the University of Michigan also deserves special recognition for providing informal and formal feedback and support.

The prepublication reviews were extremely helpful in giving us the feedback to revise and clarify the work. The following people have greatly influenced the development of this volume by providing timely and constructive input at various stages of writing: Jannah Hurn-Mather, Wilfred Laurier University; Arline Prigoff, California State University, Sacramento; Michael Reisch, University of Pennsylvania; Robert Rivas, Siena College; Lee Staples, Woodville, Massachusetts; Nancy Wall, University of Illinois at Chicago; Marilyn Wedenoja, Eastern Michigan University; and Stanley Wenocur, University of Maryland at Baltimore. Expert editorial assistance was also provided by Neysa Folmer, Molly Roth, Kylo-Patrick Robert Hart, and Greg Hubit. Special thanks must go to the staff at Brooks/Cole who made this publication possible, particularly Lisa Gebo, who had the foresight to see the potential for this work.

A final word of recognition goes to our families—particularly our partners and children—who lived with this book for many years and also came to know the many faces of empowerment.

Lorraine Gutiérrez
Ruth Parsons
Enid Cox

Part One

AN INTRODUCTION TO
EMPOWERMENT PRACTICE

In Chapter 1, we have attempted to identify and synthesize what we know about empowerment practice and present frameworks for it. As the theory and the practice of empowerment continue to develop, one must take time to appraise this literature critically and evaluate its relevance for practice.

We begin the chapter by discussing knowledge regarding the empowerment *process*—those beliefs, attitudes, and actions known to contribute to empowerment. We then relate this knowledge to empowerment *practice*—those elements of the helping relationship that can increase one's power in the personal, interpersonal, or political spheres. In this section we also relate empowerment practice in specific ways to the social work context and explore implications for social work values, sanctions, and practice settings.

We next propose a framework for practice in which workers can begin on any of four dimensions—engagement, education, environmental modification, or political action—though practice often involves movement among dimensions. We also present methods of evaluating empowerment practice that incorporate procedures and values consonant with this framework.

Many of the subsequent chapters build on, react to, or challenge the perspective we present. Because empowerment stresses the validation and recognition of multiple voices, we present in this first chapter one perspective for understanding empowerment that can contribute to the field of social work. While reading this chapter, you may want to think about the following:

1. *How does the empowerment perspective depart from other ways of thinking about practice? How is it similar?*
2. *To what extent is empowerment practice relevant to all populations, communities, or issues? Are there some populations or communities for which this method would be inappropriate? How can an empowerment perspective be applied to work in settings with which you are familiar?*
3. *How can social workers most effectively evaluate empowerment in practice? Can they use methods for empowerment in designing this research?*

Chapter 1

A MODEL FOR
EMPOWERMENT PRACTICE

Ruth J. Parsons, Ph.D.
University of Denver, Denver, Colorado

Lorraine M. Gutiérrez, Ph.D.
University of Michigan, Ann Arbor, Michigan

Enid Opal Cox, D. S.W.
University of Denver, Denver, Colorado

INTRODUCTION

Empowerment has been a consistent theme within the social work profession for over a century (Simon, 1994). In the late 1800s, conditions such as the concentration of wealth, large-scale immigration, and an economic recession contributed to great social needs that existing charitable institutions could not meet (Wenocur & Reisch, 1989). Responses to these conditions included social reforms and the development of social work methods, ranging from concrete assistance to child protective services. They also reflected differences in perspective, from a focus on social control of the poor to an emphasis on self-determination and empowerment (Simon, 1994; Wenocur & Reisch, 1989).

Today the social work profession faces similar economic conditions. Over the past decade, income differentials have become more pronounced, and the proportion of the population considered middle class has shrunk (Dressel, 1994). Of particular concern is an increase of three sectors of our population that have traditionally possessed the least power or fewest social resources: people of color, older people, and people with disabilities. Within the next 50 years, immigration and fertility patterns will likely lead to an increasingly multiracial, multicultural, and multiethnic society (Gutiérrez, 1992). At the same time, conditions of economic inequality and economic stratification by gender and race have not abated (Dressel, 1994; Simon, 1994). Because both women and people of color continue to experience disproportionate economic and social disadvantage, these demographic projections have led to concerns that the United States could become a nation of poor children, youth of color, and older European Americans, with none of those groups capable of producing the economic resources necessary to support existing social services or other social goods (Ozawa, 1986; Sarri, 1986; Williams, 1990). The empowerment perspective proposes that social service programs, policies, and practices that address issues of power can help deal with these changes.

This book and others (Lee, 1994; McWhirter, 1994; Miley, O'Melia, & DuBois, 1994; Pinderhughes, 1990; Rees, 1991; Simon, 1994; Solomon, 1976) identify many methods of empowerment practice that enhance the ability of individuals, families, groups, and communities to develop the power to act on their own behalf in society (Gutiérrez, DeLois, & GlenMaye, 1995; Parson, 1991). In this, they present a vision of ways that social work policy and practice can work toward positive social change. This chapter and those that follow will specify how practitioners can carry out these methods with different populations, fields of services, and forms of practice.

THE EMPOWERMENT PROCESS

Empowerment practice strives to develop within individuals, families, groups, or communities the ability to gain power. Research and practice on empowerment have identified a specific process that contributes to this change (Cox, 1988, 1991; Cox & Parsons, 1994; Gutiérrez, 1994; Kieffer, 1984; Parsons, 1991; Simon, 1994; Torre, 1985). This literature has identified the following components as particularly significant:

1. *Attitudes, Values, and Beliefs.*   Beliefs regarding self-efficacy—a sense of self that promotes action on one's behalf, a belief in self-worth, and a sense of control—affect the empowerment process. Psychology views these attitudes as the sole component and primary goal of empowerment. However, empowerment in our sense goes beyond developing feelings of individual control to affecting larger social systems.

2. *Validation Through Collective Experience.*   In collective experience, the self and others recognize shared experience; i.e., that some of one's perceptions about oneself and the surrounding world are indeed valid and therefore legitimate to voice. This recognition contributes to a collective

view that reduces self-blame, increases the tendency to look beyond personal failure as the cause of the problem at hand, brings about a sense of shared fate, and raises consciousness. Collective experience can motivate one to seek change beyond the individual level toward other systems, such as the family or community.

3. *Knowledge and Skills for Critical Thinking and Action.*   Through mutual sharing and support, individuals can think critically about the internal and external aspects of a problem. They can identify macro-level structures and their impact as well as explore how they have acquired their values, beliefs, and attitudes and how these affect the problem. Increasing power includes learning to think critically, learning how to access information and take action, actually taking action, and assessing the outcome. The process of placing problems in a sociopolitical context reduces self-blame and helps individuals see the roots of their problems in society. Through consciousness raising, people come to see how their problems are similar to those of others. They also begin to notice common experiences that help them collectively to understand and take action.

4. *Action.*   Through reflective action (*praxis*), individuals can develop action strategies and cultivate the resources, knowledge, and skills necessary to influence internal and external structures. Psychologically, they learn to assume responsibility for their actions. Behaviorally, they become willing and able to act with others to attain common goals and social change, as well as reflect on and learn from those actions.

Though these four components are necessary for empowerment, no linear relationship among them is assumed and none is considered more important than any other as a place to begin work. In empowerment practice, as in any other context, one must start where the client system is to define its needs and goals. Therefore, social workers should know all the dimensions of the empowerment process.

ELEMENTS OF EMPOWERMENT PRACTICE

Empowerment practice draws from social work and other disciplines such as health education, community development, and community psychology. As a practice model, it involves a value base, sanctions for intervention, a theory base that guides practice, guidelines for the client-worker relationship, and a framework for organizing the helping activities. Figure 1.1 describes these elements and their interrelationships.

FIGURE 1.1

Components of a Practice Model

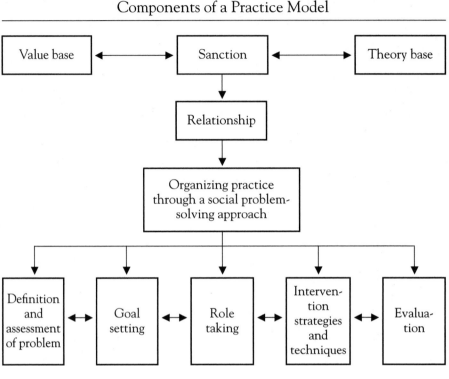

Value Base

Empowerment practice incorporates the basic values of the National Association of Social Workers' (NASW) Code of Ethics. Several commitments outlined in the code are particularly important to this practice. First, clients and workers must effectively engage in the creation of an environment compatible with human needs; this is congruent with social work's commitment to promote social justice as reflected in the code of ethics. Next, the professional commitment to self-determination and self-actualization stressed in the code also plays a significant role in empowerment. Finally, the involvement of client systems to the fullest extent possible in planning for and controlling their lives creates an opportunity for them to develop themselves to their fullest throughout the lifespan.

Sanctions for Intervention

Sanctions for empowerment practice come from varied sources, such as the professional value base from which social workers derive their assumed right to engage with clients and pursue goals. Other sources include the laws, rules, and regulations of agencies, as well as client requests. These sources often compete for priority, with many in direct conflict. For example, the beliefs of women clients about their rights to protection from violence may conflict with the regulations of a specific agency or with a social policy provision. Workers are often concerned about the lack of sanctions for specific resources or activities as prescribed by agency rules and regulations. For example, some agencies may not allow workers to lobby for social change.

The sanction base provided in an organizational setting is complex. Figure 1.2 illustrates various types of sanction within this context. Practitioners must assess the strength of organizational support concerning their activities. Often, workers and their clients find themselves challenging agency regulations that do not reflect the values of empowerment practice —for example, countering sexism or creating a more egalitarian distribution of resources. Agency regulations based on cost-efficiency can also conflict with the needs of client constituencies, social work values, and the principles of empowerment. When these conflicts arise, the NASW Code of Ethics clearly stipulates that social workers' main responsibility is to clients and the promotion of the general welfare of society. Therefore, social workers need to make professional decisions based on this code and the value base of empowerment.

Theory Base

Though empowerment practice builds on theoretical bases from social work and the social sciences, its roots lie in a particular political-economic perspective. This perspective assumes that social problems occur in all tiers of multilevel systems and exist in groups with varying degrees of power and

FIGURE 1.2
Strength of the Organizational Sanction Base

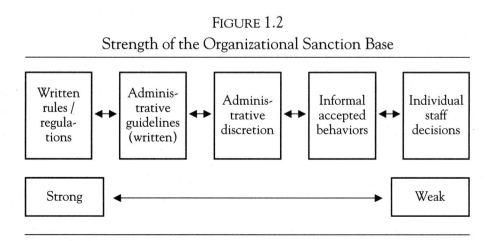

conflicting interests (Gutiérrez, 1994; Parsons, Jorgensen, & Hernández, 1994; Rees, 1991). Empowerment practice from this perspective does not aim at an ultimate fit among different groups' needs, expectations, and resources. Instead, it becomes part of a struggle to make needs and resources compatible (Gould, 1987).

Such practice requires practitioners to understand the significance of power in social relationships. The empowerment perspective has moved beyond certain negative views that present power only as an exploitative and scarce resource; rather, this perspective recognizes that social interaction can generate personal or interpersonal power (Bricker-Jenkins & Hooyman, 1986; Pinderhughes, 1989; Solomon, 1976). In its most positive sense, *power* is (1) the ability to influence the course of one's life, (2) an expression of self-worth, (3) the capacity to work with others to control aspects of public life, and (4) access to the mechanisms of public decision making. When used negatively, though, it can also block opportunities for stigmatized groups, exclude others and their concerns from decision making, and be a way to control others (Garvin, 1985; Leigh, 1985; Mathis & Richan, 1986; Pinderhughes, 1983; Weick & Vandiver, 1982).

The empowerment perspective recognizes that belonging to a disempowered group can have personal as well as social costs. Indirect and direct power blocks are the primary social mechanisms in this process. *Direct power blocks* restrict access to material resources. *Indirect power blocks* include a lack of resources and those social values that support structures of inequality (Solomon, 1976). One form of indirect power block is negative valuation, or stigma, which suggests to members of oppressed groups that they are deficient in some way. As negative valuations become part of an individual's development, they can interfere with the acquisition of adequate interpersonal, technical, and social skills. Negative valuations can also engender inaccurate beliefs regarding status, opportunities, and resistance. For example, displaced workers might think they were laid off because of their own incompetence rather than economic changes in the workforce. These beliefs could encourage them to accept social conditions rather than act to improve their lives (Freire, 1973; Gaventa, 1980; Pinderhughes, 1989; Solomon, 1976). Direct power blocks, such as inadequate health services for the poor, affect individuals in more concrete ways (Solomon, 1976).

In empowerment practice, power occurs on three levels: personal (feeling and perceptions regarding the ability to influence and resolve one's own issues); interpersonal (experiences with others that facilitate problem resolution); and environmental (societal institutions that can facilitate or thwart self-help efforts) (Gutiérrez, 1994; Pinderhughes, 1989; Solomon, 1976). As such, practice strategies must focus on all levels to facilitate empowerment in clients. Empowerment practice thus draws from systems theory and the ecological model to inform practitioners' understanding of the multilevel interventions (Simon, 1994).

Empowerment goes beyond existing systems approaches, however, by describing how issues of race, gender, class and other memberships can affect the helping relationship. Lee (1994) suggests that social workers maintain a "fifocal vision" for work with oppressed groups. This vision includes:

1. A historical view of oppression, including the history of social policy related to oppressed groups
2. An ecological view, which encompasses knowledge of individual adaptation potential, power in general, the abuse and withholding of power, structural inequities, and socioeconomic pollution
3. An ethnoclass perspective, which sharpens one's knowledge of the true effects of racism and classism and their interplay
4. A feminist perspective, which highlights in particular oppression of women but also conceptualizes phenomena in a unique voice, seeks out the unity of such concepts as "the personal is political," and envisions power itself in limitless terms
5. A critical perspective to critique all forms of oppression and develop strategies that link individual and social change

Fifocal vision is a way of organizing many dimensions of experience, serving as a lens that can help one carry out practice at different phases and levels of intervention.

GUIDELINES FOR WORKER-CLIENT RELATIONSHIP   The relationship established between worker and client is key to the success of any intervention. Empowerment-based practice requires one to redefine the helping process as one of "shared power" and "power with," and as "participant driven," with the professional becoming a "facilitator" or resource rather than a director. Roles and responsibilities become mutual and shared (Barr & Cochran, 1992). In this practice, clients and workers act as partners. Rather than owners of problems, clients are seen as resources. Problems are seen as embedded in social systems, thus affecting all aspects of society, including the worker and the client. An egalitarian relationship or balanced partnership with clients is a critical aspect of empowerment practice. A partnership in action is based on the assumptions that the client and worker are both resources, and that in the context of understanding private troubles as public issues, the client's long-range goals (social justice) are also the goals of the worker. When addressing powerlessness, authoritarian relationships must be avoided and expertise demystified wherever possible.

This partnership, however, does not suggest that the social worker unconditionally accept all attitudes, behaviors, or decisions of clients, such as abusive, addictive, or exploitative behaviors. Instead, it suggests a relationship of dialogue and critical analysis in which social workers and clients can discuss and analyze the multiple dimensions of a situation. An open and collaborative relationship can facilitate the critical awareness necessary for individuals to make effective decisions and use their power constructively.

Achieving a partnership takes time. Because of their socialization, including professional education, both client and worker may reinforce the worker's belief that expertise must be used to raise his or her status vis-à-vis the client. The empowerment orientation views expertise simply as "knowledge and skills" that the worker brings to a problem-solving situation in which the client provides an equally valid source of expertise.

Many factors affect the process of achieving a balanced partnership, including the following:

- Preconceived perceptions of roles
- Values and beliefs concerning power and status
- The ability of the worker and the client to identify and appreciate each other's strengths
- The ability of the worker and the client to accept and respect diversity
- The ability to overcome judgmental interpretations regarding weaknesses perceived in each other
- Common interests shared by the worker and client with respect to the political dimension of the problem or issues addressed

Preconceived perceptions about roles may include the belief that the practitioner holds all the knowledge and should take full responsibility for the solution of the problem. The perception that seeking help is a sign of weakness or pathology, embedded in medical-model practice frameworks (O'Melia & DuBois, 1993; Saleebey, 1992), hinders an egalitarian relationship. Workers who have learned traditional helper/helpee roles may find accepting a more equal relationship difficult.

Values and beliefs regarding status and power are closely related to perceptions of professionalism. Power in the egalitarian relationship must be understood as the collective power to achieve goals, both personal and political, rather than power over each other (Rees, 1991). The client and the worker cannot allow concerns about status to interfere with the equal exchange of ideas and efforts toward mutual goals.

Identifying strengths in each other requires sharing experiences and knowledge about subjects of mutual concern. The worker must learn about the context of the problem, cultural factors, the daily struggles of the client or group, local relationships, the past history of the problem, and many other aspects of the problem that only the client has access to, as well as the formal training and skills the client may have (Saleebey, 1992). The client will also benefit from the worker's formal training and life experience. The key lies in remaining open to these possibilities.

Respect for diversity includes an understanding of how the client and worker and their place in the social structure can affect problems, processes, and possibilities. It requires a respect for each other's strengths and non-judgmental approaches to each other's apparent weaknesses. This respect grows from sharing experiences and from an openness to learning and exploring issues. When gender, ethnic, racial, class, or other differences exist in the helping relationship, the client and worker should together analyze how previous experience and preconceived notions regarding such differences affect their ability to collaborate.

Common interest between worker and client regarding the political dimensions of problems will become more clear as the consciousness-raising process proceeds and the political dimensions of specific personal problems become more apparent. For example, common political interests between clients with disabilities and workers can include the lack of an adequate national health care system and employment discrimination. This common concern could then lead to collaborative activities to improve access to education and employment for people with disabilities.

A Framework for Practice

In empowerment practice, client and worker join to gather and evaluate data and to formulate an ongoing assessment of the internal and external components of the problem and its context. Because personal pain is often a political issue, an assessment has to include these two dimensions of experience. A focus on the client's experience, expertise, and view of the problem, as well as what the client wants, are primary issues in assessment (Compton & Galaway, 1994).

This assessment framework (see Figure 1.3) considers sources of problems from the personal to the external environment (Cox & Longres, 1981), opening up these two dimensions for consideration. The worker and client enter a dialectic process, working as partners to formulate the problem, review the action to better understand the problem, and plan strategies. They must also analyze the microsystems (individual, family, peer group) and macrosystems (service delivery, political institutions and structures) that affect the problem. For example, the worker and/or client might approach a reticent service provider with a variety of tactics; both would review their results together to help them better understand the service delivery process and plan further actions.

Acceptance of oneself is necessary, not only for the worker, but also for the client, as disempowered people often blame themselves for their own pain and stress. Though workers should consider the strengths and

FIGURE 1.3

Assessment Components

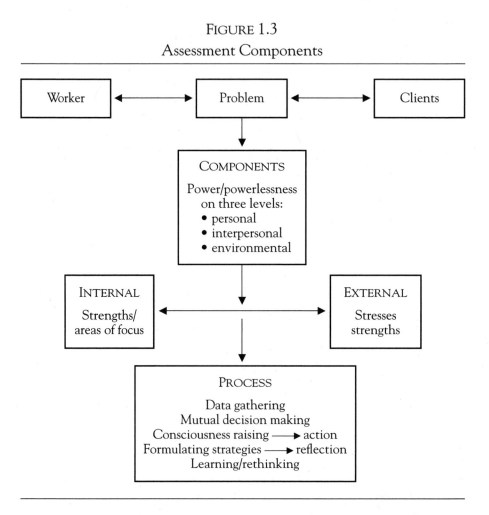

weaknesses of both client and environment, assessment must move toward personal and multidimensional environmental strengths (Cowger, 1994).

Assessment is engagement in a process of critical consciousness raising throughout all dimensions of the problem. Consciousness raising requires both reflection and action and takes place continuously throughout the intervention process. For example, in an effort to assist low-income hotel dwellers whose housing was constantly threatened by neighborhood renovation or health violations, both workers and clients participated in a daily political assessment of the situation to identify strategies that might help preserve or replace the housing. Without this daily experiential learning and mutual struggle, an awareness of the political nature of the process would have been impossible. This awareness helped the clients understand their emotional response to the helplessness they felt in the situation. No static definition of the problem existed. The participants focused on different levels of systems as they used new information to reformulate their assessment. Research on actions taken in cities throughout the nation helped them formulate a strategy toward local solution. In summary, workers and clients functioned as a team to gather information, assess the information, formulate strategies, prepare suggestions, etc. In this way, the process became a learning experience, empowering for all involved.

Specific goals stem from the general goal of empowerment: increasing the power of clients to participate in, share control of, and influence those events that affect their lives and those they care about. The goals of intervention strategies are therefore based on the client's decision, in collaboration with the worker, regarding the set of circumstances under consideration. In exploring how to help her teenage son remain in school, for example, or how to gain control over an alcohol problem, the client's perception of success is critical to goal setting. Appropriate action to solve an agreed-on problem becomes the focus of both worker and client.

Long-range structural changes in society present an immediate concern to clients and social workers alike. Because empowerment practice stresses the importance of struggle for the actualization of values that guide both consciousness raising and action, workers following this model help clients see the benefit of ongoing engagement with others to build and sustain a positive environment. This approach assumes that empowerment requires social justice and a safe environment. In summary, goal setting in empowerment practice expands the personal to the interpersonal and then to the political, meshing with values inherent in social work practice.

Directed toward achieving goals, intervention strategies include the following multilevel system strategies: one-to-one, family, group, organizational, community, and national. The appropriate levels for intervention are determined by agreed-on assessments and goals; however, participants need to emphasize multilevel system intervention, key to facilitating empowerment goals.

The primary social work roles assumed in empowerment practice are teacher/trainer, resource consultant, and sensitizer (awareness raiser) (Solomon, 1976). Themes of education and training come up often between worker and client. Other important roles for social workers include leading groups and helping clients develop group-leadership skills. Consequently, the goal of intervention becomes twofold: (1) to achieve results relative to the immediate situation and (2) to teach clients the knowledge and skills necessary to perform these interventions for themselves and others.

Solomon (1976) notes that the "practitioner must demonstrate an understanding of the dynamics of powerlessness and its consequences to develop expertise in the utilization of practice skills in the service of empowerment" (p. 26). She suggests that empowerment-enhancing interventions often have at least one of the following four goals:

1. Helping the client to see himself or herself as an agent of change relative to problems
2. Helping the client to use the practitioner's knowledge and skills
3. Helping the client perceive the practitioner as a partner in the problem-solving effort
4. Helping the client perceive the "powerlessness" as open to influence

Solomon's view reaffirms the importance of the value context in which specific interventions are implemented.

The use of mutual aid groups similar to those suggested by Gitterman and Shulman (1986) is also a common intervention of the empowerment practitioner. These authors suggest nine potentially empowering processes available through mutual support groups, including the following:

- Sharing data
- Dialectical process, entering taboo areas
- All-in-the-same-boat phenomenon
- Mutual support
- Mutual demand
- Individual problem solving
- Rehearsal
- Strength-in-numbers phenomenon (p. 9)

Other intervention strategies include plans for community organizations and the development of opportunity structures (Matura, 1986), the strengthening of mediating structures (Berger and Neuhaus, 1977), and the development of vehicles for collective empowerment in groups, organizations, institutions, or protest movements. Though such interventions are many and diverse, they share an underlying set of values that asks, "Does this action or activity help the client engage in the empowerment process?" "Will the client be better able to cope independently and participate in social change activities with the worker and with peers?"

INTERVENTION IN
FOUR DIMENSIONS

Empowerment practice centers on a continuum of factors regarding the personal, interpersonal, and political aspects of the problem at hand. Though focus on these factors may fluctuate, all remain critical to the empowerment process, which strives to achieve the most comprehensive analysis and approach for each problem-solving situation. Table 1.1 illustrates four dimensions of intervention. These represent activities focused on client systems, from individual to sociopolitical.

TABLE 1.1
PRIMARY PROBLEM-SOLVING ACTIVITIES

DIMENSION 1 Establish Worker/Client Relationship; Meet Immediate Needs	DIMENSION 2 Education; Skills Development; Self-Help	DIMENSION 3 Secure Resources; Assess Systems	DIMENSION 4 Social Action; Political (macro) Change; State/ National/ International
Linking individuals/families to existing services	Knowledge development	Knowledge development re: resources, organizations	Development of knowledge re: political-economic system, national issues
Beginning consciousness-raising process	Physical, psychological, and social aspects of problem solving	Developing skill in communications with professionals, organizations	Development of skills re: addressing national issues (macro), working with organizations
Factual learning about how to find/request resources	Developing new skills such as advocacy and mediation	Developing organizational and community-change skills	Articulation of the political nature of personal problems
	Knowledge specific to selected problems	Participating in organizational change	Letters/calling campaigns, negotiation, mediation
	Use of group to address common problems and solutions	Participating in opportunities on decision-making bodies	Lobbying, picketing
	Helping self via helping others	Creating/joining formal self-help programs and organizations	
	Skills in mutual problem solving		

(continued)

Dimension 1

Interventions consist mainly of initial work with individuals identified by themselves or by outreach or intake workers as needing assistance. The presenting problems may stem from lack of resources, interpersonal conflicts, emotional problems, specifically defined environmental problems, or any other concern of the client. With each client, the worker must first establish

TABLE 1.1
(CONTINUED)

DIMENSION 1	DIMENSION 2	DIMENSION 3	DIMENSION 4
PRIMARY PARTICIPANTS			
Individuals	Individuals	Individuals	Individuals
Families	Families	Families	Families
Workers	Small groups	Small groups	Small groups
	Workers	Large groups	Large groups
		"Problem-focused networks"	Communities
			National organizations
			Local/state organizations
PRIMARY TARGETS FOR CHANGE			
Individuals	Individual/group's situation	Organizations	Large groups
Families	"Common problem solutions"	Agencies	Communities
		Individuals	Legislation
		"Common problems"	Policy
			Local government
			State government
			National government

a working relationship and assess needs and resources. If indicated, securing entitlements is a first step in the helping process. One must do an initial assessment at this stage to determine the client's needs and goals. At this point, clients' consciousness regarding the global aspects of their conditions and circumstances may be quite limited or hidden by an immediate need for critical resources. An assessment includes clients' views of the problem and their awareness of such problems in both themselves and their families. It also includes their perceived power to manage the problem or not.

Dimension 2

Interventions are designed to provide the knowledge and skills necessary to master identified problems, such as life transitions, developmental problems, or more specific conditions. The methods suggested for this second dimension include conferences, workshops, courses, small-group formats, newspapers, telephoning, and videos. Ongoing small groups allow the formation of support networks in which individuals can discover the strength of their common interests and have their perceptions and experiences validated by one another through discussion of the content of the training (Gitterman & Shulman, 1986; Lee, 1994). Educational programs and materials must take adult learning styles into account and must be determined in part by the interests and desires of the clients.

In dimension-2 interventions, the assessment of power dynamics involves larger systems. Because clients now understand these problems as common to many others, they define problems more broadly. This comprehension of a "common issue" often leads to self-help and collective action. Self-help approaches to empowerment actually require participation with other individuals in groups focused on alleviating a shared problem, such as alcoholism, illness, poverty, fear of crime, or housing issues. Further, knowledge made available through local, state, or national networks broadens the base of individual and collective knowledge.

A key factor in self-help is the action that group members decide to take. Reisman (1965) describes the essence of this action as the helper-therapy principle. Members of the self-help group seek not only to assist themselves in overcoming or coping with a problem but also to assist other members of the group in their struggle. Helpers appear to benefit greatly from this process. The development and use of interpersonal skills such as counseling, listening, and advocacy often proceed from such participation. At this level, consciousness regarding the public nature of the problem and the political nature of causality can be developed.

Dimension 3

Interventions center on change or mediation in the immediate environment. Learning about social service and health care resources and how to access them is one key activity. This dimension often proceeds from the consciousness process through which clients and workers continue to explore the impact of the environment on personal problems. For example, a single parent seeking employment may engage in training programs and support groups in dimension 2 and become engaged in job development and exploring gender discrimination and sanctions in dimension 3. The activities of dimension 3 also include an important focus on learning about professional helpers and how to communicate with them effectively.

Dimension 4

Interventions involve clients in the political aspects of their problems. This includes social action or other collective efforts to impact environmental forces that contribute to individual problems. The knowledge base in this dimension consists of the collective intelligence of participants and sources of formal knowledge such as national social action groups and academic institutions. For example, participation in the National Organization for Women (NOW) enables a woman to address health and other issues from an informed base of social action. Besides disseminating materials about current social policy of interest to all women, NOW offers training in skills necessary for social action.

Interrelationship of the Dimensions

Though presented as separate, the four dimensions are not mutually exclusive. Tasks in all dimensions may proceed simultaneously. For example, while developing a relationship, worker and client may become involved in a discussion of national advocacy organizations or may attend a social action event. Also, while mutual support groups can be useful, many of the tasks and activities that enhance empowerment can be accomplished on a one-to-one basis when use of groups is not feasible.

These dimensions, furthermore, need be neither linear nor sequential; that is, intervention may begin in any dimension, with each dimension enhancing the others. Though dimensions 1 and 2 represent most traditional social work practice, the goals of empowerment practice necessarily include the consciousness and activities of dimensions 3 and 4. For example, financial insecurity, common to many groups such as women or displaced blue-collar workers, lies rooted in the economic structure and values of U.S. society. In dimension 1, individuals and families may somewhat alleviate financial problems by finding and securing entitlements. In dimension 2, these individuals and families may participate in discussion groups concerning rental costs in their area and learn about housing alternatives. In dimension 3, a group of community residents may implement a communal garden or a craft co-op to help alleviate financial stress. In dimension 4, community groups or individuals may identify links between personal problems and societal dynamics and participate in strategies for action such as improving the AFDC or job-training and employment policies and resources.

The social worker serves as a catalyst throughout this process by raising questions about the relationship between various private problems and related public issues, then challenging the group members to come to their own conclusions. This increases awareness of the continuum of private troubles and public issues. Empowerment often results from this process (Gutiérrez, 1995; Kieffer, 1984). Though comprehending the environmental aspects of one's struggles is often a first step in gaining control over some aspects of one's life situation, consciousness-raising activities must also focus on the internalized aspects of the problem in order to facilitate empowerment. A person may resist productive problem solving because of beliefs or values that the others involved see as nonfunctional. For example, some Latino parents who speak little English may avoid interaction with their children's teachers because of discomfort with speaking a second language. They may be unaware of the availability of Spanish-speaking staff or faculty who can assist with communication. Often a person is unaware of the source of the difficulties or is acting on ideas that have never been challenged. The group process frequently illuminates such values, providing an opportunity to reassess them in the light of new information. Consciousness raising also requires that individuals seek to understand the external aspects of the problem, such as age discrimination or lack of jobs in the economy. Working with others toward a collective understanding and alleviation of these conditions is thus helpful. The most important function of workers is to help people identify links between personal problems and societal dynamics.

EVALUATING THE OUTCOMES OF EMPOWERMENT PRACTICE

Evaluating empowerment practice is complex. Because empowerment is both a process and an outcome, evaluation approaches need to address assessment of a dynamic process at some identified state. Traditionally, evaluation has focused on ways to assess the degree of change that has taken place. But the nature of the empowerment process suggests that participants look at evaluation efforts as collaborative and ongoing. Although a social worker may end a helping relationship, the client will continue to change. In many empowerment-based programs, in fact, clients can continue their work by taking different roles in the service program or in their lives in general.

As such, ongoing evaluation ideally takes place throughout the helping process. From the beginning of work, practitioners join service consumers as scientists to determine the effectiveness of their work together. In this way clients and consumers can develop the strategies to evaluate change and monitor its direction.

One needs both qualitative and quantitative approaches to identify the process and the outcome of empowerment-based practice. Briefly, assessments of empowerment are often qualitative, using the stories and expertise of clients for both designing and implementing an inquiry. To assess the outcomes of empowerment, researchers have created instruments designed to measure attitudes, knowledge and skills, critical thinking, networking, and taking action (Zimmerman, 1990). For example, a qualitative approach to documenting such outcomes (Parsons, 1995) confirms the presence of personal, interpersonal, and political components of empowerment, as identified by clients and workers in five empowerment-based social work programs. These perceived changes in clients of empowerment programs confirm existing literature regarding the outcomes of empowerment and can provide a basis for designing evaluation approaches to empowerment practice.

TABLE 1.2
OUTCOMES OF EMPOWERMENT-BASED PROGRAMS

INTRAPERSONAL	INTERPERSONAL	POLITICAL/COMMUNITY
Self-efficacy	Knowledge/skills	Political action/participation
Self-awareness	Assertiveness	Giving back
Self-acceptance	Setting limits on	Making a contribution
Being in self	giving	Taking control (action)
Self-esteem	Asking for help	
Feeling you have	Problem solving	
rights	Practicing new skills	
Critical thinking	Accessing resources	

When evaluating the outcome of empowerment practice, one must assess whether the initial concerns of the client were addressed and whether the client gained power on the three levels suggested by Parsons (1995). Table 1.2 suggests dimensions that one could use to develop individual assessment tools. Some outcome measures for intrapersonal empowerment would tap into the client's perception of his or her own ability to make choices. Measures of interpersonal power would include a look at the degree to which the client has gained the ability to influence others in socially acceptable ways. In assessing gains in political power, the social workers and the client could examine how effectively the relationship increased the client's involvement in mutual aid groups, neighborhood groups, or political activities that could improve the status of the larger community.

SUMMARY

The empowerment process involves (1) a critical review of attitudes and beliefs about one's self and one's sociopolitical environment, (2) the validation of one's experience, (3) an increased knowledge and skills for critical thinking and action, and (4) action taken for personal and political change. A social work practice framework contains values, sanctions, a theory base, a professional relationship, and an organizing framework for identifying and assessing social problems, setting goals, planning strategies, intervention, and evaluation. Empowerment-based practice imbues these components with a common and consistent theme of facilitating empowerment in clients. Focusing on consciousness raising and education, interventive strategies are conceptualized as a continuum of the personal to the political. The four dimensions of focus for intervention activity include personal, immediate systems of family and peer group, service delivery systems, and political structures. Interrelated instead of exclusive, these dimensions serve as a continuum of consciousness raising and action taking *with* the client, not in the place of the client. Education is an inherent component of service delivery across these dimensions. Finally, the evaluation of empowerment practice needs to address both the process and the outcome of empowerment and requires both qualitative and quantitative approaches.

REFERENCES

Barr, D., & Cochran, M. (1992). Understanding and supporting empowerment: Redefining the professional role. *Empowerment and Family Support Networking Bulletin, 2*(3). Ithaca, NY: Cornell Empowerment Project, 1–8.

Berger, P. L., & Neuhaus, R. J. (1977). *To empower people: The role of mediating structures in public policy.* Washington, DC: American Enterprise Institute for Public Policy Research.

Bricker-Jenkins, M., & Hooyman, N. (1986). *Not for women only: Social work practice for a feminist future.* Silver Spring, MD: National Association of Social Workers.

Compton, B., & Galaway, B. (1994). *Social work processes* (5th ed.). Pacific Grove, CA: Brooks/Cole.

Cowger, C. (1994). Assessing client strengths: Clinical assessment for client empowerment. *Social Work, 39*(3), 262–268.

Cox, E. O. (1988). Empowerment Interventions in Aging. *Social Work with Groups, 11*(3/4), 111–125.

Cox, E. O. (1991). The critical role of social action in empowerment oriented groups. In A. Vinik & M. Levin (Eds.), *Social action in group work* (pp. 77–90). New York: Haworth.

Cox, E. O., & Longres, J. (1981, March). *Critical practice-curriculum implications.* Paper presented at the Annual Program Meeting of the Council on Social Work Education, Louisville, KY.

Cox. E. O., & Parsons, R. J. (1994). *Empowerment Oriented Social Work Practice with the Elderly.* Pacific Grove, CA: Brooks/Cole.

Dressel, P. L. (1994). And we keep on building prisons: Racism, poverty and challenges to the welfare state. *Journal of Sociology and Social Welfare, 21*(3), 7–30.

Friere, P. (1973). *Education for critical consciousness.* New York: Continuum.

Garvin, C. (1985). Work with disadvantaged and oppressed groups. In M. Sundel, P. Glasser, R. Sarri, & R. Vinter (Eds.), *Individual change through small groups* (2nd ed.)(pp. 461–472). New York: Free Press.

Gaventa, J. (1980). *Power and powerlessness: Quiescence and rebellion in an Appalachian valley.* Urbana: University of Illinois Press.

Gitterman, A., & Shulman, L. (Eds.). (1986). *Mutual aid groups and the life cycle.* Itasca, IL: Peacock.

Gould, K. H. (1987). Life model versus conflict model. *Social Work, 32*(4), 346–351.

Gutiérrez, L. (1989). *Empowerment in social work practice: Considerations for practice and education.* Paper presented to the Council on Social Work Education Annual Program Meeting, Chicago, IL.

Gutiérrez, L. (1990). Working with women of color: An empowerment perspective. *Social Work, 35*(2), 149–154.

Gutiérrez, L. (1992). Empowering clients in the twenty-first century: The role of human service organizations. In Y. Hasenfeld (Ed.), *Human service organizations as complex organizations* (pp. 320–338). Newbury Park, CA: Sage.

Gutiérrez, L. (1994). Beyond Coping: An empowerment perspective on stressful life events. *Journal of Sociology and Social Welfare, 21*(3), 201–220.

Gutiérrez, L. (1995). Understanding the empowerment process: Does consciousness make a difference? *Social Work Research, 19,* 229–237.

Gutiérrez, L., DeLois, K., & GlenMaye, L. (1995). Understanding empowerment practice: Building on practitioner based knowledge. *Families in Society, 76*(9), 534–542.

Kieffer, C. H. (1984). Citizen empowerment: A developmental perspective. *Prevention in Human Services, 3,* 9–36.

Lee, J. (1994). *The empowerment approach to social work practice.* New York: Columbia University Press.

Leigh, J. (1985). Primary prevention approaches. In S. Grey, A. Hartman, & E. Saalberg, (Eds.) *Empowering the black family: A round table discussion.* Ann Arbor, MI: National Child Welfare Training Center.

Mathis, T., & Richan, D. (1986). *Empowerment: Practice in search of a theory.* Paper presented at the Annual Program Meeting of the Council on Social Work Education, Miami, Florida.

Matura, R. C. (1986, April). *Opportunity structures for the aged.* Paper presented at the North Central Sociological Association, Toledo, OH.

McWhirter, E. (1994). *Counseling for empowerment.* Alexandria, VA: American Counseling Association.

Miley, K., O'Melia, M., & DuBois, B. (1994). *Generalist social work practice: An empowering approach.* Boston: Allyn and Bacon.

O'Melia, M., & DuBois, B. (1994). From problem-solving to empowerment based social work practice. In L. Gutiérrez & P. Nurius, (Eds.), *The education and research for empowerment practice* (pp. 161–170). Center for Social Policy and Practice: University of Washington School of Social Work, Seattle.

Ozawa, M. (1986). Nonwhites and the demographic imperative in social welfare spending. *Social Work, 31,* 440–445.

Parsons, R. J. (1991). Empowerment: Purpose and practice in social work. *Social Work with Groups, 14*(2), 27–43.

Parsons, R. J. (1995). *Empowerment based social work practice: A study of process and outcomes.* Paper presented to the Annual Program Meeting of the Council on Social Work Education, San Diego, CA.

Parsons, R. J., Jorgensen, J. D., & Hernández, S. H. (1994). *The integration of social work practice.* Pacific Grove, CA: Brooks/Cole.

Pinderhughes, E. (1983). Empowerment: For our clients and for ourselves. *Social Casework, 64,* 312–314.

Pinderhughes, E. (1989). *Understanding race, ethnicity and power.* New York: Free Press.

Rees, S. (1991). *Achieving power*. North Sydney, Australia: Allen & Unwin.

Reisman, F. (1965). The helper-therapy principle. *Social Work, 10*(2), 27–32.

Saleebey, D. (Ed.). (1992). *The strengths perspective in social work practice*. New York: Longman.

Sarri, R. (1986). Organizational and policy practice in social work: Challenges for the future. *Urban and Social Change Review, 19*, 14–19.

Simon, B. L. (1994). *The empowerment traditions in American social work*. New York: Columbia University Press.

Solomon, B. (1976). *Black empowerment: Social work in oppressed communities*. New York: Columbia University Press.

Torre, D. (1985). Empowerment: *Structured conceptualization and instrument development*. Unpublished doctoral dissertation, Cornell University, Ithaca, NY.

Weick, A., & Vandiver, S. (Eds.). (1982). *Women, power, and change*. Silver Spring, MD: National Association of Social Workers.

Wenocur, S., & Reisch, M. (1989) *From charity to enterprise: The development of American social work in a market economy*. Chicago: University of Illinois Press.

Williams, L. (1990). The challenge of education to social work: The case of minority children. *Social Work, 35*, 236–242.

Zimmerman, M. (1990). Taking aim on empowerment research: On the distinction between individual and psychological concepts. *American Journal of Community Psychology, 18*(1), 169–177

Part Two

EMPOWERMENT IN PRACTICE:
POPULATIONS

Because empowerment methods were initially developed to address the needs and conditions of women and people of color, practice has always centered on the experiences of oppressed populations. This part of the book looks closely at empowerment methods applied to four historically oppressed populations: women, people of color, gays and lesbians, and people with disabilities. These groups were selected because they make up the largest populations served by social workers. However, in reading these chapters, you should consider how other populations—such as displaced workers or the aging—could also benefit from empowerment methods. The issues and techniques presented in the next four chapters are used by other groups as well.

In Chapter 2, Linnea GlenMaye describes ways one can view women as an oppressed group because of their gender and the social conditions related to gender. She also suggests that workers recognize how the diverse experiences of women of different ages, races, social classes, and other social conditions affect their own experiences of gender discrimination. Empowerment for women includes changing thoughts and actions to improve the role and status of all oppressed populations. You may want to think about the following as you read this chapter:

1. *How do you view the role and status of women in society? In what ways do women experience oppression and discrimination?*
2. *The author recognizes that not all women are aware of their status as an oppressed group. What are the implications of consciousness-raising methods when working with people unaware of their status?*
3. *How closely do the empowerment-oriented programs described resemble other forms of social work practice? How easily could they be incorporated into the activities of most social work agencies?*

In Chapter 3, Margo Okazawa-Rey proposes a self-help model for work with poor communities of color. The author directs close attention to the ways in which people have defined *community of color* to suggest that this phrase does not recognize the wide range of populations involved. Rather than attempting to identify a method for working with this broad group, she provides a rich example of how empowerment methods have been used with a specific population (older African-American women) and a specific issue (becoming a custodial grandparent). From this specific example she identifies practice principles one could use with many other groups. When reading this chapter, think about the following:

1. *What do we mean by* community of color? *What are the positive and negative consequences of using this term?*
2. *In what ways did the group facilitators use cultural values, practices, and symbols in their empowerment practice? How might one tailor such methods to the cultural patterns of other populations?*
3. *What role did the facilitator play in moving the group members from a purely personal perspective on problems to views more directly related to social status, gender, or race? How open were members to this critical analysis?*

Kathryn DeLois, in Chapter 4, challenges readers to examine compulsory heterosexuality in their work and daily lives. This chapter describes not only the conditions of oppression that affect the lives of gay men and lesbians, but also the vibrant and supportive culture and forms of resistance within this community. She challenges readers to examine their attitudes and engage in political education and action to confront the ways in which lesbians and gay men are denied access to resources. Questions to think about when reading this chapter include the following:

1. *The author identifies the ways that agency procedures, intake forms, and symbols can be unsupportive to lesbians and gay men. Does your current practice organization reflect these conditions? If so, how?*

2. *What is the social work profession's role in advocating for oppressed popula-*
   tions? In what ways can workers step out of their official "job descriptions"
   or work roles to advocate for broader changes or against discriminatory
   policies?
3. *How can social workers tailor empowerment interventions to involve existing*
   elements of gay and lesbian culture and methods of resistance? How can
   workers act in partnership with advocates in this community?

In the final chapter of Part Two, Richard Renz-Beaulaurier discusses issues for empowering people with disabilities. With a focus both historical and contemporary, he traces ways in which social policies regarding disability have reflected societal philosophies and norms. He suggests that to empower people with disabilities, social workers need to transform their traditional relationship with this population. Important questions to think about when reading this chapter include the following:

1. *In what ways have social workers and social policies oppressed people with*
   disabilities? How has this been the case for other populations as well?
2. *How can social workers most effectively work in partnership with people with*
   disabilities? What new skills or attitudes might this require?
3. *How can the experience of people with disabilities challenge people's notions*
   of independence and self-sufficiency? How does this relate to the current
   understanding of empowerment?

Chapter 2

EMPOWERMENT OF

WOMEN

Linnea GlenMaye, Ph.D.
University of Las Vegas, Las Vegas, Nevada

INTRODUCTION

Empowerment is an appropriate goal for any community, group, or individual who experience systematic and institutionalized discrimination (Solomon, 1976). The term *empowerment* describes the transformation from individual and collective powerlessness to personal, political, and cultural power. Because women individually and collectively live under conditions of discrimination and powerlessness, the empowerment of women is an appropriate and necessary part of social work's vision of and practice toward a just society.

Talking about women as a group, however, raises complex questions about the similarities and differences among groups of women and among individual women. The concept of women as a gender and as a group is currently being redefined as a result of philosophical critiques of unifying concepts and, more importantly, the assertions of those whose experience as women of color, lesbians, women with disabilities, or impoverished women did not fit prevailing theories of women's condition in society.

In talking about women as a group, one must see *woman* as comprised of a complex set of interlocking individual and group experiences including at least race, class, and gender. Researchers and practitioners who work with women must define their own vantage point and admit they cannot speak for all or even any women. As such, you should know that my position in this chapter has been influenced by my status as a white, lesbian, middle-class, feminist academic, and I admit my own inability to speak for all women.

That women as a group are situationally and experientially fragmented is beyond doubt. I believe, though, that speaking of women in the universalizing sense is not only possible but both necessary and appropriate. Though not one, but many, *women* are nevertheless united in two fundamental ways: (1) they are a distinct and separate biological sex and, as Lerner (1986) points out, are not a subgroup or a minority but are half of the whole and (2) women as members of this sex share both the bodily experience of femaleness and the social condition imposed on them by virtue of their sex. This social condition has been variously described as the oppression, subordination, deprivation, exploitation, victimization, and powerlessness of women because of their status as the devalued half of humanity. Though each describes some aspect of the condition of women, each cannot adequately describe the total experience of women. Although I recognize the limits of any particular term to describe the social condition of women, I have chosen to use the word *oppression* to describe it, however flawed it may be in helping one distinguish between general conditions and the particular experiences of more or less privileged women.

Frye (1983) captures the essence of the experience of oppression when she describes it in terms of its root meaning of flattening, molding, and reducing:

> The experience of oppressed people is that the living of one's life is confined and shaped by forces and barriers which are not accidental or occasional and hence avoidable, but are systematically related to each other in such a way as to catch one between and among them and restrict or penalize motion in any direction. It is the experience of being caged in: all avenues, in every direction, are blocked or booby trapped. (p. 4)

When I say that women are oppressed, I do not mean that such oppression is the *only* oppression. It is, however, an oppression that cuts across every culture, system, and social relation. That is, no matter what the system —welfare, capitalism, legal, religious, or any other—being a woman in that system counts in fundamental, mostly negative but sometimes contradictory ways. A mercurial phenomenon, women's oppression defies ordinary analysis and targeted solutions. In countless and unnoticed ways, it impinges on the daily lives of women and men from every group, walk, and generation. This oppression is global and intimate. In this regard, hooks (1989) argues that the feminist struggle is of global importance for all women and men because sexist oppression is "that form of domination we are most likely to encounter in an ongoing way in everyday life" (p. 21). As she states,

> Feminist effort to end patriarchal domination should be of primary concern precisely because it insists on the eradication of exploitation and oppression in the family context and in all other intimate relationships. It is that political movement which most radically addresses the

person—the personal—citing the need for transformation of self, of relationships, so that we might be better able to act in a revolutionary manner, challenging and resisting domination, transforming the world outside the self. (p. 22)

In Frye's (1983) analysis, women's common experience of oppression comes from their confinement to a ghetto of sorts, a distinct service sector that she identifies with the service of men and men's interests as defined by men—personal, sexual, and ego-boosting. The details of this service vary by race, class, and other individual and group factors, but one can make two basic observations about this service, as Frye suggests: (1) Even though women's interests may overlap those of men, men do not serve women as women serve men, across every race/class line and (2) women are held accountable for the good outcomes of such service though they do not have enough power to achieve them.

THREE CONDITIONS OF WOMEN'S OPPRESSION

Although in one sense one can easily say that women are oppressed, as well as the oppressed of the oppressed, unraveling the threads of powerlessness that bind women proves to be difficult. It is beyond the scope of this chapter to analyze or even to describe the full extent of such oppression. Feminist theorists have labored for at least the last 150 years to describe the personal, political, economic, psychological, and spiritual forms of oppression that define, limit, and obliterate women's lives and choices, and I will not attempt to re-search that territory. Instead, I suggest three general conditions that all women largely share and that together produce and enforce the subordination and relative powerlessness of women: (1) profound alienation from the self, (2) the double-bind situation of women, (3) institutional and structural sexism.

Alienation from the Self

When I first began working with women recovering from rape and sexual assault, I was immediately struck by how often, when asked to describe their feelings and needs, they could identify neither. This lack of self-knowledge seemed to contradict directly the common thought that women have an innate ability to "get in touch with their feelings." I found that one of the most basic consequences of rape was the profound disengagement or dissociation of the self as a coping strategy. Feminist theorists have noted that this alienation from the self, most easily identifiable in victims of traumatic violence, is in fact common to most women in U.S. society. This alienation of the self has two major aspects. The first amounts to an estrangement of a woman from her inner self—the self that has individuated needs, wants, capabilities, dreams, and intrinsic worth. The second is estrangement from personhood itself. The first condition of alienation profoundly depends on the second; that is, the denial of the full personhood leads inexorably to the relative inability to identify with an inner self having worth and subjectivity.

The alienation of self is analogous to the loss of voice described by other feminist theorists (Belenky, Clinchy, Goldberger, & Tarule, 1986; Collins, 1990; Gilligan, 1982; hooks, 1989). One can describe *loss of voice* as the profound inability to articulate an integrated vision of oneself as a subject, or as Belenky et al. (1986) suggest, "an extreme in denial of self and in dependence on external authority for direction" (p. 24).

Bartky (1990) defines women's alienation from personhood experienced as an aspect of the oppression in which women internalize feelings of inferiority and exercise "harsh dominion" over their own self-esteem. Basing her argument on the concept of "psychic alienation" developed by Fanon, she claims this alienation stems from three modes of psychological oppression: stereotyping, cultural domination, and sexual objectification.

STEREOTYPING   Culturally and historically determined, the stereotypes that uphold sexism function as a whole to maintain the superiority of men and the inferiority and deficiency of women. Female stereotypes are so well known that all members of society can call them up. Bartky points out that stereotypes limit authentic choice and moral agency because the deficient and inferior self shadows and blocks the emergence of the authentic self. Institutions, of course, also use stereotypes to impede women's choices and advancement. These ideas of proper female behavior also provide the only socially acceptable standard for women's achievement and self-esteem. As such, women are held to an unrealizable model of femininity. Being a perfect mother and sex object, contradictory goals in themselves, stand as the highest calling of women.

CULTURAL DOMINATION   Bartky argues that women, like other oppressed groups, see a degraded or distorted image of themselves in the dominant culture. Unlike other oppressed groups, however, women have no alternative culture to recognize as their own. For a woman, then, the experience of cultural domination is a pervasive feature of cultural being and therefore appears natural and unchangeable. Women's cultural identity resides in patriarchal culture, even though in a basic sense women have not created or participated consciously and powerfully in the creation of that culture. Bartky points out that by not having an alternative culture, women may find it easier to identify with the oppressors of their own ethnic culture than to identify with women of another culture.

SEXUAL OBJECTIFICATION To become a sexual object is to have one's sexual parts or functions separated from the wholeness of one's person, and to have those parts regarded as if they represent the whole person (Bartky, 1990). This identification "becomes oppressive, one might venture, when such an identification becomes habitually extended into every area of her experience" (p. 26). For women this objectification is experienced as a routine, unwanted, and persistent emphasis on her sexual being, functions, parts, and role in every social situation. Though women experience this objectification as coming from the outside, they also experience it as a preoccupation with their own bodies. As Bartky states, "Our identities can no more be kept separate from the appearance of our bodies than they can be kept separate from the shadow-selves of the female stereotype" (p. 28).

These three forms of oppression—stereotyping, cultural domination, and sexual objectification—work together to deny the basic humanity of women and to bring about a fundamental alienation of women from their selves. As Bartky (1990) states, "To be denied an autonomous choice of self, forbidden cultural expression, and condemned to the imminence of mere bodily being, is to be cut off from the sorts of activities that define what it is to be human. A person whose being has been subjected to these cleavages may be described as alienated. . . . an estrangement from the self" (p. 31).

The Double-Bind Situation of Women

All women find themselves in a double bind when making decisions, important or mundane. A no-win situation, the double bind for women calls into question basic issues of identity and meaning. For example, women on public assistance who find jobs are criticized for leaving their children, while mothers who stay home are labeled lazy and self-indulgent. This double bind guarantees that no matter what a woman chooses, she will feel guilty, inadequate, and at some deep level of being, a failure as a woman.

The double bind of women takes place in a context of contradictory messages (Bartky, 1990). On the one hand society says that women are human, but on the other hand it takes away any opportunity to realize that humanity by molding women to stereotypical, unreachable standards. In this regard, Young-Eisendrath and Wehr (1990) argue,

> Until a woman is offered a feminist explanation for her felt condition
> of personal inferiority, she is necessarily in a double bind about her
> gender and her status as an independent adult. . . . If a woman behaves
> as a healthy adult, she will be criticized for being unwomanly; con-
> versely, if she behaves as an ideal feminine woman, she will be consid-
> ered childlike or worse, even mentally incompetent. (p. 123)

One important aspect of the double bind for women is the way in which they are forced to choose between their own needs and the needs of others. Being autonomous, self-determining, and self-actualizing is of course the mark of being fully human. Because of their role as nurturers, women are forever finding themselves in situations where self-determination seems to conflict with the demands of motherhood or any intimate relationship. To put herself above others is, for women, an act that puts her selfhood at risk.

Institutional and Structural Sexism

The institutionalized and systemic forces of sexism have been variously labeled as patriarchy, male domination, the sex-gender system, paternalism, and male supremacy. Regardless of the term, sexism comprises the mutually reinforcing mechanisms by which "men hold power in all the important institutions in society . . . and women are deprived of access to such power" (Lerner, 1986, p. 239). The unequal distribution of power is manifest in laws, economic resources, personal status, and the many ways in which women are physically and sexually victimized by male violence. That U.S. society is built on an ideology of male supremacy and dominance should be obvious to the casual observer. It is perhaps surprising then to note that the extent to which women are subordinated in this society is directly proportional to the taboo against seeing and acknowledging male domination and the relative powerlessness of women in our society. Institutionalized sexism demands the silent acquiescence of both the oppressed and the oppressor.

EMPOWERMENT
FOR WOMEN

In the previous section I outlined some common elements of the oppressive structures that define women's lives. Though every woman experiences oppression in her own way, women will generally come to a service setting because of these common elements. For example, women can face the same double-bind situation regardless of socioeconomic status, lifestyle, or ethnicity. The same consequence of losing their children can befall women who report domestic violence, choose to further a career, acknowledge their lesbian identity, or choose to divorce. For each of these women, the choice to further their own growth, safety, well-being, and authenticity contains at least the possibility of loss in other crucial aspects of their lives.

In each of these situations, social workers need to be aware of the personal dimension of oppression for each woman, which will always vary by ethnicity, age, socioeconomic status, and personal experiences of victimization. Further, workers need to bring to that setting an awareness and knowledge of how institutionalized sexism and cultural norms create a context of no-win situations and real limits to personal choices and self advancement.

Definition of Empowerment

Empowerment has been defined as "the process of increasing personal, interpersonal, or political power so that individuals can take action to improve their life situations" (Gutiérrez, 1990, p. 149). Swift and Levin (1987) imply that empowerment includes the development of a state of mind (a sense of power, efficacy, competence) and the modification of structural conditions in order to reallocate power. In an empowerment paradigm, knowledge of one's life situation vis-à-vis the power structure of society and actions taken to change that structure are linked.

Empowerment for women includes personal, interpersonal, and culture-changing thoughts and actions that together bring about real increases in the personal and political power of women. One can define such empowerment in terms of feminist goals, beliefs, and vision for a world in which no person is oppressed, suppressed, or repressed because of who they are or what they say or do. Bricker-Jenkins and Hooyman (1986) suggest that the empowerment of women involves "liberating the strength and energy of women" (p. 12). For women and all oppressed groups, securing the right to express oneself is paramount. Therefore, based on Bricker-Jenkins, Hooyman, and Gottlieb (1991), my definition of *empowerment* is

> Speaking the truth of one's life in one's own voice, and working collectively to create that possibility for all.

MODELS OF EMPOWERMENT FOR WOMEN

The literature presents ways in which empowerment can develop. Gutiérrez (1987) has identified four subprocesses that contribute to overall empowerment: enhancing self-efficacy, reducing self-blame, assuming personal responsibility for change, and developing group and critical consciousness. Swift and Levin (1987) propose a three-stage model for the development of class consciousness in which the combination of all three stages sufficiently creates a sense of empowerment. These stages are

1. Cognitive awareness of one's self-interests, one's position with regard to and knowledge of the dominant social system's distribution of power, and the position of others relative to oneself in the system
2. Affective feelings toward that cognitive awareness as well as feelings (especially loyalty vs. disaffection) vis-à-vis one's relationship to others
3. Cognitive purpose toward changing the social distribution of

power so as to improve one's social condition and advance one's self-interests to greater parity (pp. 73–74)

These two models both emphasize the development of consciousness and awareness, the need for personal and social change, and the importance of feelings and one's affective state.

One can create an empowerment model for women based on these general models by adapting them to the specific conditions of women's oppression. A three-part model of empowerment for women, then, would include the following:

1. Development of consciousness of self as a woman
2. Reduction of shame and self-blame, and acknowledgment of anger as a catalyst toward change
3. Assumption of personal responsibility for changing self and society

These three components are cumulative, circular, and ongoing. That is, there is no one moment of empowerment, but rather many moments of consciousness and action.

Development of Consciousness of Self

MacKinnon (1989) states that members of oppressed groups must become visible to themselves to discover their own identity distinct from the oppressor. In the case of women, self-identity and consciousness involves finding an authentic essence apart from the stereotypes and expectations of patriarchal society. *Consciousness* is awareness of oneself as a thinking being: that is, knowing what one is doing and why. Freire (1985) suggests that peasants did not know they had thoughts until they could stand outside themselves and view the oppressed and silent conditions of their life. Freire called this process of coming to consciousness *conscientization*.

In feminist terms, this process has generally been described as *consciousness raising*. Within this process, which generally occurs in small groups, women begin to uncover how the social forces of sexism have affected them personally. Consciousness raising is "the major technique of analysis, structure of organization, method of practice, and theory of social change of the women's movement. In consciousness raising, often in groups, the impact of male dominance is concretely uncovered and analyzed through the collective speaking of women's experience from the perspective of that experience" (MacKinnon, 1982, pp. 519–520).

Feminist theorists claim that the basis of consciousness raising is the personal experience of women. Further, the examination of their own lives and the discovery of common experiences with other women defines the theory and practice of feminism and of women's liberation from oppression (Bricker-Jenkins & Hooyman, 1986; Shreve, 1989). The main assumption of the consciousness-raising process is that the personal and the political are linked but this linkage remains hidden until women together begin to share their common experience and to see how larger social forces have shaped their lives. The personal and political aspects of consciousness raising consist of many subprocesses in women's lives.

PERSONAL   The personal dimension of consciousness raising involves (1) identifying one's own feelings, perceptions, and needs from the vantage point of one's own experiences, (2) naming or defining one's experiences in one's own language, and (3) telling one's own life story (Mies, 1989). My work with rape survivors showed me that women often find it difficult to identify feelings. It is not unusual, in fact, for women to draw a blank when asked to describe feelings. This seems especially true when women are asked to describe their feelings about a situation where they have been victimized or treated unjustly. In consciousness raising, the feelings and experiences shared revolve around the daily and routine aspects of women's lives, because this reveals the commonalties of oppression and the reality of women's lives. The power to name their own experience in their own language has been previously denied to women, oppressed by silence or being forced to use the language of the oppressor.

POLITICAL   The political dimension of consciousness raising involves (1) linking one's personal experiences to one's position as a woman in a male-dominated society, (2) identifying oneself as a woman who shares a common fate with all women, and (3) taking action to change oneself and the social structures that oppress women.

Such work involves at its core the development of a feminist consciousness, or the belief that all women's lives matter, and that no woman is free until all are free. The vision of a society where women are free guides action toward making that liberation real. As Dworkin (1983) states, "To be a feminist means recognizing that one is associated with all women not as an act of choice but as a matter of fact" (p. 221).

The personal and the political aspects of consciousness raising cannot really be separated. They exist as a dialectic in which personal experience and social reality are discovered, tested, and recreated. The full meaning of feminist consciousness resides in apprehending the complex reality of one's situation as a woman with the faith in one's ability and right to a fully human existence. As Bartky (1990) suggests,

> Coming to have a feminist consciousness is the experience of coming to see things about oneself and one's society that were heretofore hidden. . . . We begin to understand why we have such depreciated images of ourselves and why so many of us are lacking any genuine conviction of personal worth. . . . Coming to see things differently, we are able to

make out possibilities for liberating collective action and for unprece-
dented personal growth, possibilities which a deceptive sexist social
reality had heretofore concealed. (p. 21)

BARRIERS TO CONSCIOUSNESS FOR WOMEN Coming to a feminist consciousness of self involves ignoring all evidence of women's marginality and
instead putting women at the center of one's vantage point. To step outside
of patriarchal thought means adopting a stance of skepticism toward known
systems of thought and testing all statements in light of the female experience. This stance involves "developing intellectual courage, the courage to
stand alone, the courage to reach farther than our grasp, the courage to risk
failure. Perhaps the greatest challenge to thinking women is the challenge
to move from the desire for safety and approval to the most 'unfeminine'
quality of all—that of intellectual arrogance, the supreme hubris which
asserts to itself the right to reorder the world" (Lerner, 1986, p. 228).

Lerner (1986) identifies a factor that, in my view, is missing from
much of the literature on empowerment and consciousness—the great risk
involved in this process. My own experience in becoming a feminist tells
me that the decision to accept my own self as worthy and equal has been
fraught with anxiety, dread, and fear. In fact, several types of fear can block
the process of empowerment and development of consciousness for women:
fear of rape and physical violence, fear of losing relationships with men, fear
of losing children or the possibility of having children, religion-based fears,
fear of their own power, and fear of losing the only identity they know.

Another barrier is the reluctance of women to identify themselves as
members of an oppressed group. Frye (1983) offers an explanation for the
fact that many people, including women themselves, do not accept that
women are an oppressed people. In Frye's analysis, the dispersal of women
throughout systems of race and class makes it difficult for women to recognize the commonality of oppression. Further, these divisions of race and
class create situations of interest that compel women to ignore the elements
of a common oppression. Women of color, for instance, are often made to
feel that identifying oneself as an oppressed woman is antithetical to identifying oneself as racially oppressed. Describing the ambivalence that black
women feel toward the acknowledgment of sexism in black families and
communities, hooks (1989) argues,

> To acknowledge then that our families and communities have been
> undermined by sexism would not only require an acknowledgment that
> racism is not the only form of domination and oppression that affects us
> a people; it would mean critically challenging the assumption that our
> survival as a people depends on creating a cultural climate in which
> black men can achieve manhood within paradigms constructed by white
> patriarchy. . . . Until black people redefine in a nonsexist revolutionary

way the terms of our liberation, black women and men will always be confronted with the issue of whether supporting feminist efforts to end sexism is inimical to our interests as a people. (p. 178)

Most people feel, furthermore, a basic aversion to seeing themselves as victims. In the minds of many women, identifying oneself as oppressed because of one's sex may appear to be an admission of weakness and vulnerability. Related to this reluctance is the assumption that one must name the oppressor, which for women sounds like male-bashing; to be perceived in this way is threatening on many levels.

Reduction of Shame and Self Blame; Acknowledgment of Anger

In Western societies, women are viewed as sexual objects, flawed beings, and the originators of sin. As such, they are the primary bearers of shame. Society also encourages self-blaming behavior in women because of the responsibility they carry for the success of relationships, marriages, and child rearing. In coming to consciousness of self, women begin to see how the social forces of patriarchy, more than personal failings, instill feelings of inadequacy and lack of worth. Awareness of the political and social dimensions of women's experiences and problems leads away from shame and self-blame. That is, the diminishment of shame occurs only as women see how unjust their treatment as women has been. Injustice incurs anger, which may serve as a catalyst of action. This process can occur individually or be shared in a group. Collins (1990), for instance, shows how in some blues songs, as the singer grows in self-awareness and defines the oppressive situation, the listener may be inspired by anger to take action.

Collins's observation captures a core component of consciousness for women: acknowledgment of their anger toward the system that devalues them, and more importantly, anger toward individual men in their lives. This awareness of anger is necessary whether one is working with obvious victims of male violence or with women in need of general services or counseling. Because anger, especially anger toward men, is the one emotion denied women, the acknowledgment of anger is especially threatening and can take place only in an atmosphere of trust and safety.

Assumption of Personal Responsibility for Change

The assumption of personal responsibility for changing self and society can occur only in a context where women have a sense of personal and political power. Having a sense of this power requires a self-image and an image of women that radiates power and the ability to change oneself and one's world. For this image to emerge, women need to take an action never allowed under patriarchy: the act of believing in their own goodness, strength, energy, wisdom, and reality on the basis of their own lived experience as women.

Learning to believe in oneself as a women, a lifelong process full of conscious volition, is key to women's empowerment. Such action finds its force expressed in the definition and origins of *belief*: the state of believing; conviction or acceptance that certain things are true or real. Its roots lie in the composite meanings of its two parts: be-lief. *Be* means to exist, to live, and is derived from a word meaning to grow or to become. *Lief* is related to *life* and *love*, which means to be fond of, to desire, to be valued, to be dear or beloved.

By believing in herself, a woman loves herself, a seditious act in the woman-hating world of patriarchy. In loving herself, a woman also creates the primal I-Thou relationship, which is the pattern for all empowering relationships—that is, all loving relationships. In loving herself, a woman shows herself to be and relates to herself as a subject and not an object.

Speaking to the necessity for love, hooks (1989) says,

> In reconceptualizing and reformulating strategies for future feminist movement, we need to concentrate on the politicization of love . . . in a critical discussion where love can be understood as a powerful force that challenges and resists domination. . . . That aspect of feminist revolution that calls women to love womanness, that calls men to resist dehumanizing concepts of masculinity, is an essential part of the struggle. (pp. 26–27)

The assumption of personal responsibility for self- and social change must involve, for women, a conscious choice to be their own protectors. Women have been told to rely on men for protection, and this reliance is reinforced through socialization into gender role behaviors and supported through reliance on institutionalized male protectors such as police and the military. Every aspect of male-dominated society, in fact, projects the message that not only do women need protection, but that their only competent protectors are men. To successfully assume responsibility for changing themselves and the conditions of oppression, women must believe in their power and act on it to protect themselves and other women from personal and social harm. Assuming this responsibility involves, perhaps, the most fundamental shift of all in consciousness and volition for women.

A shift of this magnitude presents the possibility for women to leave abusive situations, fight abuse, and preserve their own lives and those of others. For example, in domestic violence, women are held accountable for the protection of their children, but in reality women often lack the resources—economic, legal, physical or emotional—to be protectors. By taking on the role of protector, a woman becomes aware of what needs to change for her actually to protect herself and others.

Taking on the responsibility to protect self and others is a crucial empowering act for women because it is, at once, an act of resistance to gender norms and expectations and a fundamental assertion of the right to be and to live. More than an act of self-sufficiency or independence, the act of taking on the role of protector represents an existential declaration of one's worth, so that attacks on one's body or soul will be met with speech and action rather than silence and paralysis.

EMPOWERMENT IN PRACTICE

In light of the oppressive forces that effectively disempower women, where can social workers find examples of programs or strategies that aim at empowering women? Since the 1970s, thousands of organizations and programs have been developed by women and for women to bring about changed lives and end oppression on many levels. Empowerment as a philosophy and a goal has been a foundation of almost every effort within the women's movement to realize the liberation of women from oppressive structures and beliefs. One such program, which I think especially illustrates the concepts discussed in this chapter, is the organization *Model Mugging*, or as it is known in some locations, *Powerful Choices*, *A-Step*, or *Intu-Action*.

Model Mugging

Model Mugging was created several years ago by Matt Thomas, a karate expert, who was enraged by the rapes of two women friends who had training in karate but could not fight off an attacker. In his anger, he realized that he "couldn't always be there to rescue people, that true self defense demanded that women defend themselves" ("Kicking and Screaming," p. 63). The program teaches women how to channel their fear and anger into self-defensive acts designed to disable their attacker, showing women how to transform a freeze response into an action response. This course is built on an awareness that men attack women differently from the way they attack other men, a difference not addressed in traditional martial arts or self-defense courses. Model Mugging teaches women how to use their areas of greatest physical strength, which for most women lie in the lower body, to protect themselves fully. The empowerment-based program operates under the assumption that transformation requires

1. An experience of safety that allows a great risking
2. An experience of success that encourages more risking

3. Acknowledgment that the success comes from one's own power and nowhere else (Cirie, 1990)

At its core, Model Mugging exemplifies the process of consciousness raising for women in which women fully acknowledge their vulnerability to male violence but can confront that reality by believing in their own ability to protect themselves and others. This program does not engender a false sense of security in terms of the risk of sexual assault in our society; rather, it encourages a realistic appraisal of risk and a sense of shared fate with all women. The acknowledgment of the true risk of being a woman enables women to bond with one another and to encourage each other toward the development of the skills and knowledge necessary for self-defense and safety. Research has verified that though participants of the program recognize that the overall risk of attack has not changed, they feel empowered and liberated by having acquired the skills necessary to fend off an attack (Ozer & Bandura, 1990).

Model Mugging incorporates many critical aspects of the empowerment model, including the following:

1. Self-defense training takes place in a highly supportive atmosphere where women encourage each other in the successful disabling of the attacker.

2. Integral to the act of self defense is the use of the woman's voice to authoritatively assert her resistance. She does this by saying "No!" in a loud voice that comes from her center. As she says "No," the other women say it with her. This group support not only gives her strength, but also validates her right to say "No" and provides a memory of support that she can take with her into any future violent encounter.

3. As women, the instructors for the program model empowerment by going through the same surprise attacks the learners must successfully negotiate. In so doing, they become an example of how women can emerge as victors rather than victims.

4. The attack situation is modeled on a realistic appraisal of the forms that men's violence take and that effectively disable women, such as the use of profanity to demoralize women in the attack. The setting of the attack itself, whether outdoors or in, standing or pinned down, is chosen by the woman, giving her the opportunity to conquer her own worst fear.

5. Women receive the opportunity to experience their real power not only to fight off an attack, but also to hurt and disable their attacker; that is, to deliver a knockout punch.

6. That men act as the attackers creates a realistic instance of oppression for women; it also suggests a model for how men can

actively participate in the empowerment of women. Men do this by acknowledging in a real way their role as victimizers and oppressors and doing what needs to be done to encourage powerful actions by women.

7. In the program, the route to power involves restoring a vital connection to the strength of a woman's body, thereby making the body a subject rather than an object. This embodied empowerment shows thought and action united in an act of self-preservation and integrity.

According to the testimony of women who have completed the program, the self-confidence gained in the area of self-defense affects other areas of their lives. The program's literature alludes to many of the concepts discussed earlier in this chapter. For instance, one participant describes how her own empowerment is related to the empowerment of all women: "I believe that the only way we can end oppression of women is if each of us takes control of our own lives. We *can* make changes. I certainly see the changes in myself. I never before realized how much power I have within me, and how strong my will to survive is" (Zinnon, 1990).

In most respects, the paradigm represented in this program conveys the essence of women's general empowerment. Though the program tends to focus on victims of sexual assault, I suggest that the emphasis on finding voice, physical power, and responsibility for one's own protection are fundamental to any empowerment agenda for women. Whether or not this particular program is used, I believe that these emphases could help women of all ages, starting from early childhood. Moving from fear to anger to empowered action is the fundamental transformation that all women must undergo to live freely and safely.

Empowerment for Victims of Domestic Violence

The battered women's movement was one of the earliest outgrowths of the 1970s women's movement. Programs and services for battered women grew astronomically during the early 1970s and 1980s (Schechter, 1982). The empowerment-oriented shelter movement exemplifies the use of consciousness-raising techniques in empowering women who have been abused and battered. As Schechter (1982) states,

> Before the growth of shelters, many people viewed battered women as passive, dependent, or aberrant. Shelters offered the supportive framework through which thousands of women turned "personal" problems into political ones, relieved themselves of self-blame, and called attention to the sexism that left millions of women violently victimized.

> Temporarily freed from threats of retaliation and danger, battered
> women in shelters could display their long-ignored energy, rage, and
> coping abilities and reveal their similarity to all women. (p. 2)

The Eastside Domestic Violence Program (EDVP) of the Seattle metropolitan area offers one example of an empowerment-oriented program for battered women and their children. Begun in 1982 with a support group and two safe homes, the program now includes several safe homes and support groups, as well as other services such as a children's counseling program, a transition program for battered women, groups for adolescent victims of domestic violence, services for the hearing impaired, and legal advocacy. Early in its development, EDVP began offering training on domestic violence to local police departments and other community agencies. The mission of EDVP is to provide direct services and advocacy for victims of domestic violence and to change societal attitudes and institutional behaviors that perpetuate violence.

The empowerment philosophy of this program for battered women centers on an awareness of oppression based on race, sex, age, class, sexual orientation, and disability. Recognizing the interlocking nature of oppression, this program acknowledges that domestic violence requires a comprehensive, coordinated response. They therefore work toward building coalitions with other organizations and community groups to promote advocacy and education concerning domestic violence. Empowerment within this program occurs through advocacy-based counseling, described as "The involvement of a client with an advocate counselor in an individual, family, or group session with the primary focus on safety planning and on empowerment of the client through reinforcing the client's autonomy and self-determination" (Eastside Domestic Violence Program, n.d.).

The advocate counselor facilitates immediate emotional and physical support; reestablishes self-esteem and self-awareness; identifies problems, choices, and goals; and helps victims take an active part in their own recovery. Of course, confidentiality and safety are central to the clients' empowerment. Further, rather than try to make decisions for clients, counselors support them in the decisions they make for themselves.

Within a small-group setting, consciousness raising occurs through education and the sharing of stories among the women. The advocate counselors provide labels for the women's abusive experiences, which leads to increased awareness of violence, reduces self-blame and shame, and eases the sense of craziness they feel when trying to understand what has happened to them. As one participant explained to me, "I felt empowered when I left because I knew what to call it, and I had ideas and plans for keeping myself safe" (name withheld, personal communication, March 22, 1995).

Beyond the Personal

Women who participate in Model Mugging and in the domestic violence programs offered by EDVP experience change mostly on the personal level. Changes in individual women tend to ripple throughout society: As women change themselves, their relationships, both personal and institutional, also begin to change. However, this kind of program, though entirely necessary and appropriate, stops short of making the kind of political and social changes necessary for full empowerment.

The need for women to work together for large-scale social changes has never been greater. Hard-won improvements for women are being whittled back in this age of backlash and government retrenchment. While continued efforts towards empowering women as a group have never been more necessary, the enormity of the task has never seemed more daunting. One can only blanch in realizing that *The Year of the Woman*, in breathtaking swiftness, became the year of the *Contract with America*. To take the empowerment of women past vision to political reality, practitioners committed to the empowerment of women must be willing to do the following:

1. They must commit to making women the center of their support and analysis. They need to be women-centered (Lerner, 1986) for their own support needs and as a lens through which they view their practice. In this way, practitioners can begin to see beyond distorted views of social reality. Social workers, for example, need to acknowledge fully and integrate into their practice the fact that women make up an overwhelming majority of clients as well as the profession itself. But acknowledging this fact is not enough. In working toward empowerment, practitioners must see women as a strength and a source of new wisdom and solutions.

2. Practitioners cannot do the work of empowerment alone. They must have the support and encouragement of women to maintain their commitment to struggle, to increase their stores of energy, and to mount a concerted effort to change institutions, beliefs, and the culture itself. Because this support must include the voices and insights of *all* women, practitioners must bring to the center the lives and experiences of the most marginalized women —women of color, lesbians, women with disabilities, and women of low income and no income.

3. One woman cannot do everything, but one woman can do something. That is, each woman, acting in an empowered way, can make changes in individual lives and in the larger society. Social work, for example, offers inspiring models of women with a vision of what could be, who did what needed to be done to bring about that vision—Jane Addams, Florence Kelly, and Bertha Capen Reynolds, to name a few. Many thousands of women follow their example every day in less publicized ways. Each woman needs to believe in her unique contribution and take the risk to act on her own vision.

No doubt, many programs throughout the world incorporate these and other principles of an empowerment paradigm for women. A third example of an empowerment-oriented program is unusual because, although run by a social worker, it is a church. I present it here because it illustrates how both the personal and the political aspects of empowerment for women can be implemented in practice.

Empowerment for Homeless Women

In Seattle, one social worker, Jean Kim, has waged a coordinated effort to improve the lives of immigrant and homeless women. A homeless war refugee in Korea, Kim immigrated to the United States in 1970. Since she earned her M.S.W. in St. Louis, she has worked in the mental health field as a therapist and social worker. In 1987, she became the second woman ordained by the Presbyterian Church/USA. In 1991, she fulfilled her dream of opening a women-only church, the Church of Mary Magdalene. Here, she incorporates an empowerment approach that includes the spiritual dimension she believes traditional clinical approaches do not offer (Strickland, 1995). Having committed her life to working with women who find themselves in the homeless and destitute situation she transcended, Kim describes her work as sharing with other women the empowerment she has experienced (personal communication, February 1995).

Kim's work involves empowerment on the personal, interpersonal, political, and spiritual levels. The central aspect of empowerment in her work with homeless women involves restoring pride, self-worth, and dignity, as well as helping them become more productive (the Church of Mary Magdalene, n. d.). The specific empowerment strategies are holistic in the sense that activities and services encompass every aspect of their lives in which their dignity was formerly denied and in which they were formerly powerless.

The numerous activities and services offered follow a structured social-club model, often led by volunteers from the community. Every activity has an empowerment theme and purpose. Though skill-building activities such as sewing and typing are offered, these skills are intended to empower women to see and restore gifts and talents that have lain dormant or been denied. The skill-building and craft activities also focus on art as a way to help women express their goodness and beauty. The women also receive opportunities to sell their creations, which not only provides spending money, but also demonstrates that what they produce has value.

The church service serves as the linchpin of the empowerment paradigm at Mary Magdalene. Every aspect of the day-long service works to undo the harm done to homeless women through abuse in relationships and on the street. In contrast to the way religion has traditionally dealt with women, Kim's approach is to empower women in worship by actively encouraging their refusal to be treated as inferior and empowering them to be their own theologians. Kim offers a "talk-back" sermon during the service. As she says, women have been preached at all their lives so it is time for women to use their own spiritual talents and insights.

The liturgy provides opportunities for the women to express their angers and frustrations. This is done through singing and through a ritual in which their specific angers about being poor, homeless, or sick are written down then burned. This ritual is central to empowerment because, for many of these women, acting out anger and resentment elsewhere has often led to their being denied housing in shelter and residences. After this offering, the women write down all the positive things in their lives—their dreams, their visions, their belief in themselves as good and loved—as an affirmation of their goodness and dignity. An integral part of empowerment for these women is building a sense of community and belonging that is both spiritual and social.

Empowerment in this setting also includes concrete steps that women can take to move out of homelessness and to restore individual dignity. One program, for instance, is the "ministry of the lingerie," launched to provide women, many for the first time in years, with new and properly sized underwear. Other such offerings include use of a telephone for personal and job calls, nutrition and exercise classes, medical consultations, and celebrations of birthdays, sobriety, and reaching personal goals.

Embedded in these activities is a central focus on housing as the source of empowerment for homeless women—indeed, for all people. In making housing the source of healing and empowerment, Kim's ministry aims intently at raising the consciousness of homeless women and society so that homelessness is seen as political, social, and economic oppression —the sin of society, not of the women. In so doing, the women of her congregation can free themselves of self-blame and shame regarding their situation and can take action to change the situation. The women of the congregation are invited to take part on the political level by letter writing, picketing, and other efforts toward gaining housing for homeless women. As part of her ministry, Kim educates homeless women and the public about the ways that homelessness, prostitution, and sweat-shop exploitation among immigrant women form part of the worldwide sexual and economic oppression of women—an oppression that must end before any women can be liberated. The ministry challenges communities, churches, and policy makers to see their own part in maintaining the conditions that foster homelessness and to take the steps necessary to find or create homes for the homeless.

Within this empowerment model that links spirituality and social justice, the participants—homeless women, volunteers, the community, and Kim herself—act as full partners in the work. The women are seen as sisters, rather than clients, and empowerment is based on the recognition that acts of love and solidarity among women bring them power.

CONCLUSION

Women come to the practice setting bearing the scars of oppression. In this chapter I have attempted to outline briefly what I see as some of the commonalities of women's lives. Empowerment practice for women necessitates a working knowledge of the many forms that oppression takes—sexism, racism, classism, heterosexism, ableism—and how these affect the individual and collective lives of women. This knowledge also includes understanding how women come to the practice setting faced with double-bind situations and in a state of self-alienation. Practitioners can take the role of educator in helping to make clear the links between women's state of being and the larger social forces that mold and oppress women. Although this role can appear as another version of the "expert" role, practitioners do not act as experts. Knowledge of women's oppression is fundamentally derived from the practitioner's own experiences of consciousness raising and commitment to her or his own and others' empowerment.

For practitioners then, empowerment is more than a goal—it is a way of being. Those committed to working toward the empowerment of all women must have a commitment to, and faith in, their own empowerment and must live it out: to speak the truth of one's life in one's own voice and work collectively to create that possibility for all. To live as if empowered is to replace the concept of professional practice with the notion of revolutionary praxis—the authentic union of action and reflection (Freire, 1985). Lived empowerment suggests the following:

1. To work *with* women in a full relationship, recognizing their fully human and self-authenticating lives.
2. To reflect the power that still remains hidden in the lives of women. By admiring and respecting them, practitioners can reflect the inner power of women who don't know or who don't believe that they have power. This process lies at the heart of a strengths-based perspective in which the untapped potential of clients emerges. Admiration, as Freire (1985) points out, is fundamental to understanding anything and any person. *Admiration* has the same root as *mirror*, indicating that in the process of admiring another, one holds up a mirror that reveals the inner self of the other. This original empowering act paradoxically empowers

another through that other person's *glimpse* (a brief sudden shining; related to *gleam*: a brief manifestation, as of hope or understanding) of their own true power and self.

3. To liberate one's own voice and the voices of women that have been silenced and suppressed. Practitioners must resolve to speak out on their own behalf and that of others in a voice reflecting their own experiences, struggles, and victories. Because finding and using that voice is necessarily a creative act, workers need less emphasis on the tried and true and more on the new. Further, in finding this voice, practitioners must struggle to be people of their words, bearing witness to the ongoing and lifelong struggle to transform themselves and the world (hooks, 1989).

4. To liberate the many and varied voices of women by listening: To hear is to empower. Hearing the voice of another takes effort, concentration, and the willingness to affirm difference. As hooks (1989) states, "While feminist women (many of whom are white) often say that they want to hear from women who have not spoken, they do not always want to hear what we have to say" (p. 154). Truly hearing another person means that one cannot be hung up on one's own labels. For instance, although I may believe that *feminism* is integral to empowerment for women, it helps me to know that the word may be a barrier for others.

Practitioners must be willing to listen, hear, consider, and affirm each woman's act of naming and of defining her own reality. They must also work with women as well as each other to create that possibility for all. Additional practice principles of empowerment for women include the following:

1. Practitioners must acknowledge and understand the role of oppression in the lives of women. This understanding will grow as practitioners themselves undergo the process of personal and political consciousness raising.

2. The empowerment of women requires an environment of safety, trust, and support in which women are encouraged to believe in themselves and their own reality and to find their voice to speak their truth. The presence of other women is integral to the creation of this environment.

3. Women must be given concrete opportunities to experience their own capability, strength, and worth. For instance, women who have experienced physical assault should be encouraged to find ways to experience bodily and emotional strength, and women who have experienced social indignities and assaults, such as homelessness, poverty, or racism, should be presented with opportunities to regain dignity and worth.

4. Though empowerment for women is fundamentally related to autonomy and self-determination, women must also work together to change themselves and society. Rather than work merely for individual solutions to individual problems, practitioners must find ways to bring women together and to work with women clients toward social change.

5. The many roles of the practitioner in empowerment practice include educator, supporter, advocate, activist, option clarifier, facilitator of concrete experiences of power, and model of lived empowerment.

REFERENCES

Bartky, S. L. (1990). *Femininity and domination: Studies in the phenomenology of oppression*. New York: Routledge.

Belenky, M. F., Clinchy, B. M., Goldberger, N. R., & Tarule, J. M. (1986). *Women's ways of knowing: The development of self, voice, and mind*. New York: Basic Books.

Bricker-Jenkins, M., & Hooyman, N. R. (1986). A feminist world view: Ideological themes from the feminist movement. In M. Bricker-Jenkins & N. R. Hooyman (Eds.), *Not for women only: Social work practice for a feminist future* (pp. 7–22). Silver Spring, Maryland: National Association of Social Workers.

Bricker-Jenkins, M., Hooyman, N., & Gottlieb, N. (1991). *Feminist social work practice in clinical settings*. Newbury Park, CA: Sage.

The Church of Mary Magdalene. (n. d.). Programmatic materials. (Available from the Church of Mary Magdalene, P.O. Box 359, Seattle, WA 98111.)

Cirie, J. (1990). "Transformation at the deepest level . . ." *Model Mugging News*, 4(1), 7.

Collins, P. H. (1990). *Black feminist thought: Knowledge, consciousness, and the politics of empowerment*. New York: Routledge.

Dworkin, A. (1983). *Right-wing women*. New York: Perigee

Eastside Domestic Violence Program (EDVP). (n. d.). Program description and brochures. (Available from Eastside Domestic Violence Program, P.O. Box 6398, Bellevue, WA 98008.)

Freire, P. (1985). *The politics of education*. New York: Bergin & Garvey.

Frye, M. (1983). *The politics of reality*. Trumansburg, NY: Crossing Press.

Gilligan, C. (1982). *In a different voice: Psychological theory and women's development*. Cambridge, MA: Harvard University Press.

Gutiérrez, L. M. (1987). *Toward a model of empowerment for social work practice*. Unpublished paper. University of Michigan, Ann Arbor.

Gutiérrez, L. M. (1990). Working with women of color: An empowerment perspective. *Social Work*, 35(2), 149–153.

hooks, b. (1989). *Talking back: Thinking feminist, thinking black*. Boston: South End.

Kicking and screaming, women master Matt Thomas' get-tough tactics for self-defense. (1988, July 18). *People Weekly*, pp. 62–64.

Lerner, G. (1986). *The creation of patriarchy*. New York: Oxford University Press.

MacKinnon, C. A. (1982). Feminism, marxism, method, and the state: An agenda for theory. *Signs, 7*(3), 515–544.

MacKinnon, C. A. (1989). *Toward a feminist theory of the state*. Cambridge, MA: Harvard University Press.

Mies, M. (1989). Towards a methodology for feminist research. In G. Bowles & R. D. Klein (Eds.), *Theories of women's studies* (pp. 117–139). London: Routledge.

Ozer, E. M., & Bandura, A. (1990). Mechanisms governing empowerment effects: A self-efficacy analysis. *Journal of Personality and Social Psychology, 58*(3), 472–486.

Schechter, S. (1982). *Women and male violence: The visions and struggles of the battered women's movement*. Boston: South End Press.

Shreve, A. (1989). *Women together, women alone: The legacy of the consciousness raising movement*. New York: Fawcett Columbine.

Solomon, B. B. (1976). *Black empowerment: Social work in oppressed communities*. New York: Columbia University.

Strickland, D. (1995, January 2). Minister brings church to women on the streets. *Seattle Times*, pp. B2–B3.

Swift, C., and Levin, G. (1987). Empowerment: An emerging mental health technology. *Journal of Primary Prevention, 8*(1/2), 71–94.

Young-Eisendrath, P., & Wehr, D. (1990). The fallacy of individualism and reasonable violence against women. In J. C. Brown & C. R. Bohn (Eds.), *Christianity, patriarchy, and abuse: A feminist critique* (pp. 117–138). New York: Pilgrim.

Zinnon, K. (1990). From graduates. *Model Mugging News, 4*(1), 7.

Chapter 3

EMPOWERING POOR COMMUNITIES
OF COLOR: A SELF-HELP MODEL

Margo Okazawa-Rey, Ed.D.

San Francisco State University, San Francisco, California

INTRODUCTION

"Communities of color" is a generic term used to name large, diverse groups of African Americans, Asian Americans, Latinos, and Native Americans who comprise various racial, ethnic, and class backgrounds and who live in many parts of the United States. Social workers and care providers most often come into contact with people in poor, urban communities of color. Typically, these professionals are trained to prioritize the direct service needs of clients such as material or counseling needs. As such, practitioners focus on the exigencies of delivering such services in this era of diminishing resources and accept the prevailing paradigm of locating the source of poor people's problems within individual psychology. Neither emphasis advances the notion or practice of empowering whole communities, although rhetoric about "empowerment" abounds in the human services and health care fields (Simon, 1994).

This chapter describes one way that social workers and health care providers at community-based health centers, in partnership with their clients, are responding to the multiple needs of poor people of color in an urban area by using a self-help practice model. The goal of this chapter is twofold. First, it will show the importance of acknowledging and addressing the connections between the direct and nondirect service issues related to the overall needs of their clients. Second, this chapter will assert the potentially powerful, and ultimately healing, alliance that can result when professionals and clients collaborate as capable and knowledgeable partners. In this discussion, I will use the work of the Grandparents Who Care Support

Network of San Francisco to illustrate my points. At the end, I will delineate practice principles that one may apply to other communities of color.

THE NATURE OF
THE PROBLEM[1]

The crack-cocaine epidemic affects practically every aspect of existence in poor, urban, African-American communities throughout the nation. The most dramatic effects of the epidemic are clearly visible: Infants simultaneously inhale their first breaths and experience withdrawal from drugs; youngsters "run" illegal substances for their older peers and "mentors"; men murder one another over deals gone sour; women sell themselves wholesale for a smoke of dope.[2] The less dramatic, often publicly invisible consequence of the crack-cocaine plague is the countless number of grandparents who must care for their grandchildren because the parents cannot.

Although in African-American communities the extended-family's care of children is not new, the current trend defies traditional arrangements. For example, whereas parents of the children used to be active partners in the child-rearing, crack-using parents of this generation of children and infants participate often erratically or not at all.

Social workers and health care providers in urban areas were among the first group of professionals to identify this wave of grandparents suddenly becoming parents. For instance, health care providers working in San Francisco observed a dramatic increase in the number of missed doctors' appointments and acute aggravation of previously controlled chronic physical illnesses, such as diabetes and high blood pressure. It seemed that the added daily child care and homemaking responsibilities often prevented the patients from keeping medical appointments, and the stress related to their new roles aggravated their illnesses. For example, having to transport small children by public transit to school or doctors' appointments generates stress, especially for an elderly person. According to the providers at San Francisco

---

[1]From "Grandparents Who Care: An Empowerment Model of Health Care for African Americans," by M. Okazawa-Rey. In A. Dula and S. Goering (Eds.), *It Just Ain't Fair: The Ethics of Health Care for African Americans*. Copyright © 1994 Annette Dula and Sara Goering. Reproduced with permission of Greenwood Publishing Group, Inc., Westport, CT.

[2]A smokable form of cocaine, crack is highly addictive and inexpensive. Available in most states in the country, its principal users are urban African Americans. Since its introduction into urban areas, crack has been associated with substantial increases in drug-related arrests, adolescent gang violence, and incidence of neonatal cocaine addiction and syphilis, gonorrhea, and other sexually transmitted diseases. For more detailed information, see Nobles, Goddard, and Cavil, 1987.

General Hospital, these patients identified the increased stress as a direct outgrowth of complicated family arrangements, violence associated with the drug-using lifestyles of their adult children, and the assumption of primary or sole responsibility for their grandchildren (Miller & Trupin, 1990).

Poor and working-class, middle-aged and elderly African-American women constitute a significant proportion of grandparents who have assumed such responsibility. These women range in age from the mid-forties to the early seventies, many are single by divorce or death, and many were employed full- or part-time, in traditional female service occupations and professional occupations, until forced to quit because of difficulties such as unaffordable child care. Miller and Trupin (1990) cite the most common reasons for the women taking over their grandchildren's care:

1. Involvement of the adult children with crack cocaine or alcohol and the resultant neglect of their children
2. Incarceration of the adult children on drug- or alcohol-related charge(s)
3. Reluctance to surrender their grandchildren to the state foster care system

After having raised their own children, often under difficult circumstances and sometimes not long ago, the grandmothers are ambivalent about their new role. On the one hand, they believe themselves to be fully capable and willing to fulfill their obligations to family, and they are satisfied knowing the grandchildren are now living in safe, comfortable, and loving surroundings. Many are willing to take on the responsibility of parenting because of their strong belief in keeping the family intact—not surrendering the children to state social services officials—and their undying faith in the ability of their adult children eventually to resume fully functional lives. On the other hand, these grandmothers also are frustrated and angry about having lost their independence—even on the most basic level, such as private bathroom time—and their hopes of fulfilling personal dreams. As one grandmother exclaimed, "I was ready to go on a two-week cruise before I got these grandchildren!"

Though the initial point of contact between the grandparents and professional providers is health-related, the problems experienced by the former extend far beyond particular health concerns. They desperately need day care, special education services, transportation, respite care, and money. They must learn how to negotiate complicated and sometimes resistant social service, educational, and criminal justice bureaucracies. Finally, they must address the intrafamilial issues related to the problems, such as dealing with the erratic behaviors of their drug-using adult children or the emotional injuries experienced by the grandchildren.

The needs of grandparents served by urban community health centers, therefore, seriously challenge the existing modes of health care service delivery and tax the already meager resources available. Thus, given the changing nature of social problems in poor African-American communities, health care organizations can no longer simply address health concerns as isolated phenomena, just as schools in those communities can no longer focus only on the "Three 'Rs."

THE GRANDPARENTS' GROUP

Health and Illness:
The Context for the Group

Although in the 1940s the World Health Organization defined health as a "state of complete physical, mental, and social well-being" (Germaine, 1984, p. 34), this holistic view is criticized as an unreachable goal for individuals and society. The prevailing conceptions of health and illness, and responses to it, reflect the values of Western medicine. Defined solely in biomedical terms, *health* is the absence of disease, and *disease* is a departure from the norm of biochemical variables (Engel, 1977). These definitions inhibit "the view of the patient as a total person in a total environment by overlooking the personal and environmental dimensions in health" (Germaine, 1984, p. 34).

Recently, some in the health care establishment have begun to rethink these definitions. Ahmed, Kolker, and Coelho (1979), for example, define health as "*a multidimensional process* involving the well-being of the whole person in the context of his environment" (p. 9). Similarly, Germaine (1984) has added the concept of "illness" to the disease model: "Illness is a sociopsychological concept [that] includes the cultural meaning of the discomfort or pain to the patient and her family" (p. 34).

Germaine cites Kleinman as suggesting that in situations where only "disease" is treated, care will be less satisfactory to the patient and less clinically effective than in situations where both "disease" and "illness" are treated together. The problems of both are complementary, and both require intervention for effective care (Germaine, 1984, p. 35).

Early on, Mechanic (1970, 1972) took the concept of illness a step further. He has cited two important aspects of illness behavior: (1) the nature and quality of the symptoms of the disease and illness and how these affect the daily function of the person and (2) the connections between the symptoms and environmental factors such as culture, life circumstances, age, gender, and access (geographic and social) to the health care facility (Mechanic, 1976a, 1976b). Although a lengthy review lies beyond this chapter, other bodies of medical sociology literature suggest the necessity of considering the social and economic conditions surrounding patients' lives if they are to be served effectively (for example, see Duff, 1993; Fox, 1989).

Two health care providers, Doriane Miller and Sue Trupin, took seriously this critical need to address the entire complex of issues—biomedical, social, cultural, and economic—surrounding the lives of grandparenting patients at San Francisco General Hospital. In 1990, they founded a formal support network, Grandparents Who Care, to help address them.

Workings and Philosophy

Ms. Johnson,[3] a typical participant of Grandparents Who Care, is a middle-aged, working-class, African-American woman. She recently shouldered the responsibility for her three grandchildren after witnessing their neglect by her adult son and his wife, who actively use crack cocaine. Her "babies" are ages 6 months, 2, and 3. At her first meeting, she described her reason for attending:

> I started havin' a lot of problems after the babies came to live with me. I tried to talk to the doctor about it but you know how they are. [She waves her arms above her head as she speaks.] They're kind of up there with it. I'm glad he told me about this meeting, though.

Ms. Johnson, who is facing "a lot of problems," feels at once a desire to confide in her physician and a sense of distance and alienation from him. Many times, patients like Ms. Johnson disclose to "The Doctor" problems they would not disclose to anyone else because physicians are often perceived as godlike. Chances are that the physician, trained in mainstream medicine and working in an already overused health center, has neither the inclination nor the time to discuss in detail problems unrelated directly to a patient's physical condition. Fortunately, Ms. Johnson's physician knew of the existence of Grandparents Who Care and referred her there.

As stated earlier, Grandparents Who Care was founded by two health care providers who observed firsthand the physical, social, economic, and emotional toll exacted on grandparents like Ms. Johnson. The founders intended the support groups to take over where the health care services ended.

The philosophy of Grandparents Who Care rests on the following assumptions:

1. The health problems of individuals are very much related to their family/home/community situations
2. Cultural and institutional barriers often impede access to necessary health care and other services

---

[3]Only pseudonyms are used throughout this chapter to insure patient confidentiality.

3. Professional health care services alone do not adequately or appropriately meet all these needs
4. Individual and collective empowerment—as African Americans, grandparents, and community members—is essential to maintaining one's health

Currently, the organization comprises five support groups, with each group meeting for one and a half hours weekly and attended by anywhere from 2 to 25 grandparents; not surprisingly, an overwhelming majority of them are women. One group specifically serves adolescents in the care of their grandparents.

The groups are based on a social support intervention model that provides emotional, informational, and practical support and are cofacilitated by two health care professionals such as a nurse, doctor, or social worker. On this base, each group develops its own features from the perspectives, skills, and personalities of the facilitators and the needs of the participants. A volunteer board, made up of grandparents, community members, and professional health care providers, advises the organization in matters such as policy formulation. Two neighborhood health centers and San Francisco General Hospital provide the rooms in which the meetings take place. In the following pages, I will provide a detailed description of one of these groups, which I cofacilitated with another African-American social worker.

Inside One Group

Our group has met since March 1991, although active outreach and recruitment efforts began in the early winter. It has a total membership of approximately 20 women and 1 man (probably the only male member of the entire network). Of these members, there is an active core group of approximately 8 women, with 3 of the longest-standing members having emerged as leaders within our group and the larger network.

Two features of this group make it particularly appropriate for meeting the needs of poor and working-class African-American women. First is the implicitly Afrocentric feminist content and approach used in the group. Second is the explicit commitment to empowerment.

Through content and process of the group, rooted in Afrocentric feminist epistemology, we confront, resist, and redefine Western male conceptions of legitimate knowledge and notions of leadership and expertise. The criteria for expertise, the power of decision making, and the "text" for discussions and exchanges in the groups flow from and toward the participants (Hill-Collins, 1990). As facilitators, we validate and attempt to deepen the belief in the grandmothers as experts about their lives and the communities in which they live. This expertise includes their knowledge of the numerous institutions, such as the city/county social services department and the school and criminal justice systems, derived from having to negotiate them in their daily lives.

The grandmothers' knowledge base is uncovered both deliberately and inadvertently. For example, when one woman faces a particular problem with her grandchild in the school system, another one will describe her dealings with this system and offer suggestions concerning the most effective ways to intercede. Or, in telling her personal experiences, a grandmother will display the range of information, knowledge, and skills she possesses. The professional facilitators attend to the more technical aspects of a problem or an issue. We, for example, use our contacts in the educational system to secure special services or to help move grandmothers through the bureaucratic red tape. Hence, the professional serves as a consultant rather than as an all-knowing leader.

The group uses primarily a modified version of the "call-and-response" mode of communication. In this kind of dialogue, "long extant in Afrocentric . . . tradition whereby power dynamics are fluid, everyone has a voice, but everyone must listen and respond to other voices in order to be allowed to remain in the community" (Collins, 1990, p. 237). Any member can call; any respond. Whoever knows about a subject or has information from any source, especially personal experience, finds encouragement to share it.

Often, the meetings assume an in-the-kitchen/on-the-porch/on-the-street/in-church tone. Each meeting begins with members "checking in" to inform each other of any significant problems and victories they experienced during the previous week, or simply to say, "Hi." Next, any woman with particularly pressing or significant concerns, as defined by the woman herself, takes the floor. At any point, other participants may ask for clarification, offer a suggestion, or add her own experiences to the story. Again, the facilitator primarily serves as technical consultant, traffic controller, and reflector—that is, someone who can mirror observations and perceptions from a relatively detached position. A typical meeting flows as follows:

Facilitator: *Good morning, ladies. How is everyone this morning? And what good thing did you do for yourselves during the week?*

                 The women slowly respond by describing briefly their condition and an act of self-care they performed during the previous week. Before everyone gets a chance to report, one grandmother is ready to share a problem she is facing.

Ms. Daniels: *I have something I wanna talk about. My grandson is having a lot of problems with his teacher at school. . . . They've suspended [him] again. . . . They don't know what to do with him. You know he's smart but he's not reading at his right level and he keeps having trouble with his teacher Ms. Anderson, a young white lady. . . . I'm not being prejudiced but I think it's somethin' racial.*

Ms. Jackson: *Un huh! These schools just don't know how to deal with these black children, especially them boys. When my son was in school, they used to call me all the time saying he's been suspended.*

Ms. Daniels: *I've been thinking about taking him out of that school.*

Ms. Brown: *Didn't he just get to that school this year? Why did they move him from that other one anyway? I remember you sayin' last year that he was doin' real good there.*

Ms. Daniels: *I don't know why they moved him. They just did.*

Ms. Brown: *They can't do that without your permission, although they will try to slip stuff past you. You have rights as a parent. They can't do anything with your child without you knowin' it or you givin' permission.*

A chorus of "Amen," "Yes, that's right!" and other responses echoes throughout the room. A detailed and lively discussion concerning the rights of parents, the faults of the schools and school system, and the ill state of special-education programs in particular dominates the next 45 minutes of group time. The facilitator stops the action when everyone talks at once and one person begins to dominate the discussion.

Ms. Brown: *You know what we need is someone to come in and tell us how the whole thing around special ed works. We need a guest speaker who can explain to us what's going on and what we can do.*

Facilitator: *That's a good idea. I'll call "Advocates for Special Ed" to see when someone could come talk to us. Does anybody who didn't get a chance to check in yet want to do that now?*

The group meeting ends with the facilitator making a few summary statements and asking someone to pray, whereby spontaneous wording or the standard Lord's Prayer is said and most people hold hands.

ACTUALIZING THE GOAL OF EMPOWERMENT

Every day, the members of the network face the issue of powerlessness rooted in racial and economic inequality; the grandmothers experience the "triple jeopardy" of racial, class, and gender-based oppression. Thus, one of the essential goals of Grandparents Who Care is empowerment.

The contemporary roots of empowerment lie in the progressive social movements of the 1960s and 1970s, such as the Black Power, Women's, and Welfare Rights movements, all founded to transform oppressive conditions in U.S. society. This version of empowerment rested on the principle of self-determination: Individuals and communities have the right to determine their own fates. From this perspective, *empowerment* denoted both micro (personal) and macro (institutional) interventions to effect changes in the lives and communities of subordinated peoples, with these interventions geared ultimately toward progressive societal transformation. The concept had an explicitly political meaning even in the context of providing social services. Thus, in working with female survivors of rape, for example, professionals immediately addressed the physical and emotional traumas of the victim (micro). In public arenas such as the courts, professionals also challenged the asymmetrical power relations between men and women, as well as the societal approval of men violating the rights and integrity of women (macro).

Empowerment has become a basic organizing principle for addressing contemporary health issues and problems. Organizations working in the AIDS epidemic, such as ACT-UP, provide one example. Another, the National Black Women's Health Project (founded by Byllye Avery, recipient of the MacArthur Award), is based in Atlanta, Georgia, with self-help-group affiliates established throughout the nation. Of course, recovery and support groups that deal with addictions, breast cancer, and incest round out the list.

To suit mainstream interests, however, the term *empowerment* has been appropriated and diluted. For example, the so-called "me generation" of the 1980s employs the term to denote furthering individualistic interests. Another distortion is exemplified by the "men's movement" in which mostly white, middle-class men gather in support groups and at weekend retreats to reclaim their "rightful" place and role as the dominant members of society (Faludi, 1991). Even social service professionals sometimes use empowerment as the 1990s euphemism for "pull yourself up by your bootstraps." These examples merely "blame the victim," and promote the self-interests of those in the dominant group.

As one means toward empowerment, Grandparents Who Care has implemented a project to train grandparents to become group facilitators. This enables them to practice and assert formally their own leadership skills and, eventually, to have all the support groups become self-sufficient. Those seasoned members of a support group interested in becoming formal leaders receive training from professionals in the basic skills of support group facilitation. After the four-week training series, each works with a professional to establish a new group, including all the outreach and initial start-up work such as making individual contacts with prospective members, speaking to church groups, and following up on referrals from health centers.

Women also become empowered through active participation in political advocacy and lobbying. Currently, for example, most grandparents receive assistance, through the AFDC, limited not only in the amount of money dispensed, but also in covered services. Though the foster care system better meets the needs of the children, most grandparents do not qualify, because they are family care providers. As such, the grandmothers collaborated recently with a state legislator to pass a bill that would make it easier for them to receive payments and entitlements under the foster care system.

This change is particularly crucial. Many children require special medical, psychological, and educational services because they suffer from the combined effects of poor prenatal care and neglect. For instance, one member of our support group cares for a 4-year-old with a tracheotomy tube who requires trained medical assistance during many of his waking hours. Many of the other grandchildren need help with manifestations of developmental disorders.

Coauthored by the women and sponsored by the legislator, this bill reached the desk of the governor, who vetoed it. The grandparents, however, have used the experience of having succeeded to the extent they did as a collective referent for empowerment.

A final example of empowerment relates directly to the grandmothers' own health concerns. Through the education and support dispensed in the group, the women can now more easily connect their state of health to the circumstances of their daily lives. For example, when Ms. Turner arrived at one meeting, she was "lookin' tired," with puffy eyes and nasal tone. She stated during check-in that she almost did not attend the meeting because of "sinus problems" over the weekend and described, in a fairly detailed way, her symptoms. Afterwards, when members probed about her weekend, she disclosed that her grandchildren had been extremely distressed by an unexpected visit from their mother. Because of the visit, they had become unruly, which then caused Ms. Turner to exert added emotional and physical energy to quiet and comfort the children.

Initially, Ms. Turner talked of her physical symptoms and the family crisis as two unrelated incidents. During the course of the meeting, however, as the other women in the group told similar stories, she herself began to make a connection. In subsequent meetings, Ms. Turner could articulate her understanding of the connections between physical illness and emotional distress.

The examples just described offer a few specific ways that Grandparents Who Care attempts to actualize the goal of empowerment. As the current membership gains confidence and skills, and the network becomes stronger and more formalized, the possibilities for expanding the practice of empowerment multiply. For instance, grandparents might organize in their own neighborhoods to address the issue of drugs.

PRACTICE PRINCIPLES

In this chapter, I have provided one example of empowerment practice from which to draw specific principles that one could generalize to other communities of color. Before one does so, however, one should consider the following cautionary notes, some of which may be self-evident: (1) No community of color is monolithic. Specific ethnic, cultural, class, and geographic factors shape the experiences of its members. (2) Simply "being one" —that is, of the same racial or ethnic group as the identified community— does not necessarily make one suitable to be a social worker in that community. Issues of identity and identification, insider and outsider status, and other factors that make up one's social location come into play. Thus, for example, being Latino does not automatically make someone an effective worker in Latino communities; conversely, being non-Latino does not automatically preclude one from serving an important role in that community. Moreover, certain structural factors influence the power relations between professional and client, regardless of professionals' desires otherwise. (3) Finally, one should apply practice principles according to each specific context. This application requires what is referred to as *praxis* (Freire, 1973) and *reflective practice* (Schon, 1983), methods that involve the integration of action and reflection.

The practice principles I have attempted to illustrate are as follows:

1. Expand the prevailing definitions of personal and community problems, from addiction and mental illness to homelessness and poverty, to include micro, meso, and macro factors. Grandparents Who Care expanded the typical biomedical perspective of health to include as central issues the social, economic, and cultural factors that shape overall health. This perspective highlights not only physical diseases, but also the social problems that indirectly affect the health of individuals and how they deal, or do not deal, with their physical conditions. One must therefore address health concerns in the context of individuals' and communities' circumstances.

2. Honor and draw directly from clients' cultural backgrounds and personal experiences. For example, our support group used the call-and-response model of communicating, included prayer, and drew heavily from the grandparents' knowledge bases and experiences.

3. Analyze and understand the structural inequalities that affect the lives of people of color. Addressing the problems in their totality also requires one to understand that their roots lie deep in economic, social, and political inequality based on race, gender, class, etc. Thus, the grandparents in our group came to see, for example, that their children's addiction and criminal behavior may be related to an overwhelming sense of powerlessness and despair rather than simply liking "gettin' high." Or that their grandchildren's difficulties in school may be due to stigmatizing and tracking of children of color into less challenging classes.

4. Promoting collective support and action. The proverbial "power in numbers" is critical to the empowerment of oppressed peoples. A grandparent who had been isolated in her new role as parent found great solace in being with others facing similar obstacles and gained power from the emotions, knowledge, and understanding generated by the members. Moreover, after engaging in a specific task, such as working with a legislator to help draft a bill, the grandparents derived a real sense of agency: They could act on their own behalf with positive results.

CONCLUSION

In an era of diminishing economic resources for human services, one creative way to help offset the shortage is to view community members as resources. Concurrent with the retrenchment in government-sponsored services to people, however, a conservative backlash fights the efforts by oppressed populations, such as women and people of color, to bring about equality. Thus the extent of progress will depend on people's ability and willingness both to care for themselves and to organize as communities to bring about the necessary societal changes. The empowerment model I have just described presents one possible way to do both.

This model also raises important questions. What are the limits of empowerment? How does one ultimately address the contradictions created when members of two bodies holding unequal power—clients and professionals—attempt to relate as equals? How do the effects of internalized racism, sexism, and classism prevent one from even seeing some of those contradictions? What role should groups such as Grandparents Who Care play in creating a mass political movement, which this country's history has shown is the only viable way to transform the society as a whole?

REFERENCES

Ahmed, P. I., Kolker, A., & Coelho, G. V. (1979). Toward a new definition of health: An overview. In G. V. Coelho and P. I. Ahmed (Eds.), *Toward a new definition of health* (pp. 7–22). New York: Plenum.

Collins, P. H. (1990). *Black feminist thought: Knowledge, consciousness, and the politics of empowerment.* Boston: Unwyn Hyman.

Duff, K. (1993). *The alchemy of illness.* New York: Pantheon.

Engel, G. L. (1977, April 8). The need for a new medical model: A challenge for biomedicine. *Science, 196*(4286), 129–136.

Faludi, S. (1991). *Backlash: The undeclared war on American women.* New York: Crown Books.

Fox, R. (1989). *The sociology of medicine.* Englewood Cliffs, NJ: Prentice-Hall.

Freire, P. (1973). *Education for critical consciousness.* New York: Seabury.

Germaine, C. B. (1984). *Social work practice in health care: An ecological perspective.* New York: Free Press.

Greywolf, E., Ashley, P., & Reese, M. F. (1982). Physical health issues. In D. Belle (Ed.), *Lives in stress: Women and depression* (pp. 211–221). Beverly Hills, CA: Sage.

Mechanic, D. (1970). *The bureaucratization of medicine.* New York: Wiley.

Mechanic, D. (1972, May). Social psychological factors affecting the presentation of bodily complaints. *New England Journal of Medicine, 286,* 1132–1139.

Mechanic, D. (1976a). *The growth of bureaucratic medicine.* New York: Wiley.

Mechanic, D. (1976b, June). Stress, illness, and illness behavior. *Journal of Human Stress, 2,* 2–6.

Mechanic, D. (1977, August). Illness behavior, social adaptation, and the illness of illness: A comparison of educational and medical models. *Journal of Nervousness and Mental Disease, 165,* 79–87.

Mechanic, D., & Volkart, E. H. (1961). Stress, illness behavior, and medical diagnoses. *American Sociological Review, 26,* 51–58.

Miller, D., & Trupin, S. (1990). *Grandparents Who Care of San Francisco: A program summary.* San Francisco: Author.

Minkler, M., & Roe, K. M. (1993). *Grandmothers as caregivers: Raising children of the crack cocaine epidemic.* Beverly Hills, CA: Sage.

Nobles, W. W., Goddard, L., & Cavil, W. E. (1987). *The culture of drugs in the black community:* Oakland, CA: Black Family Institute.

Okazawa-Rey, M. (1994). Grandparents who care: An empowerment model of health care for African Americans. In A. Dula and S. Goering (Eds.), *It just ain't fair: The ethics of health care for African Americans.* Westport, CT: Greenwood Publishing Group.

Schon, D. A. (1983). *The reflective practitioner.* New York: Basic Books.

Simon, B. L. (1990). Rethinking empowerment. *Journal of Progressive Human Services, 1*(1), 27–40.

Chapter 4

EMPOWERMENT PRACTICE WITH
LESBIANS AND GAYS

Kathryn A. DeLois, Ph.D.
University of New England, Portland, Maine

INTRODUCTION

Lesbians and gays, both collectively and individually, are already actively involved in their own empowerment. Because of my own experience as a lesbian, in graduate school I engaged in a study of how women come to identify themselves as lesbian. The research was carried out with a nonclinical cohort of 30 self-identified lesbians (DeLois, 1993). The women I interviewed shared their stories of coming out, of self-discovery, of confronting and ultimately crossing social barriers that define and constrict sex roles in U.S. society. Each described the empowerment she had experienced in the process of "becoming more and more myself" (p. 54). These women, as well as other lesbians and gay men, have become empowered to the extent that they try to resist society's constricting norms.

In spite of the general fear and loathing that we as lesbians and gay men have inspired, we have developed our own culture, complete with music, literature, theatre, and film; we have our own businesses, history, social support systems, political groups—in short, we have carved out our own space within a nonlesbian/gay society. This resilience, resourcefulness, and pride was displayed in the summer of 1993 when about 1 million of us marched in Washington, D.C., and again in June of 1994 when we commemorated the 25th anniversary of the Stonewall Riots in New York City. Everywhere a lesbian or a gay man has come out, there is empowerment at work. Being out, in and of itself, is resistance to the heterosexist oppression in U.S. society.

However, not all of us are out. And for many of us who are, the cost has been high: loss of family, loss of job, loss of child custody; retreat into depression and alcoholism; and the constant threat of verbal and physical assault. The fear of being truthful about oneself is not irrational when the potential risks are so high. Of course, one risk of not coming out is being found out.

LESBIANS AND GAYS AS AN OPPRESSED POPULATION

Oppression

Modern history shows a long tradition of treating lesbians and gays as pariahs. Known "homosexuals" numbered among those rounded up for Hitler's death camps. In the United States, the McCarthy era remains unrivaled in its drive to root out and persecute communists and homosexuals. Until the 1970s, the American Psychiatric Association defined *homosexuality* as a mental disorder. In this century, "treatment" for lesbians and gays in the United States has included both incarceration and relegation to insane asylums. Indeed, Haeberle (1989) has argued that the fate of lesbians and gays under Hitler, "when seen in the context of still-prevailing social attitudes and government policies in many countries are merely sobering examples of excess. Their underlying causes are still waiting to be removed" (p. 379). Many mainstream religions to this day consider lesbian and gay love as immoral. According to Freire (1994), the oppressors seek to change the oppressed, to push them toward adapting to society, in order to dominate them more easily. Certainly, throughout the modern era, no effort to change, correct, convert, shame, humiliate, or otherwise discourage lesbian/gay existence has gone untried. Pharr (1988) has written of homophobia, "Its power is great enough to keep ten to twenty per cent of the population living lives of fear (if their sexual identity is hidden) or lives of danger (if their sexual identify is visible) or both. And its power is great enough to keep eighty to ninety percent of the population trapped in their own fear" (p. 2).

The starting point for empowerment practice for/with lesbians and gays, then, is the dismantling of homophobia. First, one must recognize that the problem is not being lesbian/gay, but rather society's continued rejection of lesbians and gay men. This includes not only individual rejection but institutionalized homophobia, or heterosexism—that is, the system of privileges society confers on nonlesbian/gay people.

COMPULSORY HETEROSEXUALITY Rich's classic feminist essay, "Compulsory Heterosexuality and Lesbian Existence" (1993) challenges feminists to "examine heterosexuality as a political institution which disempowers women—and to change it" (p. 227). This is a critical point. Compulsory heterosexuality limits not only lesbian existence but also that of all women, gay men, and men who are neither white nor wealthy. In short, it upholds the power arrangements that benefit rich, white, nongay men. As a hegemonic system, compulsory heterosexuality has created rigid definitions of "masculine" and "feminine" behavior. Because lesbians and gays are a challenge to those definitions, the system must condemn them. This partly explains the relentless effort to eradicate or control lesbian and gay behavior, particularly in public. At the same time, the fear of being labeled "lesbian" or "gay" is enough to keep most nonlesbians/gays safely within their designated sex roles. Any system that limits the human expressions of women and men to one half their full range must be dismantled.

The empowerment of lesbians/gays therefore extends beyond the lesbian/gay population. That is, dismantling compulsory heterosexuality goes beyond simply accepting lesbians/gays as equal members of society with the same civil rights as nonlesbians/gays. It goes beyond "allowing" lesbians and gays the right to marry in imitation of nonlesbian/gay couples. An empowerment analysis of compulsory heterosexuality also requires one to look at the racism, sexism, and classism that oppress the majority for the benefit of the minority. Going beyond an assimilationist or accommodationist solution to the twin problems of homophobia and heterosexism, one must challenge the "normality" of heterosexuality and consider what the world would be like without homophobia (Pharr, 1988). Could we raise children without the labels "sissy" or "tomboy"? What might it be like to be an adolescent boy without the pressure to "prove his manhood" by proving his heterosexuality? And what energy might be released for the good of society if millions of lesbians and gays no longer expended huge amounts of time and thought to their safety, and millions more women and men no longer monitored their actions and words to avoid being labeled "dyke" or "faggot"? Empowering lesbians and gays means freeing all women and men to become fully who they are without fear of ostracism.

THE YOUTH   Consider, too, the impact of compulsory heterosexuality on lesbian/gay youth. It is estimated that such youth are two to six times more likely to attempt suicide than other youth. Although they account for only about 10% of all youth, they represent about 30% of all completed suicides (Cook, 1991a). Besides the same dangers adult lesbians and gays face, these youths face the potential of rejection from their families, on whom they depend financially, emotionally, and legally. Further, with few adult role models, fewer peer groups to offer support, and little to no accurate information available to them at school or home, young lesbians/gays can experience extreme isolation. One member of the Federation of Parents and Friends of Lesbians and Gays (P-FLAG) says, "As a society we have been slowly killing these children over a period of years. With their suicides, they are simply finishing the jobs we started" (Cook, 1991a, p. 2).

Other risks faced by lesbian and gay youth include low self-esteem, identity conflicts, and alienation from the family (Cook, 1991b). Not surprisingly, lesbian and gay youth turn to substance abuse to cope with being an object of hatred as well as self-hate. They also face the risk of dropping out of school, where harassment and abuse may be allowed. Further, they are at risk for becoming homeless because they run away from rejecting homes or are thrown or pushed away by their families; it is estimated that 25% of all street kids are lesbian or gay (Gibson, 1993).

EMPOWERMENT PRACTICE WITH LESBIANS AND GAYS

The components of empowerment practice most relevant to working with lesbian/gay clients include the following, each of which I shall address in more detail later on:

1. Providing a safe climate and a trusting relationship between client and worker (Parsons, 1994)
2. Raising and developing critical consciousness (Freire, 1994; Gutiérrez, 1990; Simon, 1990; Solomon, 1976; Staples, 1990; Swift & Levin, 1987)
3. Working toward political power and legal rights (Rappaport, 1987; Swift & Levin, 1987) as well as taking action through political advocacy and mobilization of resources (Gutiérrez, 1990; Solomon, 1976; Staples, 1990)
4. Updating practitioners' knowledge regarding the history of oppression of lesbians/gays (and other groups) in the United States (Simon, 1990)
5. Organizational change, i.e., removing impediments to nonheterosexist practice (Solomon, 1976)

A Safe Climate

Involving more than nonjudgmentalism, a safe climate provides a place to celebrate same-sex attractions. In this atmosphere, caregivers recognize, point out, and celebrate the strengths of the individual client and the lesbian/gay community. If the worker merely tolerates or accepts a client's sexual orientation, a trusting relationship will not develop. Social workers have positive mandates from the National Association of Social Workers and from the Council on Social Work Education to be proactive agents for the rights and protection of lesbians and gays.

Whether or not clients perceive caregivers as trustworthy allies is determined by their commitment to the elimination of heterosexism in their own lives and practice. Social workers must examine their own heterosexism/homophobia (all have it; all were raised with it). They must ask themselves these questions:

- Do I assume everyone is heterosexual unless they tell me otherwise?
- In what ways do I benefit from heterosexist assumptions?
- Am I comfortable talking about sexual orientation?
- Do I challenge heterosexist/homophobic jokes or remarks?
- Do I assume that lesbians and gays all have the same beliefs, problems, or agendas?

Lesbians and gays are no more monolithic than any other group. Further, because they were raised in a homophobic/heterosexist culture, they may suffer from internalized homophobia.

Consciousness Raising

Not automatically aware of the impact of heterosexism/homophobia on their lives, lesbians and gays need social workers to help them make these connections and move away from blaming themselves for not coping better. A consciousness-raising (CR) group provides the ideal vehicle for clients to share stories, draw connections, and begin to recognize the personal as political.

CR groups provide contact with role models. For those just coming out or struggling with isolation, involvement in a group—support, social, athletic, or spiritual—provides the opportunity to interact with others. Lesbian/gay novels, poetry, magazines, and films may also serve part of this function. The importance of connection with other lesbians/gays cannot be overestimated.

One women's center at a small New England college began a lesbian support group. Though the group was small and attendance inconsistent, a previously nonexistent network began. Toward the end of the spring semester, this group planned and carried out a week-long series of campuswide events to celebrate lesbians and gays. The week culminated with a "speak out" in which lesbian/gay students, faculty, and community members came out publicly. Those who participated stated that they felt their fear melt away as they stood shoulder to shoulder with their lesbian and gay colleagues.

Political Power

Lesbians and gays do not enjoy certain privileges that heterosexuals take for granted. People can legally lose their jobs or custody of their children because of their sexual orientation. Lesbians and gays cannot serve openly in the nation's armed forces. Social workers have a responsibility to work toward the liberation of lesbians and gays from these overt forms of oppression.

The many forms such political work can take include the following. People can educate their community about gay and lesbian issues. If their area lacks resources for lesbians/gays, they can start them. People can also work to have lesbian/gay affirming material included in their public school curriculum, write letters to local newspapers and the NASW chapter newsletter, or start a lesbian/gay task force for their NASW state chapter. Finally, people can stay abreast of relevant legislative issues and write their state and national representatives.

Updating One's Own Knowledge

One can begin by reading the literature and learning the effects of laws on lesbians/gays. Local lesbian/gay-friendly resources can include certain churches, bookstores that carry lesbian/gay literature, and doctors and lawyers knowledgeable about issues specific to lesbians and gays, Alcoholics Anonymous and other self-help meetings, and lesbian/gay social or political groups in one's community. Becoming familiar with lesbian/gay affirming novels, films, and magazines will also help professionals be a resource for clients.

Organizational Change

A lesbian or gay man knows within the first five minutes at a social service agency whether or not that setting is friendly. Intake forms provide a good measure of this. Categories such as "married, single-never married, or divorced" ignore the existence of committed same-sex partnerships. The absence of openly lesbian or gay staff members, of lesbian/gay literature in the waiting room, of lesbian/gay-friendly posters, artwork, or other decor all signal a heterosexist organization.

Working day after day in an unsupportive environment can demoralize and disempower a lesbian/gay staff member. In addition, many agencies with a nondiscrimination statement in their policy manuals have never stopped to consider its implications. For example, a lesbian working for such an agency applied for health benefits for her life partner. She was told that because her same-sex partner was not "legally" related to her, the benefit did not apply to her. When she took the matter to the director as an issue of discrimination, she was told that it wasn't discriminatory since the benefits applied to married partners; because she wasn't *married* to her partner, she wasn't entitled to the benefit. The fact that society denies lesbians and gays the privilege of marriage was not considered germane to the issue.

Fortunately, this individual and her partner decided to pursue the issue. Through a letter-writing campaign, the coordination of other agency branches, and thorough researching of domestic partner benefits in other states and agencies, the adoption of same-sex partner benefits has currently begun in this agency.

CONCLUSION

Empowerment practice for and with lesbians and gays stems from four perspectives:

- *It is profoundly political* in that all the major institutions of U.S. society support homophobia and heterosexism.
- *It extends beyond the lesbian/gay population* because freedom from homophobia/heterosexism is a threat to the sexist, classist, racist power arrangements under which everyone lives.
- *It is a personal issue* in that lesbian/gay individuals are at risk for conditions such as depression, substance abuse, suicide, homelessness, and injury or death from perpetrators of hate crimes.
- *There is a thriving lesbian/gay culture* in this country even in these conservative times. While it may be better hidden in some areas of the country than in others, it does exist, offering refuge, support, and strength to women, men, and youth who seek a place to be themselves while joining with others to create change.

These themes suggest how counselors can engage in empowerment practice that moves their individual clients, themselves, the profession, and society closer to the day when sex roles and stereotyping have lost their meaning.

Social workers have the power to help people—*all* people, not just lesbians and gays—to see the barriers to their own growth that exist in heterosexist social institutions. It is often easier and certainly quicker to treat only the symptoms of the oppression. Those undertaking empowerment practice must not work to integrate lesbians and gays into a mainstream culture that hates and devalues them but must instead help create an environment in which all people are valued as complete human beings and are encouraged to "find and live authentic lives" (DeLois, 1993, p. 88).

REFERENCES

Cook, A. T. (1991a). Who is killing whom? Issue Paper No. 1, Respect All Youth Project. Washington, DC: INSITE & P-FLAG.

Cook, A. T. (1991b). You can help. Issue Paper No. 2, Respect All Youth Project. Washington, DC: INSITE & P-FLAG.

DeLois, K. A. (1993). *How women come to identify as lesbian: A grounded theory study.* Unpublished doctoral dissertation, University of Washington, Seattle.

Freire, P. (1994). *Pedagogy of the oppressed* (Rev. ed., M. B. Ramos, Trans.). New York: Continuum.

Gibson, P. (1993). Gay and lesbian youth suicide. In W. B. Rubenstein (Ed.), *Lesbians, gay men and the law* (pp. 163–167). New York: New Press.

Gutiérrez, L. (1990). Working with women of color: An empowerment perspective. *Social Work, 35*(2), 149–154.

Haeberle, E. J. (1989). Swastika, pink triangle, and yellow star: The destruction of sexology and the persecution of homosexuals in Nazi Germany. In M. B. Duberman, M. Vicinus, & G. Chauncey, Jr. (Eds.), *Hidden from history: Reclaiming the gay and lesbian past* (pp. 365–379). New York: New American Library.

Parsons, R. J. (1994). *Empowerment based social work practice: A study of process and outcomes.* Paper presented to Council on Social Work Education Annual Program Meeting, San Diego, CA.

Pharr, S. (1988). *Homophobia: A weapon of sexism.* Inverness, CA: Chardon Press.

Rappaport, J. (1987). Terms of empowerment/exemplars of prevention: Toward a theory for community psychology. *American Journal of Community Psychology, 15*(2), 121–149.

Rich, A. (1993). Compulsory heterosexuality and lesbian existence. In H. Abelove, M. A. Barale, & D. M. Halperin (Eds.), *The lesbian and gay studies reader* (pp. 227–254). New York: Routledge.

Simon, B. (1990). Rethinking empowerment. *Journal of Progressive Human Services, 1*(1), 27–40.

Solomon, B. (1976). *Black empowerment: Social work in oppressed communities.* New York: Columbia University Press.

Staples, L. (1990). Powerful ideas about empowerment. *Administration in Social Work, 14*(2), 29–42.

Swift, C., & Levin, G. (1987). Empowerment: An emerging mental health technology. *Journal of Primary Prevention, 8*(1/2), 71–92.

Chapter 5

EMPOWERING PEOPLE
WITH DISABILITIES:
THE ROLE OF CHOICE

Richard Renz-Beaulaurier, Ph.D.
Florida International University, North Miami[1]

THE HISTORY OF
REHABILITATION

In this postmodern era, questioning progress has become fashionable. When one looks at the history of treating people with disabilities in the United States, important questions arise. What sort of progress has there been? What is its nature?

Historical and anthropological sources indicate that preindustrial societies acted harshly toward people with disabilities. This was particularly true with disabilities discovered at birth or with those that seemed physically limiting. In virtually all cases of severe physical disability, preindustrial peoples commonly practiced infanticide. The prevalence of infanticide may partly explain the extremely limited amount of information or historical data on disability (Neubert & Cloerkes, 1987; Oberman, 1965). Interestingly, there is also a lack of information about adults with disabling traumas or illnesses. One can ascribe this to the fact that most of these people had a low survival rate. Still, the absence of facts is striking. Biblical, classical, and other ancient sources support modern anthropological evidence gathered from nonindustrialized peoples. Virtually all such cultures castigated disabled people to some extent, often attributing disability to supernatural

---

[1]Many of the points discussed in this chapter were developed in collaboration with Samuel H. Taylor, D.S.W., at the University of Southern California School of Social Work.

causes such as demonic possession or the wrath of god(s) (Neubert & Cloerkes, 1987). The Romans, for instance, allowed fathers to expose to death any child born either "deformed or female" (Hewett & Forness). In his essay on Politics, Aristotle wrote, "As to the exposure and rearing of children, let there be a law that no *deformed* child shall live" (1943, p. 315).

To some extent, the Judeo-Christian tradition encouraged tolerance and charity toward disabled people. This orientation is still partly codified in law (Merkens, 1988). This same tradition, however, has also inspired some of the most inhumane treatment of people with disabilities, especially during the Inquisition and periodic witch hunts (Oberman, 1965). In the few places the Bible mentions people with disabilities, they are referred to as unclean (Leviticus 21), disabled as a result of sin (Luke 5), or victims of demonic possession (Matthew 12).

The industrial revolution brought about the first major change in the treatment of people with disabilities. Marxist theory has identified how workers in industrialized societies become nonhuman objects, losing their humanity in becoming merely the means of production. In these societies, people with disabilities are seen not only as a substandard "means of production" but also as an actual threat. Historically, when society could not force them to work, laws prevented them from begging (Blaxter, 1976; Oberman, 1965). One of the English Poor Laws divided people into three categories. The lowest included "those who's defects make them an abomination." It was decreed that "they shall be obliged to work, and if they refuse, a few stripes and the withdrawal of food and drink" (Oberman, 1965, p. 59).

In line with this perspective, institutions were built to force people with disabilities to work and to prevent public vagrancy and begging. Over time, the United States also embraced the two themes of shielding society and contributing to economic production. Warehousing became segregation. Work camps were located farther away from the cities, men were separated from women, and society was protected not just from the harm that vagrancy and begging were presumed to cause, but also from the "flawed" genes of people with disabilities (Wolfensberger, 1969). At its zenith, the pseudoscience of eugenics even sterilized all manner of "defectives" to protect the well-being of society (Ludmerer, 1972; Reilly, 1991). Institutions that housed indigent people with disabilities remained little better than prisons for years until the deinstitutionalization movements of the 1960s and 1970s (Hull, 1979; Wolfensberger, 1969).

Prominent supporters of both segregation and sterilization were active members of the National Conference on Charities and Corrections. Alexander Johnson, for instance, president of the National Conference in 1897, was a prominent segregationist (see Johnson, 1903; Perry 1903). Other social workers, such as Marion S. Norton, worked for organizations such as the New Jersey Sterilization League in the 1930s and 1940s, which publicly advocated the passage of sterilization laws (Reilly, 1991). While the manifest purpose of most social work practice with disabled people was to be helpful, many may have aimed primarily at social control of "defectives."

Creating economic good out of the labors of people whose economic potential has been limited by disabilities began with the founding of special training schools, which lay at the heart of vocational rehabilitation. Both strove to help people with disabilities enter the workforce and earn their keep, in either a sheltered or a competitive setting. This was accomplished through training, rehabilitating, or otherwise *altering* people to fit conditions in the workplace. Such training however, was only offered to people clearly judged to be improvable (Varela, 1983; Wolfensberger, 1969). This tendency to select only those with the best prognosis for entry into the workforce characterized vocational rehabilitation from its inception until the 1960s (Berkowitz, 1980).

Medical Rehabilitation

Beginning around the turn of the century, medical rehabilitation did not directly challenge vocational rehabilitation or segregation. It did, however, broaden the goals of medicine to include some people with disabilities. Medicine sought to "restore" patients to the fullest levels of physical functioning. Originally, professionals undertook this specifically to allow patients to engage in remunerative occupations. Even so, the concern centered not on the actual return to work, but rather on the preparation for such by way of altering the physical functioning of the patient (Berkowitz, 1980). Medical social workers of the time seemed to agree with this goal. One of the most prominent early medical social workers stated that the object of treatment with a recently disabled patient was to see "that the patient may regain in fullest extent his function as a normal person" (Cannon, 1952).

Medical rehabilitation brought social workers into the treatment arena for people with disabilities. Though led by physicians, this kind of rehabilitation favored a team approach to treatment, which often required the contributions of social workers (Berkowitz, 1980). The first professional social workers called on to assist people with disabilities were most likely medical social workers. The 1913 edition of Ida Cannon's book on social work in hospitals includes some of the first case studies of practice with people with disabilities (Cannon, 1930). The casework focused on preparing and adjusting the disabled person for life outside the hospital milieu (Bartlett, 1957; Burling, Lentz, & Wilson, 1956, p. 128; Cannon, 1930).

After World War II, that medical rehabilitators downplayed vocational goals spearheaded the provision of treatment for severely disabled individuals—people not considered viable candidates for vocational rehabilitation

(Berkowitz, 1980). As a result, people with disabilities too severe to have been accepted for vocational rehabilitation became clients of medical rehabilitation. It is interesting to note that in the disability and independent living movements that followed, many of the leaders were among the first severely disabled people to have been rehabilitated under the medical model (DeJong, 1981). Earlier, they would have been hospitalized for life. Today, Ed Roberts, who helped found the Center for Independent Living in Berkeley, uses a portable respirator and a motorized wheelchair. In the times of vocational focus, he would not have qualified as a candidate for rehabilitation services at all.

Modern Movements

During the 1960s and 1970s, people with disabilities, especially those with severe ones, began to organize for political action toward maintaining a more independent and self-determined lifestyle in the community. They formed organizations that practiced and advocated the integration of people with disabilities into the mainstream to the maximum extent possible. Such advocacy groups, formed by consumers for consumers (DeJong, 1981; Frieden, 1983; Lachat, 1988), succeeded enough to have their principles of self-determination, consumer control, and nondiscrimination codified in a variety of laws, the most important of which are the Rehabilitation Act of 1973, its amendments (1978), and the Americans with Disabilities Act of 1990. These acts mandate the fullest possible inclusion of people with disabilities into U.S. society. For example, all people with disabilities can choose active and informed involvement with the decision-making processes regarding their medical and vocational rehabilitation and treatment. While some members of the disability movement show hostility toward almost all professionals, for the most part the movement emphasizes allowing consumers the maximum self-determination in the selection, direction, and termination of their treatment.

Both the disability movement and the cited legislation center on creating change in society and in local communities to "reasonably accommodate" people with disabilities. This represents a radical departure from the past, when segregation-oriented groups sought to remove people with disabilities from the general population as well as from the rehabilitation that sought to alter them to fit into society. Partisans in the disability movement seek to alter society to accept and include them. Barriers, whether physical or attitudinal, are being challenged as discriminatory and unnecessary or harmful.

Disability advocates maintain that all the principal historical themes prevalent in the treatment of people with disabilities still exist today. Even with the passage of a premier piece of civil rights legislation, the Americans with Disabilities Act, programs that emphasize altering people still receive the lion's share of available funding. No doubt, many people with disabilities remain isolated and effectively segregated from mainstream society. Although one of the goals of the Americans with Disabilities Act is to help eliminate such isolation, Kailes, a prominent independent living consultant, has said that the Rehabilitation Services Administration would still rather fund a program to "teach paraplegics to walk on their hands" than to fund programs promoting true independent living options for people with disabilities (Kailes, personal communication, 1990).

This bias has caused some activists within the disability movement to question whether any role exists for professionals in the processes of empowerment for people with disabilities. In their view, rehabilitation professionals have tended to promote dependence rather than independence (Berrol, 1979; Zola, 1979). Zola (1983) contends that worship of the technical expert has actually slowed the progress of the movement and contributed to a lowering of consciousness concerning the social nature of disability.

EMPOWERMENT: GOALS AND IMPEDIMENTS

Social workers, especially those in health and rehabilitation settings, must operate in what has become a politically and socially charged environment. To empower clients with disabilities, social workers now must help people make the transition from medical and rehabilitation settings, where they have little ability to determine the course of their treatment, to community settings, where their self-determination can and should be maximized. Social workers must therefore insure that their clients become more capable of self-determination and try to increase the choices clients have regarding the treatments they will receive.

The role of service in the disability movement shows mostly in the growth of independent living centers and programs. Starting with the first in Berkeley, California, these centers have been operated by people with disabilities (DeJong, 1981). Such organizations expressly aim at empowering their constituents. Essentially, this movement grew from a lay self-help movement (Zola, 1979, 1983). Berrol suggests that professionals seeking to promote independent living and foster the empowerment of people with disabilities must "provide leadership in their areas of expertise without dominance, they must provide services, they must be active advocates, they must share their unique skills, and they must provide training. They must assure that there are the same opportunities to develop positive role models as are available to the able-bodied population" (1979, p. 457). To accomplish this, social workers must distinguish between the orientations of rehabilitation and independent living.

Rehabilitation versus Independent Living

The recent debate in the deaf community over cochlear implants for children offers a case in point. Some members of the medical community, as well as those of certain deaf organizations, have advocated the use of such devices even when the level of improvement in auditory functioning is only marginal. Other members of the deaf community view this as maiming innocent deaf children and potentially ostracizing them from their birthright of deafness and inclusion in the deaf community, as well as segregating them from the hearing community, which will never accept such children as "normal" (Barringer, 1993; D'Antonio, 1993). At the heart of this debate lies a basic philosophical difference about the nature of deafness. For the medical community, *deafness* is a disabling medical condition to be conquered, even if that means incurring some casualties. For some in the deaf community, deafness is not so much a disability as a difference, one with its own culture and benefits. Deaf advocates argue that the option of deafness is worthy of consideration and may well be chosen over the benefits of invasive procedures that often produce only marginal hearing ability. They argue that potential recipients of these procedures have the right to know all their options and the potential consequences of each.

Medical and rehabilitation institutions tend to view the problem of disability as the inability of a person to perform certain activities of daily living (ADLs). This perspective locates the problem within the person, as his or her *inabilities*; therefore, the individual must change. For example, recovered polio patients have usually been encouraged to walk even when they found this exhausting. Some disabled people have begun to discover that a wheelchair suits their needs far better than walking with crutches because it allows them to arrive at their destination faster and fresher. As they make the transition from crutches to wheelchair, however, they see clearly that their problem does not reside in their difficulty with walking, but rather the lack of accommodations for wheelchairs. Essentially, they discover that though they are less "mobility impaired" in their chairs, the environment has failed to accommodate their aid to mobility.

Changing the individual to improve his or her performance in ADLs requires the individual to follow a treatment plan laid out by technical experts (the rehabilitation team). Characterized by medical and technological solutions, these treatment plans often employ invasive, experimental, or even dangerous procedures, as in the case of cochlear implants. Indeed, people who have had disabilities for a long time are commonly approached by professionals with new, experimental techniques.

Medical and rehabilitation professionals also tend to define the disabled person as a passive beneficiary of their treatment regime. Control of the process lies in the hands of the technical experts who aim at maximizing physical functioning. However, because functioning cannot always arrive at "normal" standards, success is often thought of as completion of the treatment regime rather than actual "normalization." Take again the example of cochlear implants. Even when their actions will create social difficulties for the patient, many medical professionals prefer to perform surgery that provides little improvement in hearing and marginal functional benefits. Dependency on technical experts is fostered regarding not just the technology of treatment but also its goals and definitions of success. This requires people with disabilities to (1) view the rehabilitation professional as an expert, (2) view their own states as undesirable, and (3) work toward a prognosis and recovery that has been defined for them (see DeJong, 1981, p. 31).

On the other hand, organizations that operate within the independent-living disability movement emphasize empowerment through ever-increasing self-determination on the part of disabled people, rather than through reliance on technical experts. Such organizations depend on lay people with disabilities for their direction and governance, as well as for the provision of services and advocacy. Such organizations, often called *independent living centers*, emphasize social rather than medical needs. Minimally, this includes enhanced information and referral services that enable individuals to choose appropriate services. Peer counseling links the individual with the greater disability community and provides positive role models. Further, training focuses on the skills needed for disabled people to live within society. That is, rather than focus on *what* ADLs a person can or cannot accomplish, training in independent-living skills focuses on *how* to live independently in the community and society given his or her physical limitations. Finally, client as well as class-advocacy services are provided to help people overcome environmental, societal, and bureaucratic barriers. In the view of the disability movement, these services address society's failure to accommodate disabled people, which marginalizes them.

Intervention to change the functioning of the individual, therefore, is not necessarily a social worker's first step. For instance, a client may first need to find services that allow her or him to exercise the rights to live and work in the main community. Often, this requires action to combat physical, legal, and attitudinal barriers that would place people with disabilities in institutions or under the control of professionals or bureaucracies if left unchallenged. This final notion makes the principle of consumer control extremely important to organizations within the disability movement.[2]

---

[2] I have taken this characterization of independent living centers in large part from Richards and Smith (1990).

EMPOWERMENT STRATEGIES

Social workers, especially those in medical and rehabilitation settings, must refocus their activities to begin the transition toward empowerment objectives: to maximize and expand the range of life choices of clients with disabilities, to facilitate their clients' decision making with regard to life choices, and to bolster the achievement of life choices. Because these objectives will often conflict with those of other professionals, social workers must function as agents of change to empower disabled people to achieve their aspirations and exercise their newly legitimized civil rights. Social workers must use their unique skills and expertise to help clients with disabilities choose the criteria for success of the medical and rehabilitative interventions they receive. To achieve those ends, social workers must begin to move in the directions pioneered by people with disabilities through their movements and organizations.

The Nature of the Problem

Social workers should help people with disabilities redefine their problems in terms of the social and physical barriers that local communities must remove. To give a simple example, the problem of how to get up the steps (problem within the individual) changes to how to get a ramp installed (problem outside the individual). Appropriate social work technologies often include community organizing, client and community advocacy, and an understanding of bureaucracies in addition to traditional clinical skills.

Empowerment of disabled individuals also requires that they remain in control of this change. Social workers serve to facilitate a partnership for the realization of goals and solutions, *not* to set them for their clients. In general, social workers need to consider how to help individuals explore their range of choices, with an eye toward expanding their options rather than setting limits. Such goals are consistent not only with the disability movement, but also with traditional social work values that aim to foster the independence and self-determination of each client.

Self-Determination

Of course, no one can achieve complete independence. From the perspective of those within the disability movement, however, life is independent to the extent that it is self-determined. This view can free clients and social workers to define the personal criteria of success. Rehabilitation professionals have spent months at times teaching people with mobility impairments such skills as dressing themselves. Many of those who eventually manage to get dressed by themselves find that the process takes hours and leaves them physically exhausted. By contrast, many disabled people have learned that having an attendant help them dress in the morning takes just minutes, leaving them with the time and energy to pursue more rewarding activities (P. Longmore, personal communication, Spring 1992). One must view dependency and independence in terms of self-determination of life choices rather than the preconceptions of technical experts. Indeed, the German version of the independent living movement is called the movement for *selbstbestimmtes Leben*, literally, *self-determined living*.

Consciousness Raising

Social workers must raise the consciousness of disabled people, that is, help them realize that they are the definitive experts on their particular condition and the best arbiters of their own treatment. This includes making people with disabilities aware of their rights. As persons with rights, people with disabilities can come to see themselves as deserving citizens rather than a marginal people dependent on the largess of an otherwise indifferent society. As consciousness rises, disabled clients may come to realize that they are not the "half-persons" stereotypes depict them to be, but fully human. They may discover that their state is in fact unique and desirable and that a community for them exists, one of people both with and without disabilities.

Social workers need to augment their knowledge of these community networks so they can help clients avoid the isolation and disempowerment that has characterized most of the history of people with disabilities. Functional community supports that social workers can access include independent living centers founded and run by disabled people, advocacy organizations, newsletters and newspapers, electronic bulletin board services, and internet newsgroups. Beyond awareness of these groups and services, social workers need the community liaison skills to link these organizations and those in which they work.

Services

The Americans with Disabilities Act (ADA) has legitimized the idea that the fundamental problems facing people are less medical than social and structural. While ADA may be the most far reaching and important disability law ever passed, it contains little about how to provide specific social, health, or rehabilitation services. Rather, it focuses on removing social and structural barriers to the integration of people with disabilities into mainstream society. To empower people with disabilities, social workers must accept these terms. This acceptance may shift the "legitimate expertise" of social workers in health and rehabilitation from a focus on clinical and psychosocial interventions to community organizing, client and class advocacy, administration, and the manipulation of relevant bureaucracies. This marks a significant change; up to now, medical social workers have been oriented toward direct service rather than community, administrative, and planning modalities (Pfouts & McDaniel, 1990).

Even so, the adoption of different treatment methods alone will not suffice. Social workers must implement consumer control of services. For example, through periods of medically imposed isolation and lengthy stays under the control of disempowering bureaucracies, an individual client may not be fully capable of assuming control. Social workers must therefore introduce individual clients to the greater disability community, so as to "allow direction [of their efforts] to occur from within the disabled community, reflecting the unique needs of that community and its members" (Berrol, 1979, p. 457).

Specific Practice Principles

Social work practice with disabled people involves helping such clients move from being a passive beneficiary of services to being an active, informed consumer of services. As such, social workers need to help their disabled clients realize that the clients themselves are the definitive experts on their personal disabilities. To enable disabled people to participate fully in the planning and course of their treatment, social workers can and should provide encouragement and technical assistance. They also need to educate people with disabilites about their rights under the law, particularly with regard to their right to self-determination concerning their bodies and treatment. Finally, social workers must forge links between their disabled clients and organizations/resources sponsored by other disabled people and designed to support independence within mainstream communities.

SUMMARY

Throughout history, disabled people have been one of the most disadvantaged minority groups. Despite this, only recently have people begun to focus on the oppression and empowerment of this group. Social workers working with disabled people—especially in health and rehabilitation settings—must employ a conceptual framework for practice that maximizes clients' involvement in ascertaining the full range of their available options; prepares clients to deal effectively with professionals, bureaucrats, and agencies that may neither understand nor appreciate their need to be self-determining; and empowers groups of disabled people to consider policy and program alternatives that can improve their situation.

REFERENCES

Americans with Disabilities Act of 1990, Pub. L. No. 101-336.

Aristotle. (1943). *Politics* (B. Jowett, Trans.). New York: Modern Library.

Barringer, F. (1993, May 16). Pride in a soundless world: Deaf oppose a hearing aid. *New York Times*, pp. 1, 22.

Bartlett, H. M. (1957). Influence of the medical setting on social case work services. In D. Goldstine (Ed.), *Readings in the theory and practice of medical social work* (pp. 85–96). Chicago: University of Chicago Press.

Berkowitz, E. D. (1980). *Rehabilitation: The federal government's response to disability 1935–1954*. New York: Arno Press.

Berrol, S. (1979). Independent living programs: The role of the able-bodied professional. *Archives of Physical Medicine and Rehabilitation, 60,* 456–457.

Blaxter, M. (1976). *The meaning of disability: A sociological study of impairment.* London: Heinemann.

Burling, T., Lentz, E. M., & Wilson, R. N. A. (1956). *The give and take in hospitals.* New York: Putnam.

Cannon, I. M. (1930). *Social work in hospitals: A contribution to progressive medicine* (Rev. ed.). New York: Russel Sage Foundation.

———. (1952). *On the social frontier of medicine: Pioneering in medical social service.* Cambridge, MA: Harvard University Press.

D'Antonio, M. (1993, November 21). Sound and fury. *Los Angeles Times Magazine,* pp. 44–47, 60–67.

DeJong, G. (1981). *Environmental accessibility and independent living outcomes: Directions for disability policy and research.* East Lansing, MI: University Center for International Rehabilitation, Michigan State University.

Frieden, L. (1983). Understanding alternative program models. In N. M. Crewe & I. K. Zola (Eds.), *Independent living for physically disabled people* (pp. 62–72). San Francisco: Jossey-Bass.

Hewett, F. M., & Forness, S. R. (1984). *Education of exceptional learners* (3rd ed.). Newton, MA: Allyn and Bacon.

Hull, K. A. R. (1979). *The rights of physically handicapped people.* New York: Avon.

Johnson, A. (1903). *Proceedings of the National Conference of Charities and Correction at the Thirtieth Annual Session Held in the City of Atlanta, May 6–12, 1903* (pp. 245–252). Fred J. Heer.

Lachat, M. A. (1988). *The independent living service model: Historical roots, core elements, and current practice.* Hampton, NH: Center for Resource Management.

Ludmerer, K. M. (1972). *Genetics and American society: A historical appraisal.* Baltimore: Johns Hopkins University Press.

Merkens, L. (1988). *Einführung in die Historische Entwicklung der Behinderten Pädagogik in Deutschland unter integrativen Aspekten.* [Introduction to the historical development of disability education in Germany, integrating aspects]. Munich: Ernst Reinhardt Verlag.

Neubert, D., & Cloerkes, G. (1987). *Behinderung und Behinderte in verschiedenen Kulturen: Eine vergleichende Analyse ethnologischer Studien* [Disability and the disabled in differing cultures: A comparative analysis ethnographic study]. Heidelberg: Edition Schindele.

New American Bible. (1970). New York: World Publishing.

Oberman, C. E. (1965). *A history of vocational rehabilitation in America.* Minneapolis, MN: T. S. Denison & Company.

Perry, M. E. (1903). *Proceedings of the National Conference of Charities and Correction at the Thirtieth Annual Session Held in the City of Atlanta, May 6–12, 1903* (pp. 253–254). Fred J. Heer.

Pfouts, J. H., & McDaniel, B. (1990). Medical handmaidens or professional colleagues: A survey of social work practice in the pediatrics departments of twenty-eight teaching hospitals. In K. W. Davidson & S. S. Clarke (Eds.), *Social work in health care* (pp. 575–586). New York: Hayworth.

Rehabilitation Act of 1973, Pub. L. No. 93-112.

Rehabilitation, Comprehensive Services and Developmental Disabilities Amendments of 1978, Pub. L. No. 95-602.

Reilly, P. R. (1991). *The surgical solution: A history of involuntary sterilization in the United States.* Baltimore: Johns Hopkins University Press.

Richards, L., & Smith, Q. (1990). *An orientation to independent living centers: A national technical assistance project for independent living.* Houston, TX: Texas Institute for Rehabilitation Research (SERIES Bulletin Board Service, Rehabilitation Services Administration).

Varela, R. A. (1983). Changing social attitudes and legislation regarding disability. In N. M. Crewe & I. K. Zola (Eds.), *Independent living for physically disabled people* (pp. 28–48). San Francisco: Jossey-Bass.

Wolfensberger, W. (1969). The origin and nature of our institutional models. In R. B. Kugel & W. Wolfensberger (Eds.), *Changing patterns in residential services for the mentally retarded* (pp. 59–172). Washington, DC: President's Committee on Mental Retardation.

Zola, I. K. (1979). Helping one another: A speculative history of the self help movement. *Archives of Physical Medicine and Rehabilitation, 60,* 452–456.

Zola, I. K. (1983). Developing new self-images and interdependence. In N. M. Crewe & I. K. Zola (Eds.), *Independent living for physically disabled people* (pp. 49–59). San Francisco: Jossey-Bass.

Part Three

EMPOWERMENT IN PRACTICE: FOCUSING ON FIELDS

Part Three is composed of four chapters focused on other critical and challenging areas of social work in which empowerment strategies have proven effective. The authors in this section represent a great depth of both academic research and practice experience. Each chapter includes not only intervention descriptions and practice suggestions but also the theoretical reference points of the contributors. While all these authors concur with much of the practice framework outlined in Chapter 1, each brings a special emphasis to empowerment theory and practice and suggests critical challenges specific to empowerment among specific populations.

In Chapter 6, Susan Manning provides a provocative overview of the mental health system and its role in empowerment. She analyzes issues of power and powerlessness in the mental health field as she describes the impact of the medical model, diagnosis and labeling, and stigma on people with mental illness and on their social workers. Manning's insightful analysis of the process of internalized oppression can help readers understand, assess, and design empowerment-oriented service strategies. By including the "voices" of individuals suffering from mental illness, she gives special strength to her observations. Questions that may arise as you review her work include the following:

1. *What are the critical components of worker-client relationships in empower-ment-oriented practice? What organizational barriers and supports exist regarding the creation of empowerment-oriented worker-client relationships in various mental health settings?*
2. *At the organizational and political/economic level, what strategies can social workers use to address stigma associated with mental illness?*
3. *What role can self-help organizations such as the CHARG Resource Center play in the transformation of mental health services?*

In Chapter 7, Graydon Andrus and Susan Ruhlin describe the intense challenges to empowerment experienced by homeless individuals and families. These authors explore the personal, interpersonal, and environmental problems such people face. They also present the current political/economic situation and its propensity to increase the numbers of homeless. As they affirm the critical need to address these issues from an empowerment perspective, Andrus and Ruhlin discuss specific action strategies used with the homeless in terms of the four dimensions suggested in Chapter 1. The interrelationship of poverty, mental illness, unemployment, and underemployment are addressed. The authors also provide a provocative discussion of some of the issues related to establishing worker-client relationships with homeless people. Finally, they illustrate the important role of consciousness raising regarding the social, political, and economic forces in minimizing self-blame among the homeless. Critical questions for social workers suggested by this chapter might include the following:

1. *At the macro level of social policy, one may wish to consider issues such as these: Are there ways to change the way U.S. society approaches housing? Can the government be persuaded to advocate the development of affordable housing? Can people come to think of housing as primarily the provision of shelter rather than a medium for investment?*
2. *Concerning social service delivery, what are the pros and cons of using an emergency or temporary shelter system as the primary approach to homelessness?*
3. *What special challenges do workers face in their efforts to establish effective relationships with homeless individuals and families? What is the relationship of advocacy to empowerment-oriented intervention strategies?*

In Chapter 8, Stuart Rees presents an interesting overview of the social, political, and economic context of power issues as experienced by youth in several societies. He also stresses the increasing challenge to empowerment as poverty, racism, isolation, physical and psychological abuse, drug addiction, homelessness, and other stressors are added to the factor of youthful age. Rees affirms the concerns of other empowerment-oriented authors that interventions focus on the political, organizational, interpersonal, and personal dimensions of powerlessness related to problems of client populations. He also emphasizes the need for empowerment-oriented workers to examine the complexity of power and explore ways to address power in their work with youth. Questions generated from Rees's discussion might include the following:

1. *What special empowerment issues must youth address?*
2. *What are the characteristics of political literacy?*
3. *What societal changes will bring about long-term goals of social justice for youth?*
4. *In what practice settings could empowerment-oriented practitioners engage in the activities that promote the stages of empowerment suggested by Rees?*

In Chapter 9, Vanessa Hodges, Yolanda Burwell, and Debra Ortega discuss the application of empowerment theory and practice strategies to families. They acknowledge the differences in the degree and nature of oppression experienced by families who depend on factors such as economic status, race, and available community resources. By challenging social workers to acknowledge the potential strengths of extended family resources, they suggest the need to emphasize not only strengths but also community supports in the assessment process.

Questions that may emerge from the discussion for social work practitioners include the following:

1. *How do current political and economic factors affect families in the United States? What common needs and challenges do families of any race or class face?*
2. *What possible strategies and barriers exist for strengthening extended family networks among families of different ethnic and socioeconomic class?*

Chapter 6

EMPOWERMENT IN MENTAL HEALTH PROGRAMS: LISTENING TO THE VOICES

Susan S. Manning, Ph.D.
University of Denver,
Denver, Colorado

INTRODUCTION

People who live with a severe and persistent mental disability experience oppression and exclusion. The nature of mental disability, the societal stigma, and the worldview of the psychiatric community profoundly affect the personal and political power of this group. Repressed or ignored, their voice has largely remained unheard. Chamberlain (1990), a former patient and longtime activist in the ex-patients movement, states that the "madman" is part of our cultural heritage. Whether defined as possession, as disturbance of the public order, or as mental illness, "the mad themselves have remained largely voiceless" (p. 323). To understand their unique experience, then, I bring their voices forward here.

This chapter discusses the power and powerlessness in relation to people with mental disabilities. Specifically, it explores the components of empowerment identified by consumers of mental health services and the relationship of empowerment issues to social work attitudes and roles. Incorporating these discussions, a service model of empowerment emerges. Finally, this chapter presents issues related to empowerment as a technology in mental health.

POWER AND
POWERLESSNESS

The Medical Model:
"Power Over"

Issues of power and powerlessness lie embedded in the nature of mental ill-ness and the history of psychiatry—decades of research and theory have focused on treatments for various mental and emotional disorders. Tradi-tionally, care has followed a disease model envisioned through the relation-ship between doctor and patient (Segal, Silverman, & Temkin, 1993). This model presents the mental disability as a disease; the doctor or mental health practitioner as the expert who will cure, or at least lessen, the symptoms of the disease; and the client as a passive, often powerless participant. These roles—"expert helper" versus "inadequate help receiver"—create a differ-ence in status and self-esteem, and thus a difference in power (Boltz, 1992).

Other models, such as psychotherapy (based on resolving internal problems through dialogue with a therapist), also place the most authority with the provider, who must deliberately keep an objective distance from the consumer in the relationship. These models effect a relationship in which the professional has "power over" the consumer (Segal et al., 1993).

DIAGNOSIS AND LABELING   The disease model includes the practice of label-ing, or diagnosing. Through assessment and diagnosis, the professional defines the nature of the consumer, and what the consumer needs (Boltz, 1992). Each person must have a diagnosis in order to receive services. The individual's behavior, feelings, and attitudes become interpreted as this diag-nosis, which then becomes a form of identity (Segal et al., 1993). Because subsequent behaviors and experiences are often interpreted via the label rather than the person, labels can prevent care-givers from knowing him or her. One consumer case manager (Manning & Suire, 1996) described it as follows: "I am so conscious of it. I'd better not act like a client—too emo-tional, or too dramatic, or too impulsive, or irresponsible" (p. 940).

These labels stigmatize clients; the terms attached to them (such as *chronic*) increase the stigma. A social work author (Anonymous, 1990) dis-cusses the stigma of the label from her own experience: "I do not reveal my past diagnostic status at employment interviews. . . . Would you hire a 'chronic schizophrenic-undifferentiated' for anything more than sanding furniture or sorting screws?" (p. 391).

Labels also promote distancing by providers. When a consumer is referred to as "schizophrenic" or "borderline," providers can more easily dis-tance themselves from the experience of that person than when these labels do not interfere.

Learned Helplessness

Mental health consumers often experience a personal sense of fear and a pervasive sense of helplessness (Deegan, 1992). These feelings proceed from a history of feeling powerless and being acted on in the mental health and judicial system. Previous involuntary hospitalizations, electroconvulsive treatments (ECTs), forced medications, lack of control over treatment planning, and the absence of informed consent reinforce a loss of control over life choices. A consumer in a recent study on consumer empowerment (Manning, Zibalese-Crawford, & Downey, 1994) says, "Consumers have been in a system for years. . . . They're scared having been through shock therapy. . . . They tend to be totally intimidated by the system . . . [which wants] to break their will to change their behavior" (p. 44).

Deegan (1992) argues that consumers experience this loss of control over their lives because of a "central attitudinal barrier." This barrier is the assumption that "people with psychiatric disabilities cannot be self-determining because to be mentally ill means to have lost the capacity for sound reasoning" (p. 12). Therefore, the system takes control. A process of dependency, irresponsibility, and despair—learned helplessness—soon develops. As consumers become "experts in being helpless," the attitudinal barrier is reinforced.

IATROGENIC EFFECTS OF TREATMENT This cycle illustrates the iatrogenic effect, or the negative unintended results, of hospitalization and treatment programs, where compliance and adaptive behavior are expected (Chamberlain, 1978; Ludwig, 1971). The very behaviors that work well for institutional treatment prove the least effective for self-determination and community living. According to one consumer (Manning et al., 1994), "Motivation and independence have been educated out of individuals in the mental health system. . . . They are educated to follow the decisions and instructions of many other people, not to follow their own instincts" (p. 14). Further, practitioners then interpret the symptoms of learned helplessness—apathy, submissiveness, anger, depression, and withdrawal—as the typical negative signs of the mental disorder rather than a normal reaction to a disempowering situation (Deegan, 1992).

Blaming the Victim

The theory and interventions that guide work with consumers in the mental health system are developed, conceptualized, and researched from professional perspectives. Most of this research, however, reflects a deficit ideology. Examples include viewing the problems of consumers as "lack of skills, lack of work histories, lack of interpersonal or daily living skills, lack of symptom control, lack of compliance with medication" (Rapp, Shera, & Kisthardt,

1993, p. 728). The families of consumers have also had to deal with this attitude. Accusations that they have caused their family member's disability, that they have pathological traits, or that they contribute to the problem rather than the solution are not uncommon (Kagle and Cowger, 1984). Language used in the mental health system—*schizophrenegenic mother, enmeshment, toxic family*, and *high EE* (expressed emotion) *families*—conveys blame. This blaming creates an imbalance of power, whereby research enterprises and professionalization define the parameters of consumers' problems, while consumers have no voice in that definition (Rapp et al., 1993; Segal et al., 1993).

Stigma

A recent survey found that 65% of the respondents believe there is still a great deal of stigma about mental illness ("Mental Illness Remains," 1991). Stigma occurs when a label represents a deviation from expected normal behavior. First, stereotypes develop from the label—for example, crazy people are dangerous, bizarre, unpredictable. Then, people interpret a person's behavior in terms of the label (Boltz, 1992). For example, when a consumer case manager (Manning & Suire, 1996) advocated for a client, the staff thought she was displaying "aggressive tendencies. . . . They think I'm crazy."

   People with mental disabilities view stigma as a major barrier to empowerment. In a study on the daily hassles of such consumers, Miller and Miller (1991) have found that the items most bothersome to them center on stigma (someone rejects you, is angry at you, yells at you, etc.). In contrast, bothersome items for the general population include things like not enough leisure time, or crime. Further, the coping issues for people with mental disabilities revolve around surviving the social/interpersonal world as a member of a stigmatized group.

   Stigma especially pervades rural areas. Consumers and family members agree that accessing services in a rural community is made difficult by the public perception of mental illness. Examples from a rural consumer and family member include the following (Manning et al., 1994, p. 8):

- I feel like I have something contagious like AIDS . . . or like I have leprosy. (consumer)
- It's the smallness, it's the publicness. When the sheriff comes to get your mother, everybody knows . . . and when the sheriff comes to get your mother, it's a big problem . . . a biiiiiig problem! (family member)

INTERNALIZED OPPRESSION Individuals with mental disability internalize these norms and stereotypes. They then experience shame, lowered expectations of themselves, and fears of rejection (Boltz, 1992). As one person explains, "We stigmatize ourselves through denial, lack of acceptance, language and isolation. . . . We picked up the language of the professionals and use it to stigmatize each other" (Manning et al., 1994, p. 8).

Consumers and professionals alike sometimes blame the disability for behaviors and problems that are normal. Struggles to develop leadership, organize groups, and cope with life's problems are too often explained by the convenient scapegoat of mental disability. Subsequently, consumers find it hard to trust their own strengths and identify normal responses to their environment. For example, one consumer says, "We either make too much allowance for the illness or not enough . . . still looking for middle ground" (Manning et al., 1994, p. 9). The internalized oppression of stigma further reduces the consumer's power and increases the professional's power as expert.

Impact of Mental Disability

POVERTY The residual effects of severe and persistent mental disability also affect the process and outcome of empowerment for consumers. These consumers' quality of life, from their own evaluation, is substantially lower than the poorest groups in the general population (Lehman, Ward, & Linn, 1982; Rosenfield, 1992). For the most part, consumers live in poverty, with substandard housing, low rates of competitive employment, inadequate medical and dental care, and isolation because of limited opportunities for social and recreational activities (Link, 1983). Nearly one-third of the nation's homeless have a mental disability (Bachrach, 1987; Belcher, 1989). Access to services and support groups, particularly in rural areas, may not be within financial reach because of poverty or transportation issues.

Poverty affects both consumers and families. For example, one consumer says, "Poverty is our biggest problem." And, a family member notes, "Our son is on medicare and what a time I had getting supplemental insurance for him. . . . Try and get a doctor is hard enough for mentally ill, but with no insurance it's almost impossible. Couldn't even get a physical for him . . . a real struggle for two old people and a bi-polar son, wouldn't you say?" (Manning et al., 1994, p. 27). Poverty is thus a critical barrier to resources and contacts that increase personal power, reinforcing the debilitating effect of a severe and persistent mental condition.

LOSS OF SELF The mental condition is also disempowering because it includes a loss of self in several important dimensions (Estroff, 1982, 1989). The "narrative of loss" begins with the loss of personal history: those who did not know the consumer before the disability (such as providers, who do not know the person prior to their psychiatric disability). Then, a "cultural and symbolic" change in self from the effects of the condition, as well as others' reactions to it, takes place (Chesler and Chesney, 1988; Estroff,

1982, 1989). Finally, consumers go through the loss of a social place and space normally determined through roles that help people feel they belong in family, community, and society (Estroff, 1989).

A consumer researcher made the following observation after participating in a consumer-run support group: There is humor from the stronger ones and sympathy and empathy all the way around, but it doesn't make up for the lack of jobs, the extreme shaking of hands and fingers from medication, the repeated loss of jobs, the interruptions of careers, some permanently, never to return to their fields again, the lack of self-esteem and poor physical condition from unsuccessful medications and not too good a diet, the bloating and inactivity, restlessness, shaking, poor memory, lack of concentration, lack of connection, fear and withdrawal from others, the inability to reach out and say what they're going through and get some actual help (Manning et al., 1994, p. 9).

INSTITUTIONAL DISEMPOWERMENT Finally, community institutions can disempower people with mental disabilities (Chesler and Chesney, 1988). Failure to guarantee the legal and humane rights due any citizen; deprivation of adequate medical and psychosocial care; and lack of fair access to education, employment, and public/private services all reinforce the disempowerment of mental health consumers. Abuse of the rights of the mentally ill is well documented. Wilk (1994) has found that social workers support rights conceptually but not in actual practice. Similarly, a landmark study on informed consent in psychiatric institutions (Lidz et al, 1984) has found that true informed consent is not practiced at all.

In summary, issues of power and powerlessness rest on what Saleebey (1992) refers to as "the language of pathology and deficit" (p. 3). This language and understanding rests on certain assumptions and leads to particular purposes in practice. Stigma from professionals, society, or the individuals themselves about the "master status" of the label of their mental disability, in combination with the real consequences of a severe mental condition, create negative expectations about consumers' capacity to respond to the demands of their environment (Becker, 1963). As a detached, objective expert, the provider exerts "power over" consumers and family members, effectively negating opportunities to become empowered through their own lived experience (Goldstein, 1986).

EMPOWERMENT IN THE
MENTAL HEALTH SYSTEM

Empowerment in mental health results from a change in provider and consumer attitudes, perhaps the most difficult kind of change to accomplish.

This section addresses consumer perspectives of empowerment followed by social work attitudes and roles that can enhance empowerment.

Consumer Perspectives of Empowerment

Drawn from a recent study on consumer participation and empowerment (Manning et al., 1994), the following discussion presents the voices of people with mental disabilities.

DECISIONS AND ACTION   Here, consumers speak on their power of choice:

- "Empowerment is related to individuals directing their own life. This includes making choices, being responsible for the results of those choices—successes and failures—and learning from the results. Choice increases the control over one's life."
- "Traditionally we have felt a failure at making choices. . . . The goal is to have control over our own lives, belonging, and the right to get a level of competence and self-esteem . . . and enough resiliency to accept a failure" (Manning et al., 1994, p. 12).
- "Empowerment comes to people by doing. . . . [We] learn that risks take choices and make decisions. . . . People become more motivated . . . take action" (Manning et al., 1994, p. 13).

The opportunity to decide does not necessarily come easily. Providers, family members, and consumer leaders sometimes have difficulty letting go of the decision-making role even to promote the empowerment of another. For example, they may think, " 'I'll do it', rather than taking the time to find out what people can do . . . educating them about passing on the power . . . learning to take a little time to let someone else help them" (Manning et al., 1994, p. 13).

RESPECT   Mental health consumers also view respect as an important element of empowerment. They have described it in general ways, such as "Most important, people need respect," and also in terms of behaviors and attitudes that convey respect. In particular, "being listened to" and "being heard" were central to feeling respected. As one consumer has said, "Just hear me out. . . . We really do have something to offer." Another has expressed the lack of respect that comes from the impoverished status of being a mental health consumer. "Power is in status and financial ability. . . . I know that if I go with my Father who is a mechanical engineer, I can get a lot more done than if I were to do it myself. . . . If I have a grievance with my mental health system, I'll use my Father so I can get something done . . . because the air of respect is there. As a consumer, I have less respect . . . because of my financial ability, I assume" (Manning et al., 1994, p. 16).

Consumers also discuss the importance of self-respect in relation to empowerment. In their view, self-care, through wellness activities, living their own values, and committing to long-term relationships, all promote self-respect.

COMING OUT Related to self-respect is the importance of "coming out" about one's mental disability. Consumers and family members relate a sense of relief, freedom, and empowerment as they experience being more public. One rural family member notes, "You can't remove stigma unless you come out" (Manning, et al., 1994, p. 22). Coming out allows them to reach out to others, and it reduces isolation.

INVOLVEMENT AND BELONGING Empowerment occurs through involvement in a community. Relationships ameliorate the isolation created by disabilities and society's response to them. As one consumer says, "Relationship is the cause of a person getting better rather than meds . . . a community to belong to" (Manning et al., 1994, p. 17).

Involvement in a group or community also promotes a sense of history with others. Membership opens up new avenues for support and exchange of information, providing the chance to find new resources.

CONTRIBUTION TO OTHERS Through relationships and community, mental health consumers experience their ability to help others, that is, to contribute to the healing by becoming a helper. Consumers view this contributing as essentially empowering. For example, one person has said, "There is something about being able to help that makes you feel better and stronger yourself" (Manning et al., 1994, p. 23).

INFORMATION AND EDUCATION Consumers and family members continuously identify the role of information in empowerment. One consumer has described it this way: "I knew very little about my illness. . . . Manic-depressive . . . scares people at cocktail parties. Education with doctors is very important. . . . I never knew there were any books, never knew what I had. . . . It opened my eyes about what was possible . . . how much information was out there" (Manning et al., 1994, pp. 12–13).

Understanding the diagnosis and symptoms of mental disability, as well as learning helpful coping skills, empowers consumers and family members to manage the condition and to work with mental health professionals from an informed position. As one family member in the study has noted, "One of your jobs as a family member is 'getting professional' about the illness" (Manning et al., 1994, p. 12).

This discussion from the voices of people with mental disabilities corresponds to the empowerment process delineated in Chapter 1: self-determination, community, critical thinking, and action. The emphasis on self-determination and choice affects the individual's attitudes, values, and beliefs—her or his sense of self. Self-determination promotes self-efficacy, increases confidence in self-worth, and provides a sense of control over one's own life.

Consumers have expressed the importance of involvement and belonging to a community. Relationships provide, among other things, validation through collective experience. They also provide support, sharing of information and resources, and opportunities to experience respect from others, which in turn reinforces self-respect.

Consumers claim that the knowledge and skills for critical thinking and action, discussed in Chapter 1, develop through the education, information, and resources available in relationships with others. In addition, the opportunity to contribute to the well-being of others promotes knowledge and skill development. Obtaining knowledge about mental conditions and strategies to cope effectively with the condition promotes "coming out," which reduces stigma and shame, and increases self-respect.

Finally, consumers' emphasis on the role of decision maker highlights the discussion of action in the first chapter. Making a decision makes one responsible for it. Deciding and working with the outcomes of a decision provide the opportunity for reflective action and learning. This combats the iatrogenic effects of mental disability discussed earlier in this chapter.

Professional Attitudes and Roles

In the mental health system, the components of empowerment are inextricably connected to the consumer's relationship with providers. Because the traditional professional role is based on disempowering attitudes and methods, social workers must radically change it so they can practice from an empowerment perspective. The following discussion will focus on how to create a conversation between consumer and worker; that is, how to make room for the voices of people with mental disability through a shift in worker attitudes and roles.

SOCIAL WORK ATTITUDES Barr and Cochran (1992) delineate a "fundamental shift" in thinking relevant to empowerment work with consumers. This shift must occur for both consumers and social workers. Through empowering activities, consumers must change their view of themselves from hopeless, self-doubting, and blaming to hopeful, believing in self and "what's possible," and taking charge of their lives.

Social workers must move from a deficit model of thinking to one based on strengths. This move shifts workers away from the traditional view of consumers as pathological, unmotivated, and incompetent. According to Rose (1992), workers must focus on their clients' strengths and must expect them to grow; they must also understand that consumers' experience differs from that of others mainly because consumers have less access to the resources and opportunities necessary to reach aspirations. This shift reinforces a contextual view of people with mental disabilities as "whole human beings" who live in a social context that influences the quality of their lives.

In addition, social workers must shift from seeing themselves as experts to embracing the knowledge that consumers bring to the helping process. This validation of the consumer's experiential knowledge facilitates the legitimacy of that knowledge (Yeich & Levine, 1992). Respect for the knowledge of the consumer takes place through dialogue, which provides the opportunity to define what is meaningful within the relationship.

This shift emphasizes consumer norms and goals, with consumers making choices for themselves instead of responding to the bureaucratic norms and goals of the traditional mental health system. Thus, the provider-driven model of care becomes a client-driven model (Rose, 1991). Frequently, social workers are constrained by the limits or boundaries of their agency; what is available is considered sufficient for all consumer needs. In contrast, the client-driven model advocates for services and resources from the perspective of clients' lives and goals, achieving those both within the agency, and "in vivo," using the natural community.

Finally, the shift involves moving from "power over" to "power with and among" consumers, respecting their contribution as different but equal to that of the worker (Barr & Cochran, 1992). These issues of attitude play a key role in social workers' definitions of the boundary between their professional responsibility and "taking control" (Freund, 1993). Social workers must trust the internal motivation of individuals—that consumers will "learn from their own experiences" and have the ability to "chart their own life course" (Freund, 1993, p. 67).

The attitudes of workers are expressed through their formal role as providers in the mental health system. The next discussion is directed toward the social work role.

Social Work Role in Empowerment

The shift in attitudes reinforces the notion of a partnership between social worker and consumer. The partnership becomes one of mutual contribution, with each person having an equally valid voice. Relationship is an element common to all empowerment models.

RELATIONSHIP *Relationship* is a partnership that rests on active participation from both the social worker and the consumer. Whether in a worker-consumer dyad or in a larger collective effort, such as a group or program, the practitioner actively works with the consumer to participate in purposeful opportunities that assist in achieving his or her life plan. For example, the mutual empowerment of the clubhouse model rests on participation, role, and purpose—people with places to be and roles to play experience themselves as valued, contributing members of a community (Gramps, 1986).

The work with consumers involves an understanding of context—the concrete, material resources and the social/emotional support needed to grow (Rose, 1992). Therefore, the worker has a responsibility to the whole person, and to what each needs to lead a satisfying life, rather than to a "patient" (Rose, 1991). The relationship is directed toward enhancing consumers' ability to change their environment rather than adapting to an environment that restricts or inhibits growth.

The discovery of power is not something that can be given (Gramps, 1986). Instead, it happens in the process of being needed and being asked to help (Rappaport, Reischl, & Zimmerman, 1992). Focused on engaging consumers to take risks and be involved (Glickman, 1989), the social worker uses transformative leadership—"exercising leadership in order to give it away"—rather than "holding and stratifying leadership," which frustrates growth (Anderson, 1985).

Sensitivity to the distribution of power in the relationship is paramount. In contrast to the traditional model of objectifying and distancing from the consumer, the social worker must deemphasize the professional role. The relationship thus becomes a friendship in daily interaction, with workers using clinical skills when needed (Freund, 1993). Spontaneous and genuine rather than remote and clinical, workers are human beings who, though fallible, can offer some expertise. Experts on themselves and their environments, consumers can also offer expertise in other areas (McWhirter, 1991).

Empowerment also stresses the need for education and the sharing of information in order to increase the consumer's power to cope with the environment (McWhirter, 1991). Because skill building is a critical component of empowerment, the worker actively informs, teaches, and links the individual to others who can add to his or her repertoire of skills to achieve personal goals.

Promoting empowerment requires social workers to tolerate ambiguity, form trusting relationships, and work actively to develop an individual's strengths and social support networks, in the agency and in the natural community (Freund, 1993). The social worker has a personal commitment to the consumer that goes beyond agency roles, funding issues, and needs assessment (Rose, 1991). The worker is the "human link" between the person and the formal system. As individuals become increasingly independent and interdependent, the social worker moves to a less central position in the relationship (Freund, 1993).

The next section integrates the attitudes, practices, and roles just discussed into an actual model of empowerment practice in mental health.

A PROGRAM OF EMPOWERMENT

Many programs and methods reflect empowerment practice. These include consumer-run programs such as the Independent Living Model (Deegan, 1992), self-help groups (Silverman, Segal, & Anello, 1992), and GROW (Rappaport et al., 1992). Case management strategies include the Strengths-based Model developed by Rapp (Kisthardt & Rapp, 1992), the Advocacy/Empowerment Model (Rose, 1992), and the Partnership Model (Shera, 1993). Finally, some programs based on the psychosocial rehabilitation model are partnerships between professionals and consumers (e.g., Fountain House and other clubhouses). All these programs may be freestanding or associated with mental health centers.

CHARG[1]

A unique form of empowerment practice occurs in centers with a partner-ship governance structure, in which consumers and professionals together manage and direct the agency. One example is the Capitol Hill Action and Recreation Group (CHARG) in Denver, Colorado. Established to improve the quality of life and functioning capacity of people with severe and persis-tent mental illness, CHARG strives to empower mental health consumers through managing their own program and learning new skills. It also pro-vides needed resources and services that consumers cannot obtain else-where (CHARG brochure).

The center provides comprehensive services—drop-in socialization, psychiatric care and counseling, medication evaluation and follow-up, learn-ing and vocational programs, basic needs resources, advocacy, and outreach. In addition, consumers and professional staff at the center engage in public education about mental disability and in organizing consumer groups to advocate for their own needs.

CHARG has a unique governance structure in that it is a joint ven-ture of two nonprofit organizations: Heart of Boardwalk and CHARG. Heart of Boardwalk comprises mental health professionals, family members, and community supporters. CHARG is made up of mental health con-sumers. Further, "the combined gifts of this partnership provide a unique framework within which consumers find the support, community, and struc-ture they need to implement a successful program" (CHARG brochure). Each board of directors has 50% of the decision-making power. Both boards must approve every policy. Because equality in power defines the relation-ship between the boards as peers, each maintains an independent status.

---

[1] Adapted from *A Matter of Community I & II* by Lynn Jones. Copyright © 1984 and 1992 Lynn P. Jones. Adapted with permission.

That is, neither partner works on activities for the other (Jones, 1992). However, they share equal responsibility for the results. This arrangement provides for the decision-making opportunities identified as critical to empowerment by consumers (Manning et al., 1994). It also prevents co-optation by professionals, however well-meaning their intent.

The sharing of power between consumers and professionals is rational-ized clinically and in terms of "common sense" (Olsen, 1993). The clinical rationale for sharing power is that it promotes good mental health by enhancing communication between consumers and professionals and by increasing opportunities to assert consumer rights. The commonsense ratio-nale is that it leaves the consumer free to grow, empowers consumers to operate their own program, and closes gaps in the mental health system by providing needed services. This lived philosophy incorporates the compo-nents of empowerment discussed in Chapter 1: values, attitudes, and beliefs; collective experience; knowledge and skills for critical thinking and action; and the opportunity for action.

Jones (1984, 1992), a founding member of Heart of Boardwalk, argues that traditionally consumers have not had real power in the mental health system that provides their services. Though input on boards and commit-tees has increased in recent years because of consumer and family activism, such input does not equal the power of making decisions. Conflict still emerges from this persistent powerlessness. According to Jones, people can usually only experience power by refusing treatment rather than by partici-pating in treatment. The CHARG model, in contrast, incorporates full consumer power and participation into the governance and programming of the center.

Concepts integral to the operation of the center include community, structure, expectations, flexibility, respect for the individual, balance, and just "being there" (Jones, 1992). Referred to as a "community," the program environment is a network where people are accepted, wanted, and needed —where people experience belonging. The center is a gathering place that becomes a community for individuals who live in a variety of residences. People individually decide whether and when to attend; their ability to know what is best for themselves is respected. The community becomes a collective in which each person's sense of self and individual experience is validated.

The nature of mental disabilities makes it difficult for consumers to establish and maintain structure. CHARG provides a place where con-sumers can have a meaningful structure, can do things, and can participate. The *structure* can be another person, buildings, rituals, pastimes, activities, etc. Jones (1992, p. 10) notes that the "key word is meaningful." The devel-opment of structures ranges from intensive residential settings to employ-ment support in the community. Each structure is provided as long as necessary. Depending on their own needs, consumers can move among structures while maintaining existing friends and activities. The focus on developing structure emphasizes the skill building, sharing of information, and relationship building noted earlier as empowering activities.

Participants select activities assessed as possible and meaningful. *Possible* means that the individual can accomplish the activity. Gradually, opportunities for new experiences are presented, with success leading to further positive risk taking. There is always, though, a range of activities that accommodate a person's functioning at any level. This demonstrates the strengths-based perspective—building on strengths and providing opportunities to develop skills to continue to grow. Possible activities also support the shift in consumer attitudes from self-doubting or blaming to feeling hopeful and responsible.

Meaningful activities have a purpose—they are real, not contrived. Learning, producing something worthwhile, improving health, and having fun serve as examples of meaningful activities. These are defined in the partnership and based on the active participation of the consumer. In short they are relevant to the lives of those involved.

Rather than artificial expectations, or "expectations that are not produced from the natural process of each person" such as a treatment plan developed by staff for clients, social workers encourage the consumer to achieve those expectations that flow from the natural life process and from what the consumer wants. The professional is a "motivator and a supporter, not a judge" (Jones, 1992, p. 13). This role is congruent with the client-driven model discussed earlier, in which the worker is responsible to the whole person and helps him or her lead a satisfying life within a particular context.

Flexibility is important. One must allow time for a process to occur, not force it. A long-term effort, working with people with mental disabilities sometimes takes years rather than months or weeks to produce change. Because they are not natural to growth, time limits are not imposed in this program. Further, involvement and belonging sometimes mean lifelong commitments.

Participants do not discount but recognize the stresses of coping with a severe mental disability. When things do not go well, the consumer is not blamed. Nor are there unrealistic expectations about everyone living independently. Instead, each individual is respected for her or his particular situation and disability. As described by consumers, this shows respect for each person (Manning et al., 1994).

To incorporate new techniques with existing technology, consumers and staff avoid latching on to a particular intervention that will work for everyone. Instead, they strive for a balance of technologies that can help a variety of people with different experiences. As such, for example, hospitalization is not viewed as bad or good but as a resource some individuals sometimes need.

Regarding "just being there," in the words of Jones (1992), "The pain which my clients have experienced as a result of their illnesses is overwhelming. The losses they have suffered are nearly unspeakable. Sometimes it's been hard for me to endure one more tragic story, to hear about one more loss. At times my urge has been to rush in and try to fix things, which would feel better than being still and hearing the pain. But such things can't be fixed, and trying to do so is disrespect for the person's pain." In the words of her friend, "Sometimes all you can do is just be there." Subject to subject, each with her or his own lived experience, developing "power with" not "power over" illustrates the shift in power from worker to consumer presented earlier.

While CHARG demonstrates the usefulness of empowerment principles at every level of service delivery, any new technology that incorporates radically different assumptions is often seen as a threat to the status quo. Adopting an empowerment perspective requires a shift in the current mental health paradigm. The final section of this chapter discusses some of the issues of and barriers to adopting an empowerment practice paradigm in mental health.

EMPOWERMENT AS A TECHNOLOGY IN MENTAL HEALTH

Because empowerment is an innovative shift in "the way we do things," certain issues affect the implementation of empowerment. First and foremost, the "theoretical world view" and underlying assumptions (Swift & Levin, 1987, p. 77) that historically have directed interventions in mental health contradict most empowerment assumptions. As such, a paradigm shift is necessary, which takes time and requires an awareness of obstacles and issues.

Systems/Structural Issues

As noted earlier, oppressed and excluded groups often fail to achieve goals because of limited access to social resources, opportunities, and decision-making power. Increasing evidence suggests that the failure is due to the structure of the system with which the groups interact (Swift & Levin, 1987). Systems, such as mental health, high in "structural inequalities" and "resistance to change" are more difficult to infuse with empowering technology (p. 83).

COMPETITION The growing consumer and family self-help structures, as well as their relationship with the formal system, embody those issues. Competitive or "conflictive" relationships develop when the traditional service system competes with empowerment programs for funding, research grants, and clients (Hasenfeld & Gidron, 1992). A consumer describes the tension like this: "We're working on a continuum of collaboration to competition. . . . It's their line item dollars. . . . The only way to bridge the gap is to work with them . . . always have to . . . plan the program so you get the right 'strings.' Working within the system means developing relationships of cooperation and coordination. While these elements improve the working relationship, there is the danger of co-optation by the system" (Manning et al., 1994, p. 47).

CO-OPTATION Co-optation occurs when service agencies control more power and resources than consumers. As the empowerment subgroup creates a "compliant" relationship with the system, at the cost of some of the empowerment philosophy and technology, the program begins to look more like the traditional system in order to survive. For example, a consumer leader notes, "The division says you have to make a connection with the mental health clinic (MHC). . . . To get funding you have to have a 'road back' to the MHC for crisis intervention. . . . Then the perception we're dealing with, with consumers is 'crisis intervention.' . . . All that crap is an extension of the MHC" (Manning et al., 1994, p. 47).

Those empowerment programs initiated by the system are the most vulnerable to co-optation (Hasenfeld & Gidron, 1992). Therefore, the level of commitment on the part of social workers to advocate for a pure empowerment approach is critical. To change the system, social workers can use the same empowerment technology for themselves that they use in practice with consumers. Mobilizing a collective made up of consumers, family members, and providers with similar interests, developing skills and knowledge, and taking action over time can together change a system. Collaboration among groups changes perceptions, increases power through unity, and helps people to focus on a common purpose. One provider involved in such a collaboration has stated, "Working on this project has changed my view of mental health consumers. . . . They have become people too" (Manning et al., 1994, p. 17).

Human Factors and Empowerment

Human beings themselves promote or resist, provide or prohibit, empowerment technology. Many human factors affect empowerment—from professionals to consumers.

PROFESSIONAL RESISTANCE Stigma abounds in the mental health system. Sometimes the people who most resist empowerment technology are providers. This resistance can be insidious. In a study of social workers in mental health, Facer (1992) found that whereas 92% of workers felt that consumers should be involved in forming their own service plan, in actual practice there was minimal consumer participation. Instead, 88% of the workers "relied on their own or colleagues' observations to assess consumer need and aspirations" (p.15). Jones (1992) found professional resistance inside and outside the CHARG program. Professionals external to CHARG seemed to perceive the model as "competition" and were threatened by the "independence" from the mental health center model. Internally, professionals had to learn how to let go of the power in decision making. In both instances, however, positive change has occurred over time.

BURN-OUT—THE METEOR METAPHOR   Initially, before skills of sharing power have been developed, a few consumers tend to provide leadership. As one provider says, "A talented person arrives on the scene and takes a leadership role. . . . There are moments of great glory followed by a crash . . . meteors who don't last long. . . . People take on a big job and burn out" (Manning et al., 1994, p. 33).

The tendency to depend on a few key consumers is related to difficulty with the delegation of responsibility by both professionals and consumers. Also, once seen as leaders, consumers find themselves in great demand for other functions. For example, an administrator states, "Consumers doing work for the state mental health system . . . takes energy away from the consumer movement. . . . Are we thieves?" (Manning et al., 1994, p. 34). The lack of training for empowerment programs means that professionals and consumers must find their own way—a time-consuming process.

PRINCIPLES FOR PRACTICE

Empowerment practice with people who have a severe and persistent mental disability is based on a fundamental redefinition of three elements related to practice: attitude, relationship, and role. This chapter has demonstrated many of the following practice principles organized by these elements.

Attitudes

1. Think of and interact with the person, not the label/diagnosis.
2. Respect the person's right to self-determination.
3. Be responsible to the "whole person," taking quality of life and environmental factors into account.
4. Focus on a strengths perspective rather than a deficit model for assessment and practice.
5. Respect the diversity of skills and knowledge that consumers bring to the relationship. Let go of being the "expert."

6. Trust consumers' internal motivation to learn and direct their lives.
7. Respect consumers' ability and right to contribute—to you, to other consumers, to the agency, and to the community.
8. Recognize the individuality of people, respecting each person's unique qualities, values, and needs.

Relationship

1. Practice according to a partnership model. Develop "power with and among" rather than "power over" in relationships with consumers.
2. Allow time for a process of relationship building and growth. See the relationship as ongoing, not time limited.
3. Deemphasize the professional role. Be genuine, spontaneous, and real.
4. Work for active participation from consumer and practitioner.
5. Share leadership; value the leadership the consumer brings to the relationship.

Social Work Role

1. Develop a client-driven model of care focused on the goals and values held by the consumer.
2. Emphasize building connections through roles, involvement, and community to replace lost culture, history, and identity.
3. Develop opportunities for meaningful activities that help to build skills, knowledge, and reflexive thinking.
4. Enhance consumers' ability to transform their environment rather than adapt to it.
5. Engage consumers in taking risks, making decisions, and learning from them.
6. Emphasize information, education, and skill-building that increases self-efficacy.
7. Involve consumers and family members in decision-making roles in the relationship and within the organization.

CONCLUSION

The consumer voice is intensifying. With that voice comes an increasing emphasis on the philosophy and technology of empowerment. The philosophy of the community support system movement in mental health is based on principles of consumer empowerment and involvement in one's own care (Chamberlain, Rogers, & Sneed, 1989). Within provider-run and client-run mental health programs, the concepts of self-help not only empower consumers but also combat stigma. The empowerment model of practice for social workers in mental health offers an opportunity to embody the moral teleology of the profession in practice—actively working to enhance the self-determination of consumers. In her address to the state mental health conference, a consumer from CHARG says, "I have a life turned around. When I came to CHARG Resource Center, I had lived decades of complete disability and helplessness. I am now off neuroleptics and working and an active member of our CHARG Board. It is the only psychiatry which has actually worked, to give me a lot of support so I feel I am important to people, and then give me all the responsibilities I feel I am ready for" (Jones, 1992, p. 23).

REFERENCES

Anderson, S. (1985). The role of staff at Fountain House. *The Fountain House Annual, 3*, 9–13.

Anonymous. (1990). My name is legion, for we are many: Diagnostics and the psychiatric client. *Social Work, 38*(2), 391–392.

Bachrach, L. (1987). The homeless mentally ill. In W. Menninger & G. Hannah (Eds.), *The chronic mental patients* (pp. 65–92.). Washington, DC: American Psychiatric Press.

Barr, D., & Cochran, M. (1992). Understanding and supporting empowerment: Redefining the professional role. *Networking Bulletin: Empowerment and Family Support, 2*(3), 1–8.

Becker, H. (1963). *Outsiders: Studies in the sociology of deviance.* New York: Free Press.

Belcher, J. (1989). On becoming homeless: A study of chronically mentally ill persons. *Journal of Community Psychology, 17*, 173–184.

Boltz, S. (1992). *Creating partnerships with self-help: Differences in the self-help and professional roles.* [Center for Self-Help Research, Working Paper series.] Berkeley, CA: Center for Self-Help Research.

Chamberlain, J. (1978). *On our own: Patient controlled alternatives to the mental health system.* New York: McGraw-Hill.

Chamberlain, J. (1990). The ex-patients' movement: Where we've been and where we're going. *Journal of Mind and Behavior, 11*(4), 323–328.

Chamberlain, J., Rogers, J., & Sneed, C. (1989). Consumers, families, and community support systems. *Psychosocial Rehabilitation Journal, 12*(3), 93–106.

Chesler, M., & Chesney, B. (1988). Self-help groups: Empowerment attitudes and behaviors of disabled or chronically ill persons. In H. Yuker (Ed.), *Attitudes toward persons with disabilities* (pp. 230–247). New York: Springer.

Deegan, P. (1992). The independent living movement and people with psychiatric disabilities: Taking back control over our own lives. *Psychosocial Rehabilitation Journal, 15*(3), 3–19.

Estroff, S. (1982). *Making it crazy.* Berkeley, CA: University of California Press.

Estroff, S. (1989). Self, identity, and subjective experiences of schizophrenia: In search of the subject. *Schizophrenia Bulletin, 15*(2), 189–196.

Facer, J. (1992, March). Room to consume. *Social Work Today,* pp. 14–15.

Freund, P. (1993). Professional role(s) in the empowerment process: "Working with" mental health consumers. *Psychosocial Rehabilitation Journal, 16*(3), 65–71.

Glickman, M. (1989). *What if nobody wants to make lunch? Bottom line responsibility in the clubhouse.* Paper presented at the Fifth International Seminar on the Clubhouse Model, St. Louis, MO.

Goffman, E. (1974). *Stigma: Notes on the management of a spoiled identity.* New York: Aronson.

Goldstein, H. (1986). Toward the integration of theory and practice. *Social Work, 31,* 352–357.

Gramps, M. (1986). *Mutual empowerment.* Paper presented at the Fourth International Seminar on the Clubhouse Model, Seattle, WA.

Hasenfeld, Y., & Gidron, B. (1992). *Self-help groups and human service organizations: An inter-organizational perspective.* Berkeley, CA: Center for Self-Help Research.

Jones, L. (1984). *A matter of community I.* Denver, CO: CHARG Resource Center.

Jones, L. (1992). *A matter of community II.* Denver, CO: CHARG Resource Center.

Kagle, J., & Cowger, C. (1984). Blaming the victim: Implicit assumptions of social work research? *Social Work, 19,* 82–89.

Kisthardt, W., & Rapp, C. (1992). Bridging the gap between principles and practice: Implementing a strengths perspective in case management. In S. Rose (Ed.), *Case management and social work practice* (pp. 112–123). New York: Longman.

Lehman, A., Ward, N., & Linn, L. (1982). Chronic mental patients: The quality of life issue. *American Journal of Psychiatry, 139,* 1271–1276.

Lidz, C., Meisel, A., Zerubavel, E., Carter, M., Sestak, R., & Roth, L. (1984). *Informed consent: A study of decision-making in psychiatry.* New York: Guilford.

Link, B. (1983). Mental patient status, work, and income: An examination of the effects of a psychiatric label. *American Sociological Review, 47,* 202–215.

Ludwig, A. (1971). *Treating the treatment failures: The challenge of chronic schizophrenia.* New York: Grune & Stratton.

Manning, S., & Suire, B. (1996). Bridges and roadblocks: Consumers as employees in mental health. *Psychiatric Services, 47*(9), 939–943.

Manning, S., Zibalese-Crawford, M., & Downey, E. (1994). *Colorado mental health consumer and family development project: Program evaluation.* Denver, CO: University of Denver, Graduate School of Social Work.

McWhirter, E. (1991). Empowerment in counseling. *Journal of Counseling and Development, 69,* 222–227.

Mental illness remains a source of stigma. [News and notes]. (1991). *Hospital and Community Psychiatry, 42,* 310.

Miller, S., & Miller, R. (1991). An exploration of the daily hassles for persons with severe psychiatric disabilities. *Psychosocial Rehabilitation Journal, 14*(4), 39–51.

Olsen, Z. (1993, February). *Sharing power in the mental health community.* Paper presented at the Annual Conference of CHARG Resource Center, Denver, CO.

Rapp, C., Shera, W., & Kisthardt, W. (1993). Research strategies for consumer empowerment of people with severe mental illness. *Social Work, 38*(6), 727–735.

Rappaport, J., Reischl, T., & Zimmerman, M. (1992). Mutual help mechanisms in the empowerment of former mental patients. In D. Saleebey (Ed.), *The strengths perspective in social work practice* (pp. 84–97). New York: Longman.

Rose, S. (1991). Strategies of mental health programming: A client-driven model of case management. In C. Hudson & A. Cox, (Eds.), *Dimensions of mental health policy* (pp. 138–154). New York: Praeger.

Rose, S. (1992). Case management: An advocacy/empowerment design. In S. Rose (Ed.), *Case management and social work practice* (pp. 271–297). New York: Longman.

Rosenfield, S. (1992). Factors contributing to the subjective quality of life of the chronic mentally ill. *Journal of Health and Social Behavior, 33,* 299–315.

Saleebey, D. (1992). Introduction: Power in the people. In Saleebey (Ed.), *The strengths perspective in social work practice* (pp. 3–17). New York: Longman.

Segal, S., Silverman, C., & Temkin, T. (1993). Empowerment and self-help agency practice for people with mental disabilities. *Social Work, 38*(6), 705–712.

Shera, W. (1993). *Assessing the efficacy of a partnership model of case management.* Paper presented at the Education and Research for Empowerment Conference, Seattle, WA.

Silverman, C., Segal, S., & Anello, E. (1992). *Community and the homeless disabled: The structure of self-help groups.* Berkeley, CA: Center for Self-Help Research.

Swift C., & Levin, G. (1987, Fall–Winter). Empowerment: An emerging mental health technology. *Journal of Primary Prevention, 8*(1/2), 71–94.

Wilk, R. (1994). Are the rights of people with mental illness still important? *Social Work, 39*(2), 167–175.

Yeich, S., and Levine, R. (1992). Participatory research's contribution to a conceptualization of empowerment. *Journal of Applied Social Psychology, 22,* 1894–1908.

Chapter 7

EMPOWERMENT PRACTICE WITH HOMELESS PEOPLE/FAMILIES

Graydon Andrus, M.S.W.
Health Care for the Homeless, Seattle, Washington

Susan Ruhlin, M.S.W.
Fremont Family Shelter/Bethlehem House, Seattle, Washington

INTRODUCTION

Being without a home is not an intractable condition. The government and people of the United States have proved this well in their response to disasters, perhaps most notably hurricane Andrew in 1992. With over 200,000 people left homeless, material aid flooded in; within a few months, the vast majority no longer remained homeless (Blau, 1992).

Hurricane Andrew showed people's willingness to help those they considered deserving and able to resume financial independence with limited help. However successful, these efforts do nothing to change the complex and entrenched reality of homeless people, who suffer difficult personal conditions and societal shortcomings. The homeless population is often misrepresented and misunderstood. One of the reasons is that policy makers, program developers, and service providers have not learned to truly listen. For many reasons, they do not address the circumstances and conditions of most homeless people. The United States, as a nation and as individuals, can nonetheless employ sustainable solutions to homelessness using empowerment practice methods. As two social workers who work with homeless people in Seattle, Washington, we shall focus on working with homeless individuals residing in large warehouse-type shelters and on working with homeless families residing in motels and apartments. But first, a review of the major causes and characteristics of contemporary homelessness will help to frame this ominous social problem.

CAUSES AND CHARACTERISTICS
OF HOMELESSNESS

Many definitions of homelessness have been generated, each with its own set of statistics. Regardless of the debate about the numbers of homeless people in the United States, one cannot deny that the number is growing. Schutt and Garrett (1992) identify three primary sources of homelessness: *chronic homelessness*, which occurs among those unable to maintain any social or financial supports; *episodic homelessness*, which stems from crises and problems less continuous than those marking the chronic condition; and *temporary homelessness*, which stems from natural disasters or other calamities such as domestic violence.

The Stewart B. McKinney Act defines a homeless person as "one who lacks a fixed permanent nighttime residence or whose nighttime residence is a temporary shelter, welfare hotel, or any public or private place not designed as sleeping accommodations for human beings" (Blau, 1992). This definition falls somewhere in the middle of the spectrum of definitions. The U.S. government tends to adopt definitions that reduce the count of homelessness, while the Canadian definition of displaced person is far more inclusive.

Perhaps more important than these definitions is the context of homelessness—poverty and its causes. The homeless have become an increasingly visible sector of the poor in the United States. With certain economic causes of poverty worsening and the concurrent reduction of services aimed at preventing or ameliorating the consequences of poverty, the outcome is obvious.

Most fundamentally, one can view homelessness as a product of an economic system unwilling to distribute resources equitably. The current period of what Blau calls contemporary homelessness can be viewed historically as the fifth major period of homelessness (Blau, 1992). This period is distinguished by deindustrialization and the transition to a service economy. The shift from livable wages and benefit packages available in manufacturing jobs to lower-paying service jobs that don't provide benefits (Wagner, 1991) has left many people more vulnerable to the harsh realities of living on the edge. Over the past 20 years, the average income of a family with children headed by a person less than 30 years old dropped 24%, with young African-American family incomes dropping 33%. By the beginning of this decade, more than 12 million children, one in every five, were living in poverty (Seltser & Miller, 1993). Social welfare cutbacks, reductions in affordable housing, and the sharp increase in low-wage jobs have also exacerbated homelessness. Blau (1992) distinguishes contemporary homelessness from other periods by these characteristics: (1) growth in homelessness during economic recovery, (2) decline of social networks, (3) high incidence of mental disorders, (4) rise in homeless women and children, and (5) rural homelessness.

The recent growth in homelessness has occurred during a period of economic recovery. As such, fewer people are controlling more of the money. The purported benefits of "trickle-down" economics promoted during the Reagan era have defied gravity by trickling up. Though many people earned lower wages, rents increased. During the past 20 years, rental costs rose 13% faster than inflation; 26% faster in the western states (Seltser & Miller, 1993). In the same period, the median price of a house rose by more than 20% while median income rose by less than 1%.

With the decline of social networks and community cohesion, fewer people can turn to others in times of need. Traditional values of families, neighborhoods, and larger communities continue to erode. The trend is particularly worrisome because it indicates a cultural change that one cannot fully address simply by providing entitlements or revising policy. Principles of empowerment practice seek to reverse this alienating and frightening trend by promoting collective efforts and cooperation rather than each person for herself or himself.

A relatively high incidence of mental disorders among the homeless exists. One cannot say to what extent homelessness causes those disorders. This, combined with wide-ranging ideas of what constitutes mental illness, makes it difficult to define its prevalence in this population. People with mental disorders form a distinctive and significant group within the homeless population. The high prevalence is due partially to the development of antipsychotic drugs and the subsequent discharge of many thousands of chronically mentally ill individuals from state mental institutions. Indeed, the development of antipsychotic medications set the stage for large-scale deinstitutionalization of mentally ill people from 1955 onward. This new policy created the need to develop large numbers of community mental health centers and supportive housing.

The Mental Retardation Facilities and Community Mental Health Centers Construction Act of 1963 projected the funding of 2000 community mental health centers. By 1980, only 789 had been funded (Blau, 1992). Even if all the 2000 centers had been funded, they would not have adequately addressed the treatment and service needs of the chronically mentally ill population. The woeful inadequacy of these services left many without the essential services and support they needed. While some had family or friends to take them in, others had to fend for themselves. The streets and shelters became the daily reality for many.

There has also been a rapid rise in the numbers of homeless families, mainly comprised of single women with children. Though the single adult man is still the most common type of homeless person, this seems likely to change if the trend in homeless families continues. Welfare hotels, emergency shelters, and transitional housing have provided an effective response in some cases but have not sufficiently stemmed the tide. When domestic violence forces women to flee an abusive relationship, they lose their housing and support. In many cases, mothers lack the job skills and ability to pay for child care necessary to obtain financial independence. Given their limited options, many turn to Aid to Families with Dependent Children (AFDC). Low-income citizens living in unsubsidized housing spend approximately 50–70% of their income on rent; single mothers with children spend even more (DeWoody, 1992). With an obvious shortage of affordable housing, shelters become the only choice for many. Comprehensive services and resources are needed to address effectively the chaos and instability of homeless families. Tragically, the current political climate does not make such services a priority.

The rural community, perhaps the last bastion of traditional mutual support, has succumbed to the pressures brought about by low wages, personal economic crises, and the shortage of affordable housing. Adding to the problem, few social services are available to rural residents. Further, even available services are often difficult to access because of distance.

In discussing the causes and characteristics of contemporary homelessness, one must mention alcoholism and other chemical dependencies. Though the increased use of alcohol and other drugs is predictable for many after they become homeless, chemical dependency also contributes significantly to becoming homeless in the first place. Crack cocaine use is increasingly prevalent among shelter residents and in low-income neighborhoods. The topic deserves much consideration as there are those who would simply dismiss the entire population of chemically dependent homeless people as unworthy of services—a clear example of blaming the victim. Chemical dependency has long been considered a disease: While alcoholism and other chemical dependencies are difficult to effectively treat, so are many forms of cancer. Yet no one with cancer would be refused treatment.

Short of fundamental change in the way the United States mitigates the effects of its capitalist economic system, the homeless population will continue to rise. The remainder of this chapter will examine issues of powerlessness and empowerment-oriented practice with homeless individuals and families. Examples of empowerment-based practice with each population will be described.

ISSUES OF POWERLESSNESS

Issues of powerlessness pervade the experience of being homeless. Meeting the basic needs of food, shelter, clothing, and health care often means standing in countless lines to receive modest assistance. Dependence on others for so many needs combined with the restricted ability to control one's time, space, and options can create a general sense of powerlessness.

Chapter 1 presented three levels of powerlessness: personal, interpersonal, and environmental. This framework can help one understand the experiences of homeless people and families.

Personal

Personal powerlessness refers to the feeling and perception that one cannot influence and resolve issues in one's own life. Though limited self-esteem and self-confidence are part of the process leading up to homelessness, they are also products of finding oneself in an overwhelming and uncontrollable situation. Clients regularly remind us that we cannot possibly know what it is like to be homeless. However, the effort to understand such feelings is a worthwhile beginning for the worker. Imagine the effects of losing control of your living space, losing the freedom to come and go as you please, losing your belongings or a place to put them, and losing your health. These losses and many others contribute greatly to a sense of powerlessness, not to mention grief and depression.

Although individuals and families suffer similar types of loss, some issues are unique to families. For example, homeless children often change schools many times and have to adjust to new friends, teachers, and situations. Such children often experience increased fears, nightmares, and bed-wetting. In a shelter setting, parents often experience powerlessness because they must conform to the shelter's rules about parenting and other life tasks. When children sense their parent's loss of power, they in turn feel more insecure. The loss of home, predictability, and familiar routines has significant social and emotional consequences for the entire family.

Interpersonal

On an interpersonal level, most people try to solve problems the way they have in previous experiences. A newly homeless person's recent interpersonal experiences are likely to have been unfulfilling, thus reflecting unsuccessful attempts at meeting needs. A person homeless for an extended period has also quite likely had relationships unhelpful to their self-efficacy. Many homeless individuals face interpersonal violence daily. This threat requires an inordinate focus on maintaining one's safety, thus inhibiting personal growth and the ability to work effectively on other goals.

In a shelter setting, the power differential between a person seeking housing and a worker in a position to offer, limit, or refuse services can lead to the avoidance of such relationships. Anticipated or actual, this dynamic has a chilling effect. With increasing demands on shelter services, housing programs, and support services, the tendency to screen clients for eligibility increases. This reality does not escape the perception of most people needing the assistance. Rather than an open, honest and collaborative exchange with a worker, the conversation is loaded with fear, mistrust, and tension. In contrast, though, some people enter shelters with a minimal history of satisfying relationships, but they can find connection with other shelter residents. This connection can provide a sense of place and purpose in a community that has well-defined boundaries and shared common experience. Occasionally, power arises from unexpected places.

Families experience similar fears of shelter workers and other social service providers. Additionally, parents must deal with the power dynamic of the school system. Relationships with peers expand the interpersonal dimension to another dimension of practice as parents advocate for their children's needs and attempt to make changes in their social environment.

Further, when families enter social service systems—shelters or welfare—they relinquish much of their power as their family's life comes under the scrutiny and judgment of social workers. Parents receiving public assistance live from check to check, balancing their families' needs. Families in shelters spend much time planning for their next move, whether to another shelter, housing they cannot afford, or subsidized housing. Often shell-shocked, confused about their next step, and embarrassed by their situation, families may choose not to reveal all aspects of their situation; honesty often gets them screened out of receiving services (i.e., still using drugs, abuser may be pursuing them).

Many women have felt powerless over their situation for a long time because of childhood physical or sexual abuse or other family dysfunction. The chaos brought on by childhood abuse has affected the early development of many homeless women, which in turn has caused them to have trouble establishing themselves as independent adults (Baum & Burns, 1993). More than one-third of the homeless mothers in one study reported being abused as children; 50% of the mothers in another could not identify any adult on whom they could call for help (Baum & Burns, 1993). Many women who have suffered abuse as a child have low self-esteem and enter into abusive relationships as adults. When they leave their abuser, they have not only their own pain and healing to address but also that of their children.

When faced with the prospect of homelessness, some mothers cannot "go home" because of the small size or geographic dispersion of their relatives, their kin's lack of control of housing resources, or estrangement (McChesney, 1992). When families become homeless, they often become disaffiliated from their community, family, friends, and other social supports; they also experience a continuing marginalization and loss of identity as a family (Baum & Burns, 1993). People need to connect, to feel part of a family, a society. When people become alienated, they find it difficult to reestablish a connection with their community. As discussed in Chapter 1, a sense of positive identity promotes action and efficacy.

Environmental

The third level of powerlessness occurs at an environmental level. Some of the societal institutions one needs to get out of homelessness present barriers that discourage self-help efforts. For example, the banking industry works against establishing a safe place in which to save money by requiring minimum starting balances. The loss or theft of identification documents is common among the homeless. Getting a job, renting a hotel room, opening a bank account, or applying for public assistance usually requires state-issued I.D., which may in turn require a birth certificate and picture I.D. This often takes weeks or months if the person was born in another state. Interstate cooperation could reduce lag time significantly.

Vital support services may be inaccessible or inadequate. For example, the few post–high-school education and vocational training programs that exist are difficult to access and use while one is homeless. One needs such education to obtain livable wage jobs.

Though families experience the same environmental issues as individuals, they face additional ones by nature of their group composition. For example, families can experience discrimination from landlords who do not accept children or large families in their rental units. Children themselves experience the burden of transferring from school to school as the family moves to different shelters in various locations in the city or county. Reacting in fear and instability, children often fall behind in their schoolwork. Such children can also face stigmatization from classmates. The school system in Seattle has sought to ameliorate this issue through two innovative programs: First Place and Atlantic Street Center's Childrens' Futures. First Place is a private, nonprofit agency that provides educational and social services to children grades K–6 who live in any of Seattle's emergency shelters or in temporary/transitional housing. Childrens' Futures responds to children experiencing academic or social difficulties in selected Seattle public school sites. The services provided include support to families, housing and emergency assistance, tutoring, social/recreational activities, and summer school. Unfortunately, most cities do not offer this type of educational support.

According to Timmer, Eitzen, and Talley (1994), families in the United States are expected to exist as independent, self-reliant units amidst increased joblessness, declining real income, and expanding inequality. With the lack of governmental support, family social policies deny the basics of a decent standard of living such as universal health care, income security, affordable housing, and improved public education. The policies place blame on families for their supposed poverty of values rather than on the failure of social policy to support families (Timmer et al., 1994). Families feel overwhelmed and overburdened when support systems fail them. One of the main ways government and social policies have neglected families is the lack of decent, affordable housing. Needless to say, this neglect has left many families in the streets looking for shelter.

Any approach to ending homelessness must balance individual and structural causes. It is dehumanizing to blame homelessness solely on individuals. On the other hand, blaming homelessness solely on structural reasons ignores the responsibility of the individual to choose and act (Seltser & Miller, 1993). The barriers we have just discussed are just a few of the many concrete and perceptual barriers that contribute to the erosion of control over one's life and to a sense of powerlessness.

EMPOWERMENT METHODS

The ideas presented here come from the experiences and perspectives we have gained in working with homeless single adults (over 18 years of age) and with families defined as one or more adults (mainly women) caring for at least one child under 18. We did this work within the framework of a comprehensive case management model.

Few need empowerment-oriented work more than homeless people. "Selective focus" on historically disempowered groups and individuals is essential to such work (Simon, 1994). Though the prevalence of homelessness in the United States has spiked several times, the current trend is clearly enduring. Chronically homeless adults are increasingly disregarded, ignored, and viewed as beyond help by the public. Multidimensional work is needed to address chronic homelessness and the trend of increasing homelessness effectively. The primary problem-solving activities, outlined in Chapter 1, provide a helpful framework for discussing empowerment-oriented methods.

Dimension 1 Activities

In dimension 1, issues of worker-client relationships, meeting immediate needs, consciousness raising, and learning about how to request and find resources are outlined.

More than ever, human service workers must extend themselves person-to-person with profoundly disaffiliated individuals and engage them on issues that specifically concern these clients. It is crucial that the client be involved in defining the problem. When clients feel that a social worker is accepting their definition of the problem and actively involving them in the process of change, their relationship has begun on a strong foundation. Empowerment practice demands relationships based on collaboration, trust, mutual respect, and shared power, with clear communication and understanding.

The worker needs to build these relationships with sensitivity and patience. Unless there are needs requiring immediate attention, a relaxed pace will promote a thorough and accurate understanding of the client's needs and perceptions. Further, dialogue that on the surface does not seem particularly germane may contribute significantly to creating a validating and supportive relationship. This approach will also likely afford opportunities to move away from the traditional expert/nonexpert relationship and result in a more balanced power dynamic.

Social workers must often act promptly to address their clients' immediate survival and safety needs. With competition for basic resources on the rise and the increasing complexity of emergency service agencies, social workers might best choose simply to step forward and acquire that which the client needs, such as emergency shelter, food, clothing, physical and mental health care, and entitlements. Sometimes it is important simply to do something for a client. Reynolds (1951) has asked the question, "Does it weaken clients to have things done for them?" The average person receives help from many people in daily life, free of charge, without feeling disempowered. Helping a client complete an application for public assistance or accompanying the client to an initial appointment, when requested, is a helpful and appropriate service. An early success can help establish positive momentum with a client. However, clients must also have access to information regarding how to find or request housing and other resources on their own so they can act on their own behalf, if so inclined.

The social worker's agency may have policies and procedures that conflict with empowerment-oriented work, creating tremendous implications for engagement. For example, some shelters require all clients to work with a case manager on a service plan even though a client's presenting issues sometimes restrict the scope of such a plan. Perhaps the person is experiencing symptoms of paranoia and is not ready or interested in designing or following the plan. It is particularly important for people who have a mental disorder that the service be offered rather than imposed (Cohen, 1989). A mandate is hardly "participant driven" and certainly does not suggest "shared power."

Shelters with limits on length of stay do not allow for the natural development of a relationship between worker and client. Allowing the resident to enter the relationship without coercion is paramount to facilitating his or her sense of control and power. Social workers may need to reinterpret the shelter guidelines in order to achieve anything clients will experience as helpful. The goal may be as limited as developing a positive relationship with them. In working with homeless people, social workers may never see the results of their work when clients are forced, or choose, to move on. One worker's effort and sensitivity may lay the ground for the next encounter with a social worker.

When a worker finds herself or himself defining agency guidelines in favor of working in a respectful and empowering style, it is time for them to take on activities outlined in dimension 3: participating in organizational change. To maintain a consistent empowerment practice without formal agency sanction is difficult. We shall discuss other dimension 3 activities later in this chapter.

Agency administration and funding sources need to hear the worker's knowledge and insight. In some cases, the client may want to participate in this activity. Unless workers maintain their voice, they will likely become discouraged and cynical; feeling powerless to change the system in which one works can contribute to an abandonment of empowerment ideals. The worker's involvement is particularly important as agencies serving homeless people become increasingly formalized.

The experience of self-blame can run deep in some homeless people. Seeing oneself as a "screw up," stupid, incompetent, unworthy, or a chronic failure may overshadow any positive self-image. Workers must be careful to avoid acts that support a notion of superiority. They might need to antici-pate such acts because one can easily, without intention, dominate an inter-action with someone who has little self-worth. Allowing extra time for clients to express themselves before responding, scheduling an appointment when convenient for clients, having equally comfortable chairs in your work space, considering places other than your office in which to meet, sharing basic resources such as a telephone, and trying to phrase things in a way that fits the culture, style, and educational level of each client—all are examples of ways to help increase a person's self-worth.

One can integrate consciousness raising into any stage of the relation-ship. This may involve education or discussion regarding social, political, or economic forces contributing to the client's situation or the sharing of per-sonal views with the client. The timing of such conversations matters. If basic needs have not been met, the appropriateness of raising such abstract issues may seem completely irrelevant and insensitive to the client.

For families, basic needs are more complex. Once they have fulfilled the immediate need of shelter and physical safety, families may need finan-cial benefits, food, clothing, transportation, toiletries, laundry supplies, dia-pers, etc. Families must establish some structure and stability before moving on to dimension 2 activities.

Dimension 2 Activities

Dimension 2 activities focus on education, skills development, and self-help. Adding group interaction among homeless people can provide much-needed information and support. Many homeless people have amassed valuable information regarding housing resources, entitlements, job programs, and related services. A social worker can play an important role in facilitating such a group by finding space in which to meet and joining in the discussion as needed. Making resource guides available to verify the accuracy of information and to fill any gaps in the group's collective knowledge may prove helpful. Skills used in dealing with bureaucrats, landlords, and other people who control needed resources can be shared in this setting as well. When working with families, parenting classes and support groups provide an environment where parents can learn new skills, share ideas and resources, and receive support in the often stressful role of parenting.

Members in such a group may also become catalysts for similar, less organized conversations in a shelter or drop-in center. (See the discussion on the Goodwill Gathering later in this chapter.) If an individual's social confidence is too low to cope with groups, the social worker can engage in knowledge and skill building with the person one-on-one. Because no group dynamic exists to encourage participation, eliciting the client's input is particularly important. It is all too easy for the social worker to slip into a dominant role as the disseminator of information.

A method that people seem to accept well is working together to list tasks and short-term goals clients want to accomplish during their stay in shelter, as well as long-term goals for future economic and personal stabilization. The worker should provide clients with resources and referrals appropriate to their goals. One method, which exemplifies collaboration and mutual responsibility within empowerment practice, involves dividing the list of tasks into "client does/worker does" and at each meeting discussing actions and results. The worker, for example, can take the tasks the client would have difficulty accomplishing because of agency policy or access to information; the client can take tasks with which she or he feels comfortable. Control over one's life often comes when goals are accomplished and one's situation begins to improve. When faced with the frightening situation of homelessness, clients need successes as quickly as possible.

Support groups are especially important for homeless people because of the acute alienation they often feel. People usually feel validated when they talk with one another about similar experiences. When clients join mutual aid support groups, they may establish relationships that will help them in the future; they can also share resources and practice problem solving and interpersonal communication. Support groups that can help the homeless include parenting classes, depression support groups, Alcoholics Anonymous, Narcotics Anonymous, Al-Anon, and domestic violence support groups.

Another crucial empowerment practice is helping clients develop their knowledge. This help includes exchanging resource information and brainstorming options and ideas with clients. When clients develop knowledge about their situation on both a personal and a societal level, they can take responsibility for those things they can change in their own lives and recognize those that result from a system's limited resources. An example of empowerment through mutual support is a welfare-rights organizing group. This sort of group strives to educate members about the welfare system so they can distinguish individual and societal responsibility. Participants work together to affect changes in the welfare system. Such activities associated with dimension 2 often spill over into dimension 3.

Dimension 3 Activities

Dimension 3 activities focus on change or mediation in the immediate environment. As part of a goal to regain independence, finding and maintaining sobriety is a critical issue for the chemically dependent individual. If a client is ready, social workers should address the addiction with the client and discuss relapse prevention strategies as a first step. A sobriety group offers critical support for a person in recovery. In a downtown community, where shelters tend to be located, the risk of relapse is particularly high. Encouraging chemically dependent people to access groups is essential, given the stress of being homeless and struggling with an addiction. Working from a strengths perspective, the strategy of "reframing" (Saleebey, 1992) experiences and perceptions may increase the chance of success. For example, to focus on what has led to periods of sobriety rather than periods of relapse helps the client make a perceptual shift from failure to success.

Helping clients develop interpersonal skills is also important. If the client expresses frustration in dealing with landlords or others in charge of resources, the client may want help with assertiveness skills. Increased assertiveness will likely lead to greater self-confidence and success in negotiating with service workers.

Dimension 4 Activities

Dimension 4 activities focus on social action and social change to prevent future problems. At any point in the worker-client relationship, the idea of participation in social change can be initiated. In one instance, the second conversation with a 52-year-old man who had been intermittently homeless for many years led to participation in a resource support group for homeless men over age 50. This group quickly became a housing advocacy group that branched into political action. Staying involved in political action and similar groups will help keep awareness and dialogue alive between social worker and client. A homeless person who has worked with a social worker grounded in empowerment practice will more likely connect with larger advocacy and action groups than those who have not.

EMPOWERMENT-ORIENTED PROGRAMS

"The various helping programs, which on the surface seem so sensible and responsive, are nothing more than Band-Aids that have little or no long-term benefit. The homeless receive another meal or a place to sleep for the night, or a family is given one more check for another month's rent, but the underlying problems continue to go unaddressed" (Baum and Burns, 1993). Though this quote may seem somewhat cynical, programs are often driven by funding rather than clients' needs. Some programs, though, do respond to clients and go far beyond covering the wounds. Here, we shall discuss some of these programs as models of empowerment principles: Seattle Housing and Resource Effort (SHARE), The Mental Health Chaplaincy, Community Voice Mail (CVM), and Apprenticeship and Non-Traditional Employment for Women (ANEW).

Seattle Housing and Resource Effort

This aptly named organization offers an excellent example of empowerment-based work with homeless people. In 1990, Scott Morrow began showing up at a street corner to serve coffee and engage homeless people in dialogue.[1] Five years later, SHARE—a multifaceted organization run for and by homeless people—carries on.

SHARE richly illustrates many empowerment themes. Responding to the City of Seattle's efforts to clear the streets of homeless people in preparation for the Goodwill Games, homeless people in July 1990 convened their own event: the Goodwill Gathering. Homeless people peacefully convened in a city park for 20 days, providing meals, information, an opportunity to connect with others, and a forum to organize. A planning process began that would firmly establish SHARE as a significant force in city politics and the homeless service sector. Opportunities to validate each other and to engage in critical thinking were important aspects of the gathering. Following it, 70 people slept out at the site under the theme, "The gathering is over but the people aren't gone."

The day before Thanksgiving that year, a tent city was erected. In ten days, the population went from 16 to 160. Tent City provided safety for many who had been sleeping in the "urban jungle." Through collective action, Tent City residents brought the Seattle city government into negotiations. In response to Tent City residents' refusal to leave, the mayor's office offered an unused bus barn as a shelter. SHARE self-managed the

---

[1]Many people have contributed to the success of SHARE, including Stan Buriss, Doug Castle, Steve Hunt, Cathy Lyons, Scott Morrow, Mark Mullins, George Olebar, and Loretta Stiles.

shelter and ultimately negotiated with the city once again, resulting in the acquisition of the Aloha Inn to serve as transitional housing for homeless individuals. The former motel is self-managed with the support of a small, modestly paid administrative staff. By realizing and exerting their collective political strength, SHARE took what one SHARE member called "from the mud up organizing" and converted it into transitional housing for 66 people. Self-imposed rules were established to encourage successful transition out of the Aloha.

All the while, SHARE continued to develop emergency shelter through collaboration with community churches and local government. They have also established a free day-storage service and are about to embark on a permanent housing plan. The board of directors is gender and racially mixed. The criteria for joining the board are as follows: Agree to work in a cooperative manner, be currently or recently homeless, and have attended three organizational meetings in a row. While addressing the concrete and immediate needs of homeless people by homeless people, a community based on mutual support, collective action, and individual empowerment carries on.

The Mental Health Chaplaincy

The Mental Health Chaplaincy, another Seattle organization, exemplifies empowerment-based work. After 16 years as a local pastor, Craig Rennebohm went to Berkeley for doctoral studies in ministry with a special focus on pastoral care with mentally ill people. Combining his study with his experience in community organizing, Rennebohm returned to Seattle to begin his work with homeless people experiencing mental illness. His work falls into three categories: street outreach, congregational companionship, and "wider work." The first involves walking a regular route daily to meet and engage people who are profoundly isolated. By meeting people where they are and patiently learning their story, a relationship based on trust is formed. A sense of self and belief in self-worth begins to take hold.

This important connection, perhaps the first in years, facilitates the first steps toward receiving needed care and joining a supportive community. As emergent needs are met and the effects of profound isolation diminish, some consciousness raising may begin. Introductions to new members of the "treatment team" provide another step toward establishing an initial community of support. This development occurs only when people are ready to realize they have a voice and that their voice is respected. Rennebohm's work with individuals provides a base for organizing the wider network of care and community.

Congregational companionship training is the second type of work the Mental Health Chaplaincy does. Individuals greet and offer companionship to the parish member or visitor experiencing mental illness. This intervention attempts to convey a sense of belonging and affirm the individual's self-worth. The chaplaincy also works to link local congregations together in neighborhood networks of care.

The third major aspect of the chaplaincy is the "wider work," which focuses on referrals and consultation and includes service agencies, community groups, and community presentations to foster understanding of mental illness and the "spiritual journey." This work aims at creating communities that have the full range of needed resources.

Central to this work is a deep respect for each person's worth and the capacity of small communities to be agents of change. Rennebohm's view is clear: "Homelessness ends when a person has a place to come home to, a sense of family and neighborhood."

Community Voice Mail

How many times have you retrieved messages from your voice mail today? Imagine looking for work, or an apartment, trying to conduct your business, or stay in touch with family and friends without a phone in today's world. "CVM is a large computer system that can replicate a personal home answering machine for homeless/phoneless people" ("Community Voice Mail," 1995). Homeless men and women who don't have their own phone or answering machine miss housing and employment opportunities because they cannot be reached quickly. CVM provides 24-hour access to telephone messages. As one client has stated, "The most important services of Employment Security's Homeless Employment Program were voice mail and bus transportation. Without either, it's almost impossible to get an interview let alone a job. In today's market phone accessibility and transportation are necessities" ("Community Voice Mail," 1995). A case manager, using a Touch-Tone phone, can enroll a client in the CVM program within minutes. Clients make their own greeting and receive their own 7-digit phone number and private pass code to retrieve messages. Clients also receive a wallet card with instructions on how to retrieve their messages. An excellent empowerment-based program, CVM lifts clients' self-esteem because they don't have to rely on a shelter case worker to take their messages. It increases self-sufficiency and independence because they connect with employers and landlords, social service providers, and friends and family while working on stabilizing their lives. "CVM is a link to a person whose homelessness is a constant reminder of isolation and disconnection" ("Community Voice Mail," 1995).

Apprenticeship and Non-Traditional Employment for Women

The ANEW program prepares women to enter nontraditional fields of employment. Although not specifically for the homeless, ANEW serves many homeless and formerly homeless women. This program targets low-income, disadvantaged, low-skilled women who need training to be employed. A five-month, five-days-a-week, seven-hours-a-day course of study, ANEW includes trades math, blueprint reading and drawing, mechanical and electrical theory and practice, basic carpentry and construction techniques, and hands-on practice of these skills in shop projects. Women learn to work with pipe, concrete, welding, and other media that allow them to apply for a variety of entry-level jobs. The program also includes physical fitness training and job/life-skills training. Through the former, women build strength and endurance through aerobics, working out with weights, and at least one hour of hard physical work each day. In the latter, women work on personal issues and learn how to get and keep a nontraditional job or apprenticeship.

The ANEW program is empowering because it lifts women out of poverty by preparing them for higher-paying jobs. Women gain a new sense of self-esteem and confidence as they complete a physically and mentally grueling program. Many women also work on the G.E.D. while in the ANEW program. ANEW's comprehensive approach prepares women for jobs that get and keep them out of poverty.

DISCUSSION

Early in this chapter, we examined homelessness from historical and causal perspectives. With this condition and its service systems now more permanent than once anticipated, the importance of examining institutions, policies, and service delivery is clear. With "quick fix" approaches inadequate to address the complex needs of many homeless individuals, empowerment principles become ever more fundamental as part of an effective response. Some of the principles and methods for direct service work have been discussed. This final section will focus on a few other related issues and will be followed by a list of key empowerment practice principles.

Quality versus Quantity

With demand for services exceeding availability, many shelters and ancillary services must face a major dilemma: Should the basics be provided to as many people as possible, or more comprehensive help provided to fewer? While the latter is more effective in helping the individual or family break the pattern of homelessness and its causes, more people are literally left out in the cold. An empowerment perspective appears to support comprehensive services. However, reducing access to services may heighten the perception of scarcity and stimulate more competition among the homeless. Feelings of camaraderie and community may thus be jeopardized.

Some shelter providers and funders prioritize quantity by imposing limits on length of stay. For example, some emergency shelters allow families to remain for only a few weeks, making them move before they can get settled and begin working on their goals. Unfortunately, clients spend much of their time searching for the next shelter. Social workers often make referrals but cannot follow up with clients before they leave the program. A relationship with a case manager gets established only to dissolve when a client moves to another shelter. Follow-up and concurrent services allow for continued relationships and more natural transitions.

Another consequence of need exceeding resources is specialization. More and more, service organizations consider family composition or particular disabilities when determining access to shelters and related services. For example, many shelters will accept a couple only if they are legally married. Also, families with boys over age ten are excluded from some shelters because of issues of domestic violence. Clients can also be screened out because of substance abuse, active domestic violence, mental disorders, and negative references from landlords or shelters. Though specialization provides better services for clients who meet screening criteria, it also makes accessing services a more complicated process for the client.

Ethical Issues

How involved does a social worker become in a client's life in forming a supportive relationship without crossing into the "inappropriate"? Every social worker faces this ethical issue at some time in his or her career. Empowerment practice requires collaboration and mutual trust between worker and client. The social worker often becomes the client's community and part of her or his support system. When a client moves to another shelter or permanent housing, the relationship becomes vague. Though no longer part of the social worker's "caseload," the client may still consider the worker part of his or her support system.

Social workers are sometimes so nervous about being "inappropriate" or, perhaps, being perceived by colleagues as inappropriate that they behave in a sterile or clinical manner. Such workers may limit the connection, so crucial to relationship building, by overdefining appropriate boundaries. Because relationships with clients are so important, social workers need to consider the effects of such attitudes.

Policy Issues

Innumerable policy issues demand analysis from an empowerment-oriented perspective. For instance, good subsidized child care is a primary policy issue often ignored in funding decisions for social service programs. Recent

U.S. administrations have placed welfare on the chopping block but have allocated no additional moneys for training or child care. Many children will be left unattended because parents will be forced to work low-paying jobs without child-care subsidies. For example, one homeless woman was recently employed by McDonalds. She brought her two children to work with her and left them in the playground during her shift. She lost her job after two weeks when someone finally noticed the children and reported the situation. Here is a woman who wanted desperately to work but had no child-care options available.

Child care is the crucial link to a woman's economic and vocational independence, which leads to increased self-esteem, self-worth, and control over the family's life as reliance on public assistance is decreased or eliminated. Child care can make the difference in a woman's ability to sustain a family and avoid the constant threat of eviction. Many homeless women are not in the workforce because they cannot receive child-care subsidies. The ability of low-income women to join the workforce and get off welfare is unrealistic without child care.

Homeless families in particular would benefit from full-time and fully funded Head Start programs and before- and after-school child-care programs. Collaboration among communities, churches, synagogues, nonprofit civic organizations, and local, state, and federal governments is essential in meeting the child-care needs of this country. In addition to child care, a strong economic policy plan for families that includes child-support assurance, and health insurance, homeless families need pay equity and equal employment opportunity to have a realistic chance of becoming self-sufficient.

EMPOWERMENT PRACTICE PRINCIPLES

Here is a summary of empowerment principles used with homeless people.

- **Meeting the client's immediate needs.** If basic needs have not been met, the appropriateness of raising abstract issues may seem completely irrelevant and insensitive to the client. Social workers must often act promptly to address clients' immediate survival and safety needs.
- **Accepting the client's definition of the problem.** When clients feel a social worker is accepting their definition of the problem and actively involving them in the change process, a strong foundation for a relationship is being laid.
- **Shared power/sense of control.** The power differential between a homeless person seeking help and a worker in a position to offer,

limit, or refuse services can be significant. For clients to experience a sense of control, social workers need to be particularly sensitive to subtle and sometimes overt power dynamics.

- **Education regarding resources and skills.** Garnering necessary resources and developing advocacy skills are activities crucial to self-efficacy in the homeless. To this end, the social worker can make information available and model advocacy skills.

- **Creating a collaborative working relationship.** Homeless people often know of resources the social worker does not. Eliciting clients' knowledge and expertise brings new resources to each situation and shares responsibility.

- **Using mutual support groups.** Homelessness can be acutely alienating. Support groups can foster greater understanding of a homeless person's situation, as well as provide additional resources and problem-solving skills. The collective effort can reduce feelings of being overwhelmed and alone.

- **Consciousness raising.** Consciousness raising may involve education or discussion regarding social, political, or economic forces contributing to the client's homelessness. Such insights can promote an understanding of the difference between individual and societal responsibilities, thus reducing self-blame.

- **Participation in organizational development.** Social workers' and clients' participation in worker councils and advisory groups provide opportunities to change program goals and organizational culture. Former clients holding voting positions on boards of directors is perhaps the most direct and fundamental way to change mission statements and goals to create a more empowerment-based organization.

CONCLUSION

In working with homeless people, one finds no lack of opportunities to develop a social work practice based on empowerment principles. In fact, the need for such work is so apparent that a secondary challenge exists: to apply empowerment practice principles in a manner that fits the strengths and challenges of the homeless. For example, to select appropriate empowerment strategies, one must recognize the scope of loss experienced by homeless people.

Just as social workers must be committed to empowerment practice with homeless clients, they must also pursue integration of empowerment practice principles with those of the organization in which they work.

Development of an empowerment-based human service philosophy requires empowerment-based decision making. Collaboration between direct service workers and administrators is needed for this process to be sustained. Ultimately, administrations must be willing to share power.

REFERENCES

Apprenticeship and non-traditional employment for women. (1995). Pamphlet from Renton Technical College, Renton, WA.

Baum, A., & Burns, D. (1993). *A nation in denial: The truth about homelessness.* Boulder, CO: Westview Press.

Beck, B. M. (1983, October). *Empowerment: A future goal for social work.* Paper presented at the National Association of Social Workers' Professional Symposium, New York.

Blau, J. (1992). *The visible poor: Homelessness in the United States.* New York: Oxford University Press.

Cohen, M. (1989). Social work practice with homeless mentally ill people: Engaging the client. *Social Work, 34*(6), 505–509.

Community voice mail. (1995). Pamphlet from the Community Technology Institute, Seattle, WA.

DeWoody, M. (1992). *Confronting homelessness among American families: Federal programs and strategies.* Washington, DC: Child Welfare League of America.

McChesney, K. Y. (1992). Absence of a family safety net for homeless families. *Journal of Sociology and Social Welfare, 19*(4), 55–72.

Reynolds, B. C. (1951). *Social work and social living.* Silver Spring, MD: National Association of Social Workers.

Saleebey, D. (Ed.). (1992). *The strengths perspective in social work practice.* New York: Longman.

Schutt, R. K., & Garrett, G. R. (1992). *Responding to the homeless: Policy and practice.* New York: Plenum.

Seltser, B. J., & Miller, D. E. (1993). *Homeless families: The struggle for dignity.* Chicago: University of Illinois Press.

Simon, B. (1994). *The empowerment tradition in American social work: A history.* New York: Columbia University Press.

Timmer, D. A., Eitzen, D. S., & Talley, K. D. (1994). *Paths to homelessness: Extreme poverty and the urban housing crisis.* San Francisco: Westview Press.

Wagner, D. (1991). Social work and the hidden victims of deindustrialization. *Journal of Progressive Human Services. 2*(1), 15–37.

Chapter 8

EMPOWERMENT OF YOUTH

Stuart Rees, Ph.D.
University of Sydney, New South Wales, Australia

YOUTH CULTURES
AND SUBCULTURES

Before any social worker begins to work with youth, she or he would be wise to ask questions about youth cultures and subcultures, particularly regarding experiences of powerlessness. To avoid preoccupation with local issues and to give a cosmopolitan flavor to their work, practitioners of empowerment should develop an international perspective by at least mulling over some background information about youth in several countries. For example, to understand better the cultures and subcultures of youth in the developed world—their values, language, and behavior—one could set the social and economic scene by listing the constraints on young people's lives. These constraints demonstrate the relevance of empowerment; as such, the following "scene setting" should influence practitioners' preparation and readers' perceptions of issues that affect empowerment. Further, although one should never underestimate the predicament of young people in the third world, this chapter focuses on the empowerment of youth in developed countries.

Social justice for young people is not easy to achieve. Large-scale youth unemployment makes the passage from school to work difficult for those who have left school with little knowledge and no skills. In Australia, the decline in full-time employment has been greatest for young people age 15 to 19. Of these, only 22% of young men and 14% of young women had full-time employment in Australia in 1992 (Freeland, 1993). Although these figures vary from one suburb to another and from urban to rural areas, the overall trend is toward temporary and casual employment. This structural change means that even when enrolled in full-time education, young people will depend on their parents and/or on modest incomes derived from part-time jobs or social security entitlements when they reach adulthood.

Short-term, insecure, and often unrewarding jobs make young people doubt whether the labor market is really the means to well-being and happiness. Yet, governments and politicians continue—somewhat uncritically —to emphasize the value of *any* work, to cut back unemployment benefits, and to stigmatize the unemployed.

When threatened by youth's nonconformity, adult society often falls back on repressive measures, such as current policies in Australia and the United States that give police the power to return young people to their parents. These policies do not address the conditions that contribute to nonconforming behavior.

Direct and indirect violence often affects young people. In some contexts, violence becomes the accepted "solution" to social issues and personal difficulties. High rates of car accidents, suicide, and homicide—the latter two affecting young men in particular—illustrate this "vulnerability to violence."

Although arrangements for recording and collecting data affect figures showing international comparisons, trends can be observed. For example, World Health Organization (WHO) statistics show that over the past 20 years the suicide rate for young men between the ages of 15 and 24 has more than doubled. In 1992, the suicide rate per 100,000 young men of this age bracket was 38 in New Zealand, 27 in Australia and Canada, 22 in the United States, 19 in the United Kingdom, and 10 in Japan ("World Health Organization Statistics [WHO]," 1994). Except for Japan, where the rate for young women was half that of young men, young women appear to be six to seven times less likely than their male counterparts to take their own lives. With regard to the danger of being murdered, the international profiles vary. In a country or part of a country with a tradition of owning and using firearms and lax gun-control laws, young people's chances of being killed are greater than in other countries. For example, in 1992, the homicide rate per 100,000 young men age 15–24 was 2.1 in Australia, 3.2 in New Zealand, 14.9 in Northern Ireland (a country in the throes of sectarian hostilities), and 32.5 in the United States (WHO, 1994).

These points underline some aspects of the social and economic contexts that influence young people's lives, though race, class, and gender factors also affect any young person's vulnerability to being poor, unemployed, or a victim of violence. Questions about culture and subculture lead to two final introductory points, this time concerning assumptions about the merits of empowerment.

A tendency to idealize empowerment may give the impression that such work will center on success through repaired relationships. Empowerment, however, is not preoccupied with worker-client relationships; it also raises questions about the values of adult society, not least regarding the resources and constraints of social and economic policies.

One must pay attention to the possible intra- and interpersonal difficulties of young people. Such attention should resist any tendency to pathologize—to explain the difficulties of young people as only within their heads.

These general points should not obscure differences in the experiences of youth in general and disenfranchised and powerless youth in particular. For example, within the contexts of home, school, and community, young people experience gender, ethnicity, and success in sport differently (Walker, 1988). Identity, self-respect, and association within particular cultures depend on group membership and the perceived differences between one's own group and groups seen in opposition. Within their own subcultural groups, young people generate their own meanings, means, ends, priorities, and values.

In the case of youth dominated by poverty, one form of powerlessness leads to another and back, forming a circle of oppression (Coleman & Husen, 1985; Kurtz, Jarvis, & Kurtz, 1991). The effects of poverty are compounded by racism, isolation, physical and psychological abuse, drug addiction, and homelessness. Not surprisingly, in North and South America, among homeless youth in Britain, and in rural and urban Australia, intergenerational inequity and alienation have provoked young people into producing their own cultures. These cultures may be gangs with their own codes and means of solving problems. Sometimes those means are swift and fatal.

Vulnerable youth experience many feelings such as despair. Any assessment of such feelings requires practitioners to identify the personal and structural sources of problems, if indeed those two sources can be separated (Cowger, 1994; Cox & Longres, 1981). Such assessment begins an empowerment process that should lead to attributes such as safety, trust, interdependence, validation, and the "experience of having an advocate" (Parsons, 1994). Empowerment can convert despair to hope. To enable empowerment, every practitioner needs to comprehend the values and aspirations of young people, as individuals and in a wider social context, such as their membership in key groups.

USING BIOGRAPHY

In working out the step by step process of empowerment, one finds the concept of biography useful. It can capture the story of individuals over time—the longitudinal dimension—or at one point—the lateral dimension. Readers might like to think of this as a moving picture or a still shot.

Enabling young people to tell their stories and reflect on their lives begins a process of understanding referred to as "the promise of biography" (Rees, 1991). Such promise stems from the telling and reconstructing of stories, in context and over time, that reveal personal and social issues and the interaction between them (Carr, 1986; Rees, 1991). It involves an appraisal not only of traditional attitudes to authority (Hirayama & Cetingok, 1988; Pinderhughes, 1982, 1983) but also of those activities—art, poetry, music, dress, sport—cherished because they have provided a sense of identity, achievement, and well-being (England, 1986). Because people's perceptions of cultural, economic, and political constraints influence biography, so do the opportunities that affect their notion of choice. What is this biography/choice/empowerment relationship?

One can link biography and empowerment by enabling people to reconstruct the story of their lives in terms of experiences of power and powerlessness, or choices and their contexts. Put simply, with no real choices, powerlessness persists. If there is a widening choice over issues such as food, clothing, friends, work, and values, powerlessness gives way to control, opportunities to exercise power creatively, and other benefits hitherto unimagined. I shall elaborate these points in the subsequent comments of homeless youth.

THE NATURE OF EMPOWERMENT

Empowerment is characterized by treating people equitably—with commitment, skills, and often a touch of inspiration—and by struggles to achieve social justice (Rees, 1991). This latter goal includes freedom from oppressive policies and practices and freedom to achieve human potential. *Freedom from* refers to guarantees of basic civil liberties and an avoidance of conditions such as poverty and homelessness. *Freedom to* includes measures to provide equal access to education, health services, and employment. An interdependence of equitable processes and social justice could mean anything from small victories to substantial changes in social policy and consequent wide-sweeping benefits for social groups (Sen, 1992; Troy, 1981).

Interpretations of justice are usually controversial, not least in work with youth. To respond equitably to the needs of young people, practitioners must become advocates for some vulnerable groups and individuals. Justice requires a process of treating equals equally and unequals unequally (Pateman, 1981; Sen, 1992). For example, young people who live on the streets need more resources than those from homes with supportive partners. Those who can read and write to high standards will not be a social policy priority because scarce resources are being used in literacy campaigns for their peers who cannot read and write. At first sight this claim about treating unequals unequally may seem paradoxical, but it underlines the association between egalitarian treatment and social justice.

This association of empowerment with equity and social justice connects with the framework presented in Chapter 1, particularly with its emphasis on the interaction between personal and social aspects of problem solving. I also acknowledge a political-economic perspective that perceives environments as arenas in which struggles to control decisions (the political dimension) coexist with controversies over the distribution of resources (the economic dimension) and so affect people's chances of making choices to affect their quality of life. This matter of choice and quality of life can affect educators, students, practitioners, their clients, and the public. Without such a political-economic perspective, the claims about empowerment will likely be presented as another set of techniques that function in a professional vacuum. Social work theory and practice has experienced too many vacuumlike and vacuous theories. Empowerment must not go that route. The practitioners of empowerment must be politically and economically literate; otherwise the promise of empowerment will not be realized. Such literacy requires practitioners to understand the overall political and economic contexts in which all young people have to live. I shall elaborate that point in subsequent discussion of youth cultures.

Before embarking on a specific account of the empowerment of youth —and to link this chapter with others—let me clarify my use of the word *dimensions*. Chapter 1 referred to four dimensions of empowerment: (1) the worker-client relationship, (2) education and skills development, (3) securing resources and assessing systems, and (4) social action. In the following discussion I shall use the word *dimensions* in a different way, in regard to exercising power. Though I agree with the four areas of focus referred to in Chapter 1, I would emphasize that empowerment in each of these areas depends on the way in which one conceives and exercises power. Explaining and practicing empowerment depends on understanding the exercise of power. In education and in practice—and in writing about empowerment—this remains the central theoretical and political conundrum.

THE EXERCISE OF POWER

In discussing empowerment, one should never use the word *power* glibly. In social work and in other social sciences, this concept is widely discussed and disputed, hence the need for clarification (Lukes, 1986). In a brief unmasking of different means of exercising power, one can start with the distinction between *power over* others in destructive ways and the creative use of *power* exercised in association *with* others that liberates and empowers (Berlin, 1969; Fromm, 1960).

Though useful, this dualism oversimplifies the ways people exercise power. By contrast, the analysis of one-, two-, and three-dimensional ways of exercising power (Lukes, 1976) produces a continuum or a pendulum effect that practitioners, students, and educators can use in appraising their own practice (see Figure 8.1).

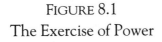

FIGURE 8.1

The Exercise of Power

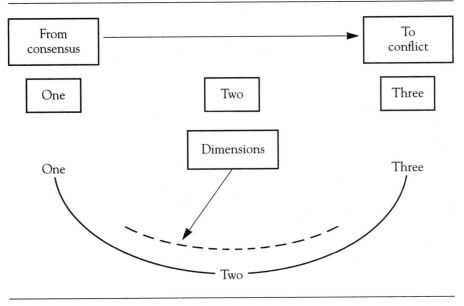

Conservative and often repressive, *one-dimensional power* imposes authority from the top down. For example, young people explain that throughout their lives they have been on the receiving end of the disempowering exercise of power. Practitioners who have experienced authoritarianism in bureaucracies will recognize it as a similar experience.

Two-dimensional power appears more democratic, encouraging at least two points of view and a setting of agendas to include official and unofficial concerns. It gives a semblance of being pluralistic and is consistent with social work traditions of openness and fairness. However, because it operates within official constraints, it will not likely give license to practitioners' and clients' creativity in seeking egalitarian, empowering ways of solving problems.

By contrast, *three-dimensional power* provides a radical alternative by asking practitioners to suspend assumptions about the conventional and approved ways of thinking and behaving. It involves a capacity for reflective thought, which Mead (1934) has called the *social mind*; it also refers to realizing the potential inherent in what the Jungian writer Hillman has called "the poetic basis of mind" (Moore, 1990). Such an exercise of power challenges practitioners and the people they work with to think and act creatively, to trespass beyond the limits of what is usually conceived as possible. Such power is crucial to problem solving and visions of social justice.

Social workers and their clients may find it difficult to reach this third dimension quickly, but its realization leads to empowerment. For example, in community work with street kids, questions about their future revolved around congenial and affordable housing. It took time to construct ideas about such accommodations that would also allow young people to remain in contact with their peers. It took even more time to encourage housing authorities to consider these points of view. In the first six months of controversy over this issue, senior bureaucrats in the housing authority refused to use their discretionary powers. Not until a social worker confronted them about their powers of discretion in policy initiatives—and thereby their interpretations of youth needs, housing, opportunity, and even "justice in the city"—did substantial change seem possible.

That process and the outcome of enabling young people to achieve a significant social policy involved a three-dimensional exercise of power by all the parties. It was not easy. It did not happen overnight, but required persistence over almost a year that involved several disappointments—the familiar one step forward, two steps back, then two steps forward and only one step back. That three-dimensional power involved establishing relationships with the young people, developing their skills and understanding about housing, identifying the systems that controlled resources, then taking action to secure those resources. This description matches the details of a model for empowerment-oriented practice outlined in Chapter 1.

EMPOWERMENT OF YOUTH: FOUR STAGES

The following comments are derived from interviews with homeless youth who participated in an action research project based in a youth refuge in a crowded inner city area of Sydney, Australia. I believe young people go through four stages of empowerment. To give an oversimplified picture of this process, I will introduce comments from a 20-year-old named Sean. The two quotations were made in July of one year and June of the next. In between occurred a process of empowerment.

> My life has nothing. It has always seemed that way. My parents were never interested. People on the streets and police, what's the difference? At least their cells are safe. You wonder, unless you can get high on drugs, what is the point of living? Death is always around the corner. . . .

> You could say, I am moving away from death, from some of the circles we move in. Life does look better now. I begin to understand what's happening. I have a place to stay, friends and this part-time job. I'm even laughing . . . well, some of the time.

Homeless for five years, Sean had lived mostly on the streets and occasionally in a youth refuge in the inner city of Sydney. However, almost any homeless youth in North or South American cities, in Europe, Australia, or New Zealand could have said the same.

Twelve months elapsed between Sean's first, pessimistic observation and his second, more optimistic attitude. During that period, he and eight young men and five young women associated with staff in a youth refuge. As a researcher and participant observer, I observed significant changes in these young people. In the following account of the processes and outcomes of empowerment, I draw freely on quotations recorded in individual and group interviews.

It is neither apt nor helpful to describe empowerment as occurring at only one time and having one set of characteristics. Empowerment goes through different stages, from an acknowledgment of powerlessness to the beginnings of awareness, from the experience of dialogue and solidarity to action and a consequent changed sense of self—toward acquiring a political identity. Taking weeks, months, or years, the process reflects different levels of consciousness and achievement at those different stages.

Stage One: Understanding Powerlessness

Young people have spoken of their hopelessness and despair. With no racist implications, they refer to a stage of blackness, not unlike the early alchemists who faced a mess in their vessels and who thought that their attempts to turn base metals into gold or silver would never materialize. Although these efforts did not lead to precious metals, they contributed to the knowledge of chemistry.

Amanda, a 19-year-old, commented, "I can only think of my home life as unhappy and scary. I was nobody. I feel that way on the streets. There's some excitement but only when I am off my face with drugs or getting money for prostitution. I mostly felt like crying. I did a lot of crying." Of his feelings of powerlessness and hopelessness, 18-year-old Kevin explained, "Since I was 7 I've never had anyone remember my birthday. Life was survival. You against them. Some fun times, mostly miserable." Kevin's reflections were echoed by his friend Ken. "Being a street kid you are nobody. But you are often scared even if you don't admit it. Death is the circle you move in. Suicide is always there. I once broke a finger. It was incredibly painful but nowhere near the pain in my mind."

This stage of powerlessness needs to be identified so that practitioners do not rush in clumsily, thinking that empowerment can begin immediately. Solomon (1976) makes the point when she stresses that "the practitioner must demonstrate an understanding of the dynamics of powerlessness and its consequences in order to develop expertise in the utilization of practice skills in the service of empowerment" (p. 26).

At this stage of powerlessness, an appropriate role for practitioners is to enable young people to find space and time to be still, to be held and supported. It is unrealistic to think that movement can always begin imme-diately, that consciousness can suddenly be raised after years of despair, that skills can be acquired overnight. Young people need a place of safety, as well as guaranteed means of regular meals and income. They need time to grieve and the opportunity to establish trust. After years of mistrust and being let down by their parents, peers, and adults in various positions of authority, young people will find it strange to be accepted, to give and receive trust let alone engage in a lasting relationship; as such, practition-ers will have to earn the right to be trusted.

The stillness involved in being available and being supportive without needing to rush, without resorting to crisis management, begins the process of earning trust. The work with Amanda and Kevin took several meetings and over three months to address their powerlessness and slowly establish trust. Discussions that led to the next stage were part of that process.

Stage Two: Awareness and Mutual Education

Enabling young people to begin to tell their stories has many benefits. First, it is a sign of taking them seriously, of "giving them a voice," an unusual experience for those seldom listened to, who have never thought their point of view worth considering. Second, the very telling of a story—referred to by some as "narrative therapy"—enables young people to see the links between their self-image and the constraints of an outside world. Third, it provides the beginnings of mutual education between practitioner and young people. Some sharing begins. The promise of biography begins to be realized.

Three months after referring to his total pessimism, Sean commented in a group discussion at the youth refuge: "It's difficult to get away from the sneers of people on the streets, the 'successful people' who look down on you. It makes you think you never want to be like them. . . . And you think the police will always be part of your life. That usually means trouble and the courts. Can you ever get control is what you wonder."

In the same small-group discussion, 18-year-old Jo, who had left home at 13, had become a heroin addict at 14, and had lived for a time with Aboriginal people in northwestern Australia, commented, "People harming me and me hurting myself. I had lots of beatings which is why I left. That's what it was like. My family would say, "I don't like your hair, I don't like your music, I don't like your friends. I don't like your clothes." The only time I felt accepted was with the Aboriginal people last year. They accepted me. They liked me. I've got some initiation scars from them [he showed the scars on his back] but they were not painful. . . . They were not people out to hurt me or me hurting myself. [At this point he pointed to his pock-marked arms.] With my tribe I felt I was someone."

This stage of awareness and mutual education provides the opportunity, in Freire's terms, of codifying themes in understandable ways that one can generalize in preparation for the next stage of consciousness raising (Freire, 1968). How does a practitioner respond to the cues in Sean's and Jo's comments? What were the general themes? How can one develop the exchange between worker and young people as an empowering learning experience for both parties?

Identifying themes will always precede the articulation of specific problems. Sean referred to the need for control in terms of his treatment by police and in courts. He also referred to control in his perception of well-dressed people passing him on the streets who seldom responded positively, let alone with money.

Jo referred to rejection and other pains of being hurt. He gave one example of the therapeutic and temporarily empowering experience of acceptance by Australian Aborigines. To him, their care and the rituals associated with their acceptance were unusual. He also acknowledged the dangers of continued heroin addiction: to his health, to his self-esteem, and to his chances of avoiding criminal behavior.

This stage of dawning awareness gives practitioners a chance to encourage young people to construct their stories so they can begin to think of different choices in their lives. Usually their stories reconstruct experiences of powerlessness. For example, a young woman who hitherto has thought of herself as incapable of assessing her circumstances can begin to spell out what has been happening. Such spelling out is a crucial part of empowerment, a small victory without which one cannot proceed to the next stage. In sharing the general themes and beginning to answer the question, "Where do we go from here?" workers offer skills crucial to enabling young people to reflect and to learn about resources and the skills to obtain them. In oversimplified terms, a dialogue between a worker and a homeless youth often sounds something like this:

Worker: *In all these conversations, you have been talking about several things: suspicion of drug dealers, the police, and your feeling about never having money or anywhere safe to sleep.*

Youth: *All of those and some more, the violence as well, the rules in the refuge.*

Worker: *Which one of those half a dozen issues is the most important?*

Youth: [after considerable discussion and disagreement] *Let's get "a place to stay" straightened out.*

In that dialogue, rapport building and mutual education occurred. This process, though, is easier to imagine than achieve. Empowerment involves a struggle for social justice. Often, the resources required to achieve this justice do not exist. They have to be conceived and struggled for, hence the need to avoid any simple notion that accessing resources is merely a question of practitioners and clients learning skills.

Stage Three: Dialogue and Solidarity

Part of the process of empowerment involves learning the language of a politics of relationships, whether in families, organizations, or a wider social theater. Some powerless youth have a limited vocabulary. They have been unwanted in families and at school, unemployable, and in many ways superfluous to conventional society's requirements. Often having a criminal record, they are perceived by police—and by themselves—as permanent deviants. They have seldom had the chance to see themselves or have others see them in another light.

Dialogue provides an experience of hearing and using the language of empowerment, thereby initiating a different set of self-perceptions. This process indirectly begins an experience of acquiring the political understanding and skills crucial for practitioners as well as clients.

One best learns a new language in solidarity with others to confirm their courage and common strategies, as when people unite to resist oppression. At this stage, the social worker best serves as a catalyst for young people to exchange views and experience solidarity. Jungian therapists have discussed this role in terms of alchemy, developing an analogy by relating chemical changes to personal and social relationships (Moore, 1990). Chapter 1 also presented the worker as a catalyst who helps clients see how private problems relate to public issues.

Kieran, a 22-year-old Maori youth who had spent several years in prison for assault and robbery, described his growing confidence in association with other young people and with some practitioners in the youth refuge. "It has taken time. Here, I am called by my first name. I like to see people. They like to see me. I belong here. The friendships are great. . . . I could deal with Social Security[1] now. I don't expect the police to stop me all the time. I could deal with them if they did: 'I have my rights. You have no right to pick on me. . . . I may have a record but I am a different person now.' My part-time job helps, but I have learned those 'right things' in here."

Susan, who had been sexually abused at home and who had survived for years through prostitution, described her growing understanding and control. Weeks before, she had painfully—at the stage of awareness and mutual education—described the pains of being a victim and the probability that she could never change how others treated her. Beginning to see

---

[1]In Australia, *Social Security* refers to social insurance payments received by unemployed individuals.

herself in a new light, she expected to make some choices, to have some influence. As she explained,

> I've heard about others being abused. I knew I was not the only one.
> I was not sure about rights . . . to Social Security, in the courts and over
> my parents. I heard it before but in one ear out the other. I have dis-
> cussed charging my parents with abuse. I learned [in group meetings]
> and from Amanda that selling my body is not the answer. You feel so
> bad when you are coming round from a high. You cannot drug yourself
> up to forget men who have you for a price. . . . You don't have to take
> what those fuckin' bastards want. I'm not frightened of courts anymore.
> . . . I don't think of a career, just having somewhere safe to live, where I
> could live with my own things, which I might call my home."

Practitioners and young people learn in a mutual way when they meet formally and informally to share experiences, talk about empowerment, *and* take action regarding rights and obligations. That is, they learn from one another. They gain confidence and give support. Hesitant at an earlier stage of association, trust becomes more solid in regard to specific activities dis-cussed over coffee, in a quiet room at an agreed time.

The practitioner's role of catalyst takes various forms. For example, the social worker brings a group together and helps to develop discussion regarding young people's civil and welfare rights: their entitlements to income, educational and job training, health services, housing rentals, and due process of law. In Australia, practitioners who work with youth but do not know about such rights prove of little use to young people (White, 1990). Worse than that, they may flatter to deceive, appearing to offer a ser-vice but ultimately disempowering clients (O'Connor, 1990).

The dialogue about rights, entitlements, and mutual obligations can be facilitated by practitioners who not only know about such rights but also have skill in ensuring that agencies provide the resources to enable empow-erment to take place. Such understanding and skill imply more than a cata-lyst. Workers need the creativity and courage inherent in that exercise of power that articulates the alternatives, which is three dimensional.

Stage Four: Action and Political Identity

Sean, whose biographical sketch was presented at the beginning of this sec-tion, spoke of his own changed identity in terms of "moving away from death." To him, empowerment meant that he no longer thought that a pre-mature death would be the only likely outcome of his life. He had begun to regain understanding and control, now rejecting the violence that had vic-timized him and that he had taken for granted. He had learned other ways of talking and behaving with the police, with hospital doctors, and during a court appearance for possession of marijuana. He had begun to develop confidence as his own advocate. As he explained, "I see myself differently now. Before, I denied that I was a street kid. It was all denial. Just surviving. It has taken me seven years to move out of it. The diagrams I drew to describe what was happening were helpful. Others could see them. Mary here [a social worker at the refuge] did arrange a meeting with a probation officer when I last went to court. She made the time. The probation officer seemed to understand. I spoke for myself. They could both see I've had more experience than them . . . but they knew things I don't."

Dean, who had been coming to group meetings for seven months, summed up his experiences of this taking-action stage. He recalled that he had previously despaired of ever having a home of this own, let alone a job. "It was not pleasant to go to that job training program. I usually never go to those things. I was 'a tough guy.' What the fuck would I need going there? They were people I despised, but I went with Kevin. We went several times. That was a new experience for me. . . . Then we had these plans about sharing a room, about budgeting for a room and a kitchen. . . . I'm still angry about lots of things, but at this moment I don't hate myself, I still dislike these yuppies on the streets. I don't want to be like them. . . . It has been good to be treated well in these training programs, and getting a regular cheque is a miracle. How long will it last?" This last question conveys that empowerment is dynamic, multidimensional, and circular. It is also mutually beneficial. The young people gained self-knowledge and political awareness in the context of relationships both healing and humorous. Practitioners gained similar benefits. As a participant observer, I also benefited from events that were sometimes inspiring and always belied the powerlessness of the initial stage.

This last stage of action and political identity describes a strengthening and flexibility, as iron becoming steel. Not an end, it feeds back into the earlier stage of awareness and mutual education.

Youth who have experienced so much violence and rejection and who see adult society as hostile, however, can always revert to powerlessness. Almost certainly, those youths need not stay in despair if they have learned some new language and roles in solidarity with others, thereby forging new alliances and understanding. Crucial to that understanding is a changed sense of self, improved relationships with friends or even relatives, and better experiences with the representatives of organizations who control information and who had previously been seen as indifferent or threatening.

SUMMARY

The practice of empowerment revolves around several key assumptions. One can think of these assumptions as principles for practice.

Assessment in Context

One should appraise the power and powerlessness of youth in general, and the biographies of individual young people in particular, regarding the interdependence of social and economic issues as well as personal and intrapersonal idiosyncrasies. One also needs to assess the resources available through policy and practice with reference to short- and long-term goals of social justice.

Political Literacy

Social workers can facilitate the self-respect and political understanding of young people and those associated with them by sharing knowledge of individual rights and conversing about opportunities and responsibilities. The knowledge and skills of empowerment depend on practitioners' political literacy, best described in terms of exercising power in a creative, three-dimensional, and liberating way.

Skills and Stages

Although empowerment involves several skills—assessment, planning, advocacy, and evaluation—work with youth suggests that negotiation is the most important skill for practitioners and young people. This skill gives empowerment practice its inherent political quality.

Empowerment usually goes through stages, from a recognition of powerlessness to a dawning of self and social awareness, from the beginnings of dialogue and experience of solidarity to taking action and achieving a sense of political identity and understanding. These stages are not linear but circular and self-reinforcing.

CONCLUSION

Perhaps the quotations used to describe empowerment have too much of a happily-ever-after feeling about them. If so, it is the wrong impression. This tough work demands commitment from individual practitioners and their organizations. It requires political literacy about the goals of social justice and the various means to attain these goals in association with young people who may have had few positive experiences with adults. Part of that political literacy involves practitioners who can learn how to obtain support and rewards for their own endeavors.

Empowerment is mutually beneficial, affecting the well-being and the identity of both practitioners and young people. The different stages present their own qualities and chemistry. Though these stages are usually worked through in progression, the characteristics of each made explicit, sometimes the practitioners and young people start at different points. If there is confidence in the three-dimensional exercise of power and if the political understanding and skills that accompany such practice can be shared with colleagues and clients, practitioners will find this work exciting and dynamic.

REFERENCES

Berlin, I. (1969). *Four essays on liberty*. London: Oxford University Press.

Carr, D. (1986). *Time, narrative, and history*. Bloomington, IN: University of Indiana Press.

Coleman, J., & Husen, T. (1985). *Becoming adult in a changing society*. Centre for Educational Research and Innovation, Paris: OECD.

Cowger, C. (1994). Assessing client strengths: Clinical assessment for client empowerment. *Social Work, 39*(3), 262–268.

Cox, E., & Longres, J. (1981). *Critical practice-curriculum implications*. Paper presented at the Annual Meeting of the Council on Social Work Education, Louisville, KY.

England, H. (1986). *Social work as art*. London: Allen & Unwin.

Freeland, J. (1993). Reconceptualizing work, full employment and incomes policy. In Australian Council of Social Service (Ed.), *The future of work* (Chapter 1). Sydney, Australia: ACOSS.

Freire, P. (1968). *A pedagogy of the oppressed*. New York: Seabury Press.

Fromm, E. (1960). *Fear of freedom*. London: Routledge & Keegan Paul.

Hirayama, H., & Cetingok, M. (1988). Empowerment: Social work approach for Asian immigrants. *Social Casework, 69*(1), 41–47.

Kurtz, D., Jarvis, S., & Kurtz, G. (1991). Problems of homeless youths: Empirical findings and human services. *Social Work, 36*(4), 309–314.

Lukes, S. (1976). *Power: A radical view*. London: Macmillan.

Lukes, S. (1986). *Power: Readings in social and political theory*. Oxford: Blackwell.

Mead, G. (1934). *Mind, self, and society*. Chicago: University of Chicago Press.

Moore, T. (1990). *The essential James Hillman: A blue fire*. London: Routledge.

O'Connor, I. (1987). Legal education for social welfare workers: Has it made a difference? *Legal Service Bulletin, 12*(3) 93–97.

Parsons, R. (1994). *Empowerment based practice: A study of process and outcomes*. Paper presented to the Council on Social Work Education Annual Meeting, San Diego, CA.

Pateman, C. (1981). The concept of equity. In P. Troy (Ed.), *A just society?* (pp. 21–36). Sydney, Australia: Allen & Unwin.

Pinderhughes, E. (1982). Family functioning of Afro-Americans. *Social Work, 27*, 91–96.

Pinderhughes, E. (1983). Empowerment for our clients and ourselves. *Social Casework, 64*(6), 331–338.

Rees, S. (1991). *Achieving power*. Sydney, Australia: Allen & Unwin.

Sen, A. (1992). *Inequality re-examined*. Oxford: Clarendon.

Solomon, B. (1976). *Black empowerment: Social work in oppressed communities*. New York: Columbia University Press.

Troy, P. (Ed.). (1981). *A just society?* Sydney, Australia: Allen & Unwin.

Walker, J. (1988). *Louts and legends*. Sydney, Australia: Allen & Unwin.

White, R. (1990). *Young people and social controls in Australia*. Melbourne, Australia: Cambridge.

World Health Organization statistics 1993. (1994). Geneva, Switzerland: World Health Organization.

Chapter 9

EMPOWERING FAMILIES

Vanessa G. Hodges, Ph.D.
University of North Carolina, Chapel Hill

Yolanda Burwell, Ph.D.
East Carolina University, Greenville, North Carolina

Debra Ortega, M.S.W.
University of Washington, Seattle

INTRODUCTION

The family is the most basic unit of socialization, education, nurturing, and care for individuals in U.S. society. As 24-hour, problem-solving, and task-oriented systems, all families face constant demands on their time, resources, and members. Each family needs information, resources, and power to make the critical decisions necessary to function as a healthy, viable unit. For example, families might choose the type and quality of formal education, social and emotional developmental activities, health care, nutrition, housing, or recreational outlets for their members. Many families, however, cannot make these critical decisions effectively, because they lack access to resources and information or lack the skills to promote healthy family development. A principal objective of social work practice, therefore, is the empowerment of families. That is, social workers should help families build on their strengths, gain access to resources, learn how to negotiate the many systems their members contact (e.g., school, neighborhood, social services), and overcome problems that affect healthy family development.

This chapter describes the principal characteristics of empowerment-based practice with families, offers examples from practice, and provides specific empowerment principles. We also discuss the barriers to full implementation of empowerment-based practice, with recommendations for future action.

THE NEED FOR COMMUNITY-BASED EMPOWERMENT PRACTICE

Empowerment of families requires that social workers quickly recognize the internal and external forces that deeply affect family well-being. While much of the literature has focused on internal family dynamics, external factors also play a significant role. Regardless of their composition, socioeconomic status, or stage of development, families are shaped by their environment. Environmental injustice, racism, poverty, unemployment and underemployment, crime, homelessness, violence against women and children, and hate-related crimes negatively affect families' well-being.

These issues particularly affect the poor, women, people of color, children, and the disabled. For example, because of their limited income, poor families have restricted choices. Those fortunate enough to have housing often live in substandard, overcrowded communities with high crime rates. These already burdened families are more likely than those with greater financial resources to be involved in public agencies with social control functions. Research indicates a link between housing characteristics (such as overcrowding) and the rate of reported child abuse and neglect (Zuravin, 1989). Other evidence indicates possible connections between child neglect and housing problems or general housing inadequacies (Zuravin, 1989).

Social problems such as inadequate housing, poverty, racism, and crime warrant community-based empowerment and empowerment-oriented practitioners (Germaine, 1991). Social service professionals and researchers have identified the need for interventions that capitalize on the strengths of a community (Cowger, 1994; Dunst, Trivette, & Deal, 1988, 1994; Saleebey, 1992). Intervention strategies, however, have historically evolved from a deficit perspective, which tends to center on the inadequacies of the individual (Saleebey, 1992). People are labeled as pathological, hopeless, and somehow responsible for their predicament. When the focus shifts from the individual to the family, the family bears the "label" of pathological, disorganized, or dysfunctional. When families and their members internalize these pathologies, they feel even more powerless over their environment, which affects their ability to overcome adversity.

Social work practice often overlooks the opportunities for intervention or other resources the community can offer to strengthen families. Because families continue to be influenced, both positively and negatively, by the communities in which they reside, this oversight hinders social work with families. Interventions with families are enhanced and more long-term change becomes possible when workers identify, target, and intervene in community problems as well as access community resources such as safety, economic development, positive role modeling, and age-appropriate recreation. The community, therefore, becomes an element in empowering the family (Dunst et al., 1994).

DEFINING EMPOWERMENT

Empowerment has been broadly defined as a theoretical framework, specific practice behaviors, and the outcome of interventions (Gutiérrez, 1990; Hasenfeld, 1987; Rappaport, 1981, 1987; Solomon, 1976). While many definitions contribute to the full meaning of the term, this chapter draws on three specific definitions concerned with individual knowledge and skills, the power of a collective or group with a common agenda, and the transaction between the individual or group and the larger community.

First, Dunst et al. (1988) define empowerment as "a person's (1) access and control over needed resources, (2) decision-making and problem-solving abilities, and (3) acquisition of instrumental behavior needed to interact effectively with others to procure resources" (p. 3). This definition addresses two critical elements of empowerment: access to resources and skills. First, for an individual or family to have control over them, critical resources must exist and be accessible. Second, the individual or family must possess certain social skills to get them.

A second definition of empowerment, offered by Deming (1984), explicates intrapersonal and interpersonal transactions that characterize empowered relationships. She defines empowerment as

> A process of discovering within ourselves and in others the capacity to bring about change. Empowerment means accepting personal responsibility to act. As we realize our power, we become free to transform ourselves and to discover untapped strengths. Our individual actions of protest and creativity create a ripple effect that empowers others. At the heart of the empowerment process is the phenomenon of helping someone else to see something he or she hasn't seen before and subsequently to act upon that insight. It is not a bullying power, not the power to make people afraid. [It is the] power to make them see new things as possible. (p. 8)

Deming's definition reinforces the notion that families have power from within to bring about positive change. It also highlights the importance of helping others, such as community members, to discover that they too possess the power and ability to effect change.

A third definition addresses capacity building. Conger and Kanungo (1988) define empowerment as "a process of enhancing feelings of self-efficacy among organizational members through the identification of conditions that foster powerlessness and through their removal by both formal organizational practices and informal techniques of providing efficacy information"

(p. 471). Shedding light on the collective notion of empowerment among group members, these authors speak of how collectives develop feelings and beliefs of empowerment (self-efficacy) by developing the capacity to identify barriers to power and then by devising strategies to remove them.

These definitions provide a foundation for understanding how to work with families from an empowerment perspective. Though many definitions of empowerment exist in the literature and field, these three present key principles of empowerment that can guide practitioners' work with families.

CHARACTERISTICS OF EMPOWERMENT PRACTICE

Empowerment practice is based on a set of beliefs and assumptions that in turn build on the values and ethics of social work and other helping professions. Collaborative relationships, capacity building, and a sense of connectedness to extended family and other networks are central themes of such practice with children and families.

Empowerment Through Collaborative Relationships

In an empowerment-based relationship, collaboration is the essence of interpersonal transactions between practitioners and family members. Collaborative relationships are characterized by trust, respect, mutual goals, shared responsibility and decision-making, and differential yet specialized knowledge. Practitioners and families find themselves in different roles, such as partner, peer, and colleague. Practitioners and families act as *equal* partners. Because these relationships depart dramatically from traditional therapeutic relationships, they require intentional and deliberate effort from practitioners and family members alike. Practitioners must work hard to push back the inclination to rescue families and solve problems without involving family members. Families must recognize the wealth of knowledge and expertise that they bring to the relationship—namely, knowledge of their family members, family history, and goals and aspirations for the family. Both must pledge to work cooperatively and relate to each other in an open, honest, and respectful manner.

While a collaborative relationship appears logical and sensible and therefore easy to initiate, practitioners and family members often have long histories of adversarial interactions that make working together difficult. Further, neither families nor practitioners are accustomed to participating as equals. For example, one of the most difficult aspects of a partnership is disagreements. Families often feel powerless and therefore obligated to follow the recommendation of the practitioners. On the other hand, practitioners are not accustomed to family members disagreeing or rejecting their recommendations or suggestions. To engage in a truly collaborative relationship, *each party* must stay open to discussing and resolving differences in an honest and respectful manner. As families and practitioners work in partnership, both gain enhanced creativity, new knowledge and skills, and —most important—the chance for enduring change and growth.

Empowerment Through Capacity Building

If collaboration is the essence of an empowerment-based relationship, then capacity building is its sum and substance. *Capacity building* refers to enabling, supporting, teaching, and encouraging family members to take control of their family and community. Empowerment-based practitioners begin with the premise that all families and communities know what they need to function in a healthy way. They also believe that families want the best for their members and community and that families do the best they can given the multiple barriers that exist between them and desired outcomes.

Empowerment-based practitioners seek to identify these barriers and work with families to remove them. Barriers may be structural, as in educational or agency policies. Other barriers might include the lack of opportunities, knowledge, or skills of family members. Still other barriers might include environmental pollution or other neighborhood obstacles.

The roles of empowerment-based practitioners generally depart from the traditional roles of therapist or counselor, although these are appropriate at times. Most often, empowerment-oriented practitioners assume roles as advocates, teachers, strategists with families, and translators of agency cultures and traditions. They also link families with formal and informal resources. In their role as brokers, practitioners must often reframe family "powers" so that agencies can better see, hear, and understand families in new and affirming ways.

This last role is particularly relevant when the system involved has a strong social control element, such as child welfare or juvenile justice. Because these systems have muted families, a large part of empowerment-based practice lies in helping families vocalize their opinion and in having other social service providers receive the opinion respectfully. Indeed, capacity building includes breaking down barriers in any service that mutes or excludes the family.

Empowerment Through Extended Family Networks

The social work profession's preoccupation with the middle-class nuclear family overlooks the importance of the extended family system, especially when one works with ethnic groups and rural families (Germaine, 1991; Martin & Martin, 1978). The extended family is a viable, resourceful, and responsive network of people and assets central to empowerment-based practice with children and families. The extended family provides a conceptual framework for understanding "family as community" and resource sharing, which demonstrate empowerment in these settings.

Martin and Martin (1978) define *extended family* as "a multigenerational, interdependent kinship system which is welded together by a sense of obligation to relatives; is organized around a 'family base' household; is generally guided by a 'dominant family figure'; extends across geographical boundaries to connect family units to an extended family network; and has a built-in mutual aid system for the welfare of its members and the maintenance of the family as a whole" (p. 1).

A key empowerment practice involves discerning the capabilities, technologies, and resources families hold naturally and informally among themselves. That is, empowerment builds on existing resource systems. The collective worth of family systems comes through in the ways they take care of each other. For example, Stack (1974) and Liebow (1966) have identified internal problem-solving mechanisms and management of resources among poor African-American families. African-American extended families have informal problem-solving "experts" who offer a variety of skills and informal assistance to other members. Usually, there is the "banker"— the person good at saving or having cash on hand—who informally gives loans when members need it. There is often a "healer" who knows the arts of herbs, remedies, or otherwise how to get kin back on their feet.

Having the final word, the "authority" is seldom questioned or disputed; little happens in the wider family scheme without this person knowing it. Often these "authorities" are elders, repositories of family history and wisdom respected by nearly everyone for their handling of delicate situations. They are the "heart beat" of extended families. Through a very informal socialization process, they also groom younger members to carry on this function.

Other "experts" as well may provide the family with invaluable resources to maintain effective functioning. This informal helping system is particularly important given the number of environmental forces that negatively affect African-American families—racism, poverty, public health problems, and high rates of unemployment or underemployment. By helping the family access needed resources and offering social support, the extended family can buffer these external forces. Though the dynamics of extended family networks can vary, empowerment-based practice recognizes the skills and resourcefulness within each extended family system and the expectations that people have of each other.

Empowerment Through
Non-kinship Networks

Non-kinship networks also provide an important component of empowerment-based practice. They can be the source of "untapped strengths" referred to by White and Van Soest in their definition of empowerment. They also offer a source of strength frequently missed by social service agencies.

Non-kinship networks are those relationships outside the extended family that provide the same kinds of supports as extended family structures. Such networks can be a part of one's culture or else created to fill a gap left by an absent or nonfunctioning extended family structure.

Latino families provide an example of the adoption of non-kin into extended family structures based on cultural norms. These families use religious tradition to bind others to their extended family through ceremonies such as baptism and confirmation. These new members enter the family structure by becoming *padrinos* or grandparents. Latino families also use a less formal adoption process to add members to their *familia*. Non-kin can be adopted by being *compadres* or confidants to family members.

The roles of *padrino* and *compadre* exemplify the incorporation of non-kin into an extended family structure. The notion of *familia*, which includes grandparents, cousins, *padrinos*, and *compadres*, moves toward a definition of the extended family that includes a communal awareness (Aragon de Valdez & Gallegos, 1982).

Other minority or at-risk groups may use less formal mechanisms for recognizing the existence of non-kin networks. African Americans refer to these network members as "fictive kin" (Stack, 1974). These network members often include "aunts" and "uncles," godmothers and godfathers, and neighbors. In another example of such inclusion, Kibria (1993) outlines three types of extended family structures in Vietnamese immigrant families. First, distant relatives with whom contact may have been limited in Vietnam are assisted, supported, and invited to live with relatives who have established homes in the United States. Second, preference generally given to paternal or maternal lineage is ignored as family members immigrate and new family networks are established. And finally, close friends are invited into family networks and supported during their immigration transition. These networks become an important component in building on the strengths and resources of families.

Social service professionals, however, often fail to assess the degree of support provided to families by non-kin members. Accustomed to the traditional structures, families may not readily identify non-kin members as part of their extended families. Empowerment practice includes the recognition, respect, and use of non-kin networks and the support they provide to families.

EXEMPLARY FAMILY
EMPOWERMENT MODELS

The empowerment of families in the child welfare system provides a challenge to the social work field. Traditionally, the child welfare worker rescues or protects the child. Family preservation and foster care reunification programs have expanded the repertoire of interventions and included the entire family as a vehicle for change. This shift, from viewing the child as completely separate from (or even without) a family to a child with an emotional connection to a family, has been a slow process. This process has been inhibited by the complex role of child welfare workers, who must advocate for the children, collaborate with families, and answer to the community. They work under risk of role conflict and may have to take on ultimate responsibility for a child's safety. To demonstrate these issues, here follow examples of two programs that embody empowerment practice with children and families in the child welfare system.

The Oregon Family Unity Model:
Kinship Ties and Non-kinship Networks

Developed by L. B. Graber, the family services manager of the state of Oregon Children's Services Division, the Oregon Family Unity Model focuses on empowering families to facilitate problem solving. The key component to the model, the family unity meeting, pursues solutions through (1) acknowledging family strengths, (2) empowering families to create change by expanding their options, and (3) including community and kinship members to advocate, support, and collaborate with families within the child welfare system.

THE MEETING The Family Unity Model begins with a family member's or the public child welfare worker's request for a family unity meeting. The family chooses participants for the meeting with suggestions from the worker. Typically, participants include extended family members, family friends, therapists, teachers, parent educators, clergy, lawyers, child welfare workers, and the client/family.

A neutral facilitator coordinates, facilitates, and documents meeting activities.[1] The meeting facilitator coordinates the negotiation of meeting times and locations, sends formal invitations, and provides a written

---

[1]Originally, the model was designed to use the child welfare worker as the meeting facilitator. A neutral facilitator allows the worker to represent his or her own position without role conflict as facilitator.

account of the meeting to all participants. Participants are invited as consultants to the family and worker.

Before the meeting, all participants receive an outline of the agenda. The agenda is divided into five parts: (1) introductions, including an explanation of the purpose of the meeting, (2) discussion of concerns, (3) an assessment of family strengths, (4) problem solving and development of a service plan, and (5) meeting closure.

The first part is self-explanatory. The second, the discussion of concerns, involves identifying areas that block the family's success. These barriers may include the drug abuse of a family member, conflicting information among providers and therapists, or communication difficulties among the caseworker, family members, and providers.

In the third part, assessment of family strengths, the family and consultants are asked to describe the family's strengths. The effect of eliciting family strengths is twofold. First, it acknowledges the tools the family already possesses to address concerns raised by the community. Second, it provides a mechanism for the child welfare worker to acknowledge strengths that the family brings to the working relationship. The inclusion of strengths in the meeting shifts the focus from problems to the hope and power of the family.

The fourth part uses family strengths for problem solving. The family and consultants, including the caseworker, brainstorm ways to meet the family's needs and facilitate their work with the child welfare system. The fifth, like the first, is self-explanatory.

The family, consultants, and case worker create a partnership of people who agree to support the family in specific areas. This partnership provides protection to the child. The group develops a visual representation of a strength-oriented service agreement to support movement toward change. This service agreement, which documents the service plan, notes the person ultimately responsible for supporting the family through change. The meeting facilitator distributes copies of the agreement to meeting participants. The creation of a service agreement through collaboration ensures that family goals are both realistic and attainable. In addition, the service plan holds the child welfare system and community accountable to the family.

USES OF THE MODEL   The Family Unity Model was developed to avoid placing children in foster care (especially when the best plan for the child and family was not clear) and to help children make the transition from out-of-home placement to their families. Currently, the family unity meeting serves families experiencing many barriers to success (S. Barrios, personal communication, March 16, 1995). Meetings assist parents and foster parents in creating smooth transitions with child visitations, encourage collaboration among multiple providers (such as therapist and parent trainers), help the family and the kinship network confront barriers in the child welfare system, and facilitate a working relationship between the child welfare worker and the family.

The Family Unity Model is designed as a framework to empower families. As with most frameworks, the success of the model partly depends on the flexibility of the meeting facilitator and caseworker. Encouraging families to become collaborators requires that professionals respect the family's rhythm of processing and problem solving.

EMPOWERING FAMILIES WITH SCHOOL DROPOUTS

School programs aimed at increasing the academic success of the students "at risk" of dropping out of school have not curbed drop-out statistics (Franklin & Streeter, 1992). Empowerment practice in school drop-out programs begins with a shift away from viewing the family as the obstacle to a student's academic success or continuation. The focus then moves to a model of family and school collaboration that can provide the best outcomes for the success of the family, including the student's academic continuation. By viewing the family as a whole and school dropout as a portion of their stress, participants can engage in optimal planning for the student.

Recently, the University of Texas implemented a multimodal systemic intervention for school drop-out prevention (Franklin, 1992; Franklin, McNeil, & Wright, 1991; Franklin & Streeter, 1992). Exemplifying the philosophical shift described in the preceding paragraph, this program creates opportunities to support families in their goals for academic success. Further, the program views the school as a partner and supporter of the family's "mission" (Franklin, 1992).

These multimodal interventions aimed at change and support target the student, family, school, and community. The program uses interventions specific to each possible level of intervention. These interventions occur on site, at the school, and in the home and community.

MICROLEVELS OF CHANGE—INDIVIDUAL AND FAMILY INTERVENTIONS
Individual students receive a variety of services. Therapeutic interventions include individual and peer group counseling. Individual counseling allows students to come to rely on the school social worker as confidant and advocate. Students can use individual counseling to address concerns related to school, family, and peers, such as substance abuse and psychosocial stress. The individual counselor also advocates for the student in larger systems such as the family, school, and community. Individual counselors can provide onsite crisis intervention, make referrals to services in the community (such as drug and alcohol treatment), and link students to mentors.

Peer group therapy creates opportunities for students to bond to their school through relationships with peers. Additionally, the group process can instill hope (Yalom, 1995). Because the group structure joins students who share difficulties at different levels of amelioration, members experience empowerment in helping others as well as themselves.

The final part of this type of intervention is alternative school programming. This program allows students to complete their education through traditional or such nontraditional means as the G.E.D. Flexible programming aimed at meeting the needs of students and families is another key of the program.

Family members participate in family therapy, a psychoeducational parenting group, and a structured self-help and parenting group. These groups offer parents a place to voice concerns for their child and family. The group format also allows families to join forces, increase social support, and develop problem-solving skills.

MACROLEVELS OF CHANGE—COMMUNITY INTERVENTION   The connection between the community and families is the final component of the school drop-out program. The school's social workers engage the community by providing mentors to students and accessing services in the community. Similarly, the student and family learn to access school personnel and peer supports to advocate for their needs in the larger community. The community then provides services outside the school setting, such as inpatient drug and alcohol treatment.

In effect, the school, family, and community become part of the student's kinship network. Support people help the student achieve academic success, improved social functioning, and increased competence in many settings. By offering services across the student's "system," the school has the resources to intervene effectively. Ultimately, the school becomes an active participant in the lives of student and family by providing educational, social, and clinical services (Franklin, 1992).

PRACTICE PRINCIPLES

Action is one of the primary elements in empowerment. Empowerment involves many processes of change. When people unite to take responsibility for transforming unhealthy or unsafe realities, they show empowerment. Building solidarity around family and community concerns holds great potential for such change. Because empowerment practice requires social workers to understand the physical and cultural environments that sustain their clients, practitioners must engage in important community processes if they want to work effectively. That is, to empower families, one must empower the communities where family members gather, live, and work.

Here are the guidelines for effective empowerment practice with children and families.

1. Begin where the client is, understanding that your client may be a family or a community.

2. Begin from a strengths perspective: Tap into the strength, resources, defiance, anger, and humor within a family or community. Family and community change must start with an identification of what is good and what is or has been done well. Building from competence not deficits offers incentives for change (Cowger, 1994).

3. Allow flexibility in service delivery. For example, families may be more comfortable meeting in their homes or in facilities such as churches and schools. Practitioners must be willing to extend themselves, perhaps even move from their own comfort and convenience zones. This flexibility goes a long way toward equalizing power in relationships.

4. Enter *and* exit relationships ethically and respectfully. If the community does so, pay proper homage to elders. Listen more than talk. Become a student rather than a teacher. Let someone "guide" you into the community, if necessary. Leave the power inside the family by enhancing existing capabilities, strengthening problem-solving technologies, and protecting families' rights to make their own decisions (Castex, 1994).

5. Look at family and community from a fresh perspective. Preconceived notions, stereotypes, and media portrayals skew reality. Remember that human beings interact and engage in many different types of relationships and settings. Where one lives, works, and sleeps (the physical) is just as significant as etiquette systems, rituals, religious beliefs, language, and customs (the cultural). Each element informs one how to be with others. Kinfolk and friends, workmates and schoolmates, neighbors and acquaintances can know, live with, and work with each other as they value their connectedness with one another. Other groups can fail to "act" as a community with each other. People experience both of these circumstances. Communities have feelings and identities just as individuals do. Communities define themselves.

6. Engender trust in your clients. Families must be able to trust that you will do what you say you will do and that you will not abuse or overextend your power as a facilitator.

7. Work as a partner with people on issues important to them. Become an ally rather than an expert.

8. Do your homework: Know the history of people and communities. Unfortunately, libraries, schools, and other traditional repositories do not carry many local histories (Burwell & Valdes, 1989). When written histories are not available, family members and community leaders can help fill in some of the gaps. These authentic histories can provide information about the families and pioneers of the community. This knowledge reframes change processes. Further, having families discover their own family's successes and struggles can motivate, inspire, and empower them.

9. Avoid negative images of families and communities. The negative connotations of living environments (i.e., trailer parks or homelessness) or family status (i.e., teenage parenting) can stigmatize families. Practitioners must also work with the media and public relations experts to correct the negative images, myths, and stereotypes. Because these social pollutants stunt empowerment, social workers should help community groups to reestablish control over the image-making processes.

10. Acknowledge each family's uniqueness. Differences exist within groups and across groups (Castex, 1994); cultural groups, families, and communities are multidimensional, dynamic, and evolving social systems. Reducing groups to one category or description denies the importance of their total experience.

ISSUES IN THE USE OF EMPOWERMENT PRACTICE WITH FAMILIES

As noted previously, empowerment practice holds great promise as an innovative approach to working with families from a strengths perspective. A number of barriers, however, prevent full implementation.

First, families spend a great deal of energy in protecting, supporting, and nurturing their members. Yet, society does not culturally support many of these methods, which mainstream service providers therefore view as "unhealthy" or "dysfunctional." Empowerment-oriented practitioners working with families and children must recognize and respect the complex, many-faceted methods of caring within families. To promote these nurturing processes and to facilitate healthy family development, they must build on existing resources and strengths within families.

Schools of social work, as well as other helping professions, must take steps to train students in these culturally competent practice methods. Training should begin with an exploration of self and an understanding of how one's own value and belief system was developed. Practitioners must learn about the migration of ethnic groups to the United States and their historical and contemporary experiences in this country. Next, practitioners need knowledge of empirically based practice models and individual, family, and community-based intervention strategies for working with families. Empowerment practice with families of color particularly requires the development of culturally competent methods. Finally, and most importantly, social workers must have a learning posture open to information about families of color. A combination of self-awareness and openness to differences of values, beliefs, and behaviors; a strong knowledge base; and a willingness to learn will enhance a social worker's ability to work with diverse families.

Second, much of the service delivery system attends late-stage and crisis interventions. This tells families they should wait and take care of their own. When families do finally enter service systems, they have become physically and emotionally drained. This depletion impedes empowerment processes, because it makes families feel hopeless, victimized, and powerless to change. Because their own attempts at change have failed, families enter the social service system feeling they don't have the ability to find workable solutions to their problems. Professionals thus need to encourage policies and practices that promote prevention and early family intervention; existing prevention-focused programs need careful evaluation, and their successes need to be replicated in other geographical locations and program areas. With prevention-oriented practice in place, families can receive the support they need *before* they enter crisis situations.

Third, the lack of opportunity for families to "self-define" their social situation also impedes the empowerment process. Traditionally, social workers have performed an assessment of family functioning based on their perceptions of their client's situation. However, what the worker might call a "crisis" the family might see as "stress." Families are much more liberal or generous in their assessments than traditional social workers. They may perceive the issues in a different light, recognizing particular factors such as strength, resources, and assets that the social worker may not see at first. Thus, the intervention recommended by the worker may not be the one needed by the family. Workers must help families to define their level of functioning, which allows families to assess their own strengths and weaknesses and engage in the problem-solving process, thus facilitating the empowerment process.

Fourth, societal images of families focus more on composition (who is present or absent) rather than on viability issues (how family members function). This image skews thinking and interventions with families. For example, by ignoring all the fascinating and competent ways extended families operate, a preoccupation with nuclear families hinders practitioners' ability to work with families from a strengths perspective. Practitioners must assess the unique strengths and resources of each family, regardless of its structure, to promote family empowerment. They should suspend preconceived ideas about what a family is and allow the family to define itself. By allowing families to define themselves, practitioners encourage members to explore resources and assets outside the bounds of the nuclear family— for example, extended family members and non-kin relationships.

Fifth, the absence of practitioners specializing in matters of due process, client rights, and ethical violations implies to families that these issues are unimportant. Nothing could be further from the truth. Empowerment-oriented practitioners must be just as knowledgeable about these issues as they are about psychosocial dynamics and family development. Practitioners who act on these matters bring a certain power to their practice with families. By remaining concerned with client rights, social workers promote client empowerment within a social welfare system that often robs clients of control and power.

Sixth, from an agency perspective, the primary obstacle in implementing empowerment practice is an inadequately trained workforce with deeply rooted beliefs and values about practice. In-service training can greatly promote an empowerment-based approach among agency personnel. However, beliefs and values are difficult to change. Practitioners will need extensive and ongoing training, good role models, mandates from the administration, and an organization that supports practitioners as they attempt to revolutionize practice.

Seventh, families often hesitate in assuming a partnership with practitioners. For one, they fear retribution: Families may wonder if they and/or their communities will experience punitive actions for assuming an equal role in the partnership. They may fear that services or income will be affected because of the new roles between themselves and the practitioner. A second reason for the hesitancy is low self-esteem among families. Because they often do not consider themselves the "experts," families tend to place control in the hands of the practitioner. Thus, the practitioners must engage families in esteem building to help them envision a relationship of equality between themselves and the practitioner.

SUMMARY

The family empowerment movement is a modern effort to reconstitute family integrity and well-being. Historically, child welfare, public assistance regulations, court orders, and mental health agendas have torn families apart. New agendas, however, have emerged to correct this assault on family life. Family preservation, family reunification, and family-life education programs are just some of the themes in this family empowerment movement. These exciting initiatives offer new paradigms, interventions, and outcomes in work with families.

Empowerment practice with families has several key characteristics. First, family empowerment models begin with a family strengths perspective. Work builds on existing and often underused natural helping systems, abilities, and other resources. Family empowerment models also take into account the various environmental contexts families experience. These models recognize that environmental factors—the community, schools, employment—influence the viability of family life just as much as family size, composition, and development. Family well-being is closely connected to community well-being. Efforts to improve living conditions, community safety, or recreational opportunities also empower families. Because building solidarity around pressing community concerns or triumphs holds great potential for change, it exemplifies one kind of social work activity in the family empowerment movement.

Finally, empowerment-based practice with families is guided by several key concepts. Practice focuses on the empowerment of families through collaborative relationships between practitioners and family members, capacity building among families, and use of the resources and support that extended family members and non-kinship networks provide. Such social work practice with families and children will help families build on their own strengths, gain access to needed resources, and develop the life skills necessary to function as a healthy family unit.

REFERENCES

Aragon de Valdez, T., & Gallegos, J. (1982). The Chicano familia in social work. In J. Green (Ed.), *Cultural awareness in the human services* (pp. 184–208). Englewood Cliffs, NJ: Prentice-Hall.

Burwell, Y., & Valdes, J. (1989). Historical discovery: Treasures of black images and resources. In *The Future of Rural Social Work Toward the Year 2000: Proceedings of the 12th Annual Institute on Social Work and Human Services in the Rural Environment* (pp. 102–110). Pensacola: University of West Florida, School of Social Work.

Castex, G. M. (1994). Providing services to Hispanic/Latino populations: Profiles in diversity. *Social Work, 39*, 288–296.

Conger, J. V., & Kanungo, R. N. (1988). The empowerment process: Integrating theory and practice. *Academy of Management Review, 13*(3), 471–482.

Cowger, C. (1994). Assessing client strengths: Clinical assessment for client empowerment. *Social Work, 39*, 262–269.

Deming, B. (1984). Empowerment: A vehicle to peace. In M. S. White & D. Van Soest (Eds.), *Empowerment of people for peace* (p. 8). Minneapolis, MN: Women Against Military Madness.

Dunst, C., Trivette, C., & Deal, A. (1988). *Enabling and empowering families.* Cambridge, MA: Brookline.

Dunst, C., Trivette, C., & Deal, A. (Eds.). (1994). *Supporting and strengthening families: Vol. 1. Methods, strategies and practices.* Cambridge, MA: Brookline.

Franklin, C. (1992). Family and individual patterns in a group of middle-class dropout youths. *Social Work, 37*(4), 338–334.

Franklin, C., McNeil, R. W., & Wright, R. (1991). The effectiveness of social work in alternative school for high school dropouts. *Social Work with Groups, 14*(2), 59–73.

Franklin, C., & Streeter, C. L. (1992). Evidence for effectiveness of social work with high school dropout youths. *Child and Adolescent Social Work Journal, 9*(2), 131–152.

Germaine, C. (1991). *Human behavior in the social environment: An ecological view.* New York: Columbia University Press.

Gutiérrez, L. (1990). Working with women of color: An empowerment perspective. *Social Work, 35*(2), 149–153.

Halley, A., Kopp, J., & Austin, M. (1992). *Delivering human services: A learning approach to practice* (3rd ed.). New York: Longman.

Hasenfeld, Y. (1987). Power in social work practice. *Social Services Review, (61),* 478–479.

Kibria, N. (1993). *Family tightrope: The changing lives of Vietnamese Americans.* Princeton, NJ: Princeton University Press.

Liebow, E. (1966). *Talley's corner: A study of negro street corner men.* Boston: Little, Brown.

Martin, E., and Martin, J. (1978). *The black extended family.* Chicago: University of Chicago Press.

Rappaport, J. (1981). In praise of paradox: A social policy of empowerment over prevention. *American Journal of Community Psychology, 9,* 1–25.

Rappaport, J. (1987). Terms of empowerment/exemplars of prevention: Toward a theory for community psychology. *American Journal of Community Psychology, 15*(2), 121–128.

Saleebey, D. (1992). *The strengths perspective in social work practice.* New York: Longman Press.

Solomon, B. (1976). *Black empowerment: Social work in oppressed communities.* New York: Columbia University Press.

Stack, C. (1974). *All our kin: Strategies for survival in a black community.* New York: Harper & Row.

Yalom, I. D. (1995). *The theory and practice of group psychotherapy.* New York: Basic Books.

Zimmerman, M. A., & Rappaport, J. (1988). Citizen participation, perceived control, and psychological empowerment. *American Journal of Community Psychology, 16,* 725–750.

Zuravin, S. J. (1989). Severity of maternal depression and three types of mother-to-child aggression. *American Orthopsychiatric Association, 59*(3), 377–389.

Zuravin, S., & Greif, G. L. (1989, February). Normative and child-maltreating AFDC mothers. *Social Casework: The Journal of Contemporary Social Work,* pp. 76–84.

Part Four

SPECIAL ISSUES IN
EMPOWERMENT PRACTICE

So that social workers can practice from an empowerment base, agency administrators, evaluators, and research directors need to support empowerment. In Parsons's study of five empowerment programs,[1] staff members state clearly the need for supervisors, evaluation personnel, administrative policies, and boards of directors to support empowerment ideas and philosophies. Chapters 10, 11, and 12 explore social service delivery and administration, research, and program evaluation as means of facilitating empowerment in clients. Chapter 13 summarizes the empowerment principles generated by all the chapters and identifies barriers to empowerment practice in human service agencies. It also identifies strategies for the profession, including professional education for facilitating empowerment.

In Chapter 10, Enid Cox and Barbara Joseph summarize the current retrenchment issues in social work programs, which inhibit empowerment of workers and empowerment practice with clients. The authors assert that given the current siege on the goals and programs of human services,

---

[1]Parsons, R. J. (1995). *Empowerment-based social work practice: A study in process and outcomes.* Paper presented to the Council of Social Work Education Annual Program Meeting, San Diego, CA.

163

empowerment-oriented strategies are needed more than ever. They identify necessary strategies to bring about empowerment practice in social service agencies, including increased participation of families and communities; egalitarian relationships among agency leaders, workers, and clients; and active interagency networks. Finally, they suggest that administrators must lead their agencies with the larger social goals in focus, visualizing the contributions their agencies make toward these goals. Questions a reader might ask include the following:

1. *Can these values and practices be carried out in mainstream and traditional agencies, or does this type of administrative process only occur in small independent agencies with private funding? How can social workers help their agencies incorporate some of the strategies identified here?*
2. *How does the the growing trend of managed care affect empowerment? How do values and practices of managed care mitigate the current characteristics listed in Table 10.2?*
3. *How can egalitarian relationships between agency leaders and workers be established in hierarchical agencies? How can egalitarian relationships between clients and workers be established in today's "professional" service delivery systems?*

In Chapter 11, Sung Sil Lee Sohng presents ways to examine knowledge that will lead to social action and transformation. By linking knowledge, power, and social movements, Sohng postulates four tenets for assessing whether research is transformative through its process and ends: antidiscrimination as ethical, research as emancipatory, research as empowering, and research as political action. The reader may want to ask these questions:

1. *Since many research funding decisions are made through the "Western-dominated world order," who will fund research specifically designated to include those who traditionally have been excluded in this paradigm, and specifically,*
2. *Will funding sources tolerate research that is openly designed to bring about social change and political transformation?*
3. *Furthermore, how can academic institutions prepare social work researchers to do such research with the current faculty who teach in schools of social work?*

In Chapter 12, Ruth Parsons suggests that one must assess client empowerment in terms of the clients' environment and worldview. She also presents the necessity of incorporating empowerment-based methods when evaluating empowerment-based practice. Finally, Parsons suggests the need for amplifying the client's voice by asking clients to identify the helping experience and the outcomes that empowerment-based programs may produce. The reader way want to ask the following:

1. *How do these types of evaluations fit with current social service delivery systems of managed care? How do they affect research in that certain accountability structures want concise outcome studies?*
2. *The evaluation designs proposed by Parsons are time consuming and process oriented. Clients must be engaged in the evaluation process and compensated for their participation. Are agencies willing to commit enough time and resources, especially considering today's shortages?*

Chapter 13 summarizes the book's intent, identifies barriers to its framework for practice, and calls on professionals to challenge current conditions and to work for positive change. The authors also call for rekindling movements for social change within the profession, rather than following the current trend of social service delivery. A reader may want to ask the following questions:

1. *Where within the profession is the leadership necessary for such action?*
2. *How in current funding structures do social work positions allow for such activities on the part of social workers?*

Chapter 10

SOCIAL SERVICE DELIVERY

AND EMPOWERMENT

THE ADMINISTRATOR'S ROLE

Enid Opal Cox, D.S.W.
University of Denver, Denver, Colorado

Barbara Hunter Randal Joseph, D.S.W.
SUNY, Old Westbury, New York

INTRODUCTION

In this chapter we shall explore the possibility of creating models of administration that empower people as subjects and actors. Energized in a dynamic, collaborative triad, administrators/clients/workers become coactivists in a process of transformation, together changing mutually oppressive conditions of work and life. We pose this egalitarian vision in contrast to the hierarchical power structures and the authoritarian, "expert" role that usually accompany service situations.

We think empowerment is a means to achieve needed social change personally and politically, in ways that meet human needs as well as ways that allow committed administrators to help design and render empowerment service models with disempowered people, both workers and clients. Given the many crises in society today and the positioning of social service workers to bear witness (Fabricant & Burghardt, 1992), such workers need to take a deeper look at empowerment theory and practice. Much like advocacy theory before it, empowerment signals the need for a response akin to a social movement. Questions of leadership and will aside, social workers are victimized by the same forces as clients. Spurred by discontent, transformation is a vision of social change as well as a process and the outcome of throwing off oppression in one's life and in one's community. According to Setleis, social workers and clients must participate in the transformation of their institutions so that institutions become just, relevant, and responsive to individual and social need. Agencies must also advocate for necessary institutional change (Lee, 1994). Hope lies in discerning how social workers can gain new consciousness, marshall their skills, and practice in collaboration with other liberating efforts.

We assume that those administrators compelled by the need for empowerment work will want to escape any training that teaches them to carry out "efficient," rationalist bureaucratic models of behavior and organization as desired ends. In its place, administrators can adopt the visionary, life-giving, need-meeting, strengths-based activities imperative in any model of empowerment. Our experience tells us that this move usually leads to a level of effectiveness (productivity and efficiency, if you will) far superior to that of the bureaucratic, authoritarian model. In this thinking, we are not Pollyannas but partisan holdouts for the basic ethics and commitments of a social work modeled long ago, which speaks to democratic self-determination and collective action, which can bring about social justice and equality for all.

Moreover, this view is bolstered by recent comprehensive efforts to define, describe, and elaborate models of empowerment practice (Cox & Parsons, 1994; Gutiérrez, 1990; Lee, 1994; Simon, 1994). These models have gained currency by exploring empowerment's many dimensions, including psychological empowerment; efforts to apply personal, interpersonal, and political aspects of empowerment; and the emphasis on egalitarian relationships among professionals and clients at all levels.

Less documented is the relationship of empowerment practice models to the organizational context of current social service delivery systems. To increase the use of empowerment-oriented models, practice settings that support this form of practice must be developed, modified, and sustained. The role of social work practitioners who serve in administrative roles— program directors, managers, administrators, supervisors, coordinators, etc. —is critical to this effort.

Philosophy and Value Base

Authors generally agree on the philosophy that guides empowerment practice. It includes the belief that the empowerment process will enhance mental, spiritual, and physical wellness as well as social justice. The values of empowerment-oriented practice, as suggested in Chapter 1, include fulfillment of human needs; promotion of social justice; more equal distribution of resources; concern for environmental protection; elimination of racism, sexism, ageism, and heterosexism; self-determination; and self-actualization.

This chapter will discuss challenges to empowerment practice at the service delivery level and the incorporation of empowerment-oriented values and interventions into the administrative process. Specific intervention strategies to support empowerment practice in current settings will also be suggested.

CURRENT CHALLENGES TO EMPOWERMENT PRACTICE IN SERVICE DELIVERY SETTINGS

The recent loss of resources and negative stigma regarding social welfare programs carry strong implications for empowerment-oriented service providers and their clients. Any discussion of empowerment strategies must include a hard look at why the profession is where it is and what is to be faced. The mid-1990s has greatly challenged government social welfare programs. Throughout the 1980s and early 1990s, the government made deep cuts in funds for the support of programs meeting human needs. Those against social welfare blame the poor for their problems. It matters little that, during this period, wages have fallen for a large segment of society as an outcome of unregulated internationalization of the economy. The need for U.S. laborers and consumers has also decreased. According to current leadership, though, the poor are poor by their own choice—a choice that includes refusal to work and failure to save for adequate retirement or unexpected disability and health-care needs.

A study sponsored by the Children's Defense Fund notes that between 1973 and 1990 the median income of all young families with children dropped more than 32%, and the poverty rate for their children doubled from 20% to 40% in 1990. (Children's Defense Fund, 1996). The minimum wage in 1992 equaled only about 80% of poverty for a family of three (Blau, 1992). The increasing percentage of women in the workforce has added income to many white middle-class homes but at the same time increased the need for caregiving resources.

The changing nature of the labor market appears to support a widening gap between people with wealth and those without adequate resources to meet their basic needs (Barnet & Cavanagh, 1994; Erickson & Vallas, 1990). By strongly challenging the bargaining power of labor, these volatile factors in the political economy weaken the cause of low-income people, whose capacity to work is their primary resource in this market/profit-driven economy.

The impact of large, comprehensive cutbacks in funding on public and private nonprofit human service programs has devastated social service agencies. Two related forces—the movement for privatization of health and social service and the increased bureaucratization of human services—have deepened the negative effects on social services that emerged in the late 1960s and the 1970s. For example, severe cutbacks in funding for child protection have led to inadequately trained and supervised case workers. This, in turn, has contributed to inadequate support for families in crisis. These problems in service delivery have been exploited—used to justify and rationalize more severe cutbacks in publicly supported human services.

Several observers have explored the changes in social services resulting from these environmental forces. However, the impact of these changes on empowerment and related social work has been analyzed less fully.

The policy proposals gaining the attention of national, state, and local decision makers call for increased inequality in income distribution, profit over human needs and quality of life, and the elimination of policies or programs that diminish racism, sexism, and heterosexism. As a part of these legislative attacks, a comprehensive movement is being organized and implemented to minimize or abolish social security, medicare, and other programs that serve the middle class as well as the working poor. Legislators now seek to remove "entitlement" from future and past social legislation even when such actions require constitutional amendments.

The political rhetoric and victim blaming surrounding this campaign has heightened competition among groups and increased negative feelings related to sex, color, and other human differences. Supported by a precarious labor market and lowering wages, the message of leadership—that resources are scarce and being used by the undeserving poor—heightens middle- and working-class fears and identifies a scapegoat for public anger. The antiwelfare rhetoric presented by leadership has combined with these factors to increase economic insecurity among groups already fearful of their ability to survive and has increased feelings of self-doubt, low self-esteem, and hopelessness for many recipients of public assistance.

Privatization and cutbacks in program resources have destroyed the sense of economic efficacy that many recipients of public programs may have developed. Privatization of public entitlement resources or services heretofore thought to be a "right" often changes the status of that resource to a "charity," provided at the will or whim of agencies and workers or for a fee beyond many clients. Privatization has undermined not only the sense of empowerment of clients but also the economic efficacy and power of social service workers (Abromivitz, 1986).

Impact at the Service Delivery Level

Under the guise of cost-containment strategies, agencies have cut entire programs and limited service in others. Increasing case loads have limited client contact and made many more holistic service interventions impossible.

Karger and Stoesz state that "as social programs deteriorated, social service delivery 'systems' were plagued by four major problems: (1) fragmentation, (2) discontinuity, (3) unaccountability, and (4) inaccessibility" (1994, p. 159).

Table 10.1 outlines the main characteristics of today's social service agencies. Clients who depend on these systems are losing their already tenuous sense of rights to services and resources. Service eligibility requirements change erratically, which increases clients' insecurity, and agencies cut programs or provide poorer and more restricted services. As both public and private agencies compete for government dollars and contracts—even for clients directly—fragmentation and inaccessibility increase. For clients, finding services becomes more difficult. Clients often must shift from service to service, because of income or government program limitations (such as the limited number of social work services available through medicare). This shifting leads to premature discharge from programs.

Impact on Social Service Workers

In the 1960s and 1970s, professionals experimented with new forms of intervention that often "fit" an empowerment practice model. However, social service workers in public and private human services agencies have experienced a shift from working in agencies (however strapped) committed to helping clients to agencies that foster cost containment or profit as primary goals. Where clients, in the worst circumstance, were once assumed to be the primary targets of agency interventions, current strategies often focus on clients who can pay or on those with relatively less serious problems.

Social workers and other human service workers have also experienced serious salary cuts, layoffs, a strong influx of the contingency market

TABLE 10.1
CHARACTERISTICS OF
SOCIAL SERVICE AGENCIES

- Deep and continuing funding cuts (cuts in programs and staff)
- Larger caseloads (increasing workloads, clients in worse condition)
- New mechanisms of internal control (decreasing the scope of professional decision making and substituting routine and specific tasks for professional judgment and holistic, creative, client-centered interventions)
- Increase in control of medical model programs over human services
- General increase in victim-blaming assessment
- Increasing hostility in worker-client relationships
- Fewer training opportunities of professional workers

Source: Cox & Parsons, 1994.

(part-time, no-benefit jobs), and devaluation of their services and per-spectives. Simultaneously, caseloads that reflect clients with increasingly severe symptoms—from being deprived of services or suffering more severe conditions—have soared.

Finally, the autonomy of social workers and their ability to use their knowledge and skills to intervene effectively in client problems has greatly diminished. Fabricant and Burghardt (1992) describe how new or increased mechanisms of control have imposed new responsibilities and redefined the tasks of social service workers. The pressures on social service workers include the following:

- Workers are to pay less attention to quality than quantity.
- Workers are to process ever greater numbers of people in far less time.
- Elaborate reporting requirements have increased paper work.
- Increasing surveillance of client-worker interactions erodes the autonomy of social service workers.
- Intervention tasks become fragmented in an assembly-line fashion, leading to routinized, quantifiable tasks.
- As tasks become specific repetitive actions, professional jobs are cut and unskilled workers hired.
- Opportunities for promotion, training, and use of new knowledge and skills have become less frequent. (Fabricant & Burghardt, 1992)

Even though they also suffer from restructuring, medically based health care services have fared better. However, social services attached to health care settings have been severely attacked and cut. Viewed as a sec-ondary service, social work has in many cases dwindled to finding commu-nity resources and assisting the discharge of sometimes very sick patients.

In summary, the current state of social services has come to represent, for many social workers, a severe loss of autonomy, status, and ability to pro-vide the interventions they find most appropriate for clients' needs. Also, they are often underpaid, working without benefits, and have few opportu-nities for training or advancement.

Client-Worker Relationships

As both clients and workers have experienced disempowering challenges, their relationship with each other has in many cases also deteriorated. Workers have been unable to help clients meet their needs; they have been forced to limit client contact and in many cases have become greatly dis-tressed or even given up with respect to their own effectiveness. Some workers have been seduced by victim-blaming arguments, which allow them to justify system failure and their own powerlessness in terms of clients' behaviors and weaknesses. On the other hand, clients experience social workers as representatives of oppressive systems, unable or unwilling to provide assistance. Too often, the conflict and tensions stemming from the worsening conditions of both social workers and clients shift onto the client-worker relationship.

In summary, social service and many health care agencies/programs end up oppressing both professionals and clients. Both struggle for survival in an atmosphere of decreasing resources and negations of their values, work, and way of life. Often, an increased sense of powerlessness and poor worker-client relationships result. The challenges to planning, management, and administrative social workers who wish to promote empowerment are complex and deeply imbedded in the larger political economy. However, neither these issues nor these challenges are new to social work. The answer may lie in preparation and the will to take them on.

Perhaps one should revisit the idea of U.S. politics as the highest art—the place to achieve human self-actualization, civic virtue, and political participation by drawing on the rich theoretical traditions that created the world's first large-scale experiment in free government. For instance, 19th-century conservatives would view politics as the arena where elected officials could protect the people from the state. Now it is the place to attain protection against the people, particularly passionate and "irrational" majorities (workers, women, people of color); this, in turn, has led people to distrust those in office. Lobbying for adequate budgets and shares of tax dollars is not simply a matter of making the most rational and compelling case; decisions are based on other factors.

Politicians count on those who can keep them in power. Even if one thinks government and politicians are mostly untrustworthy, what are the alternatives? Further, if workers and clients don't learn to speak for themselves culturally and politically, who will? Given the conditions we have just described, withdrawal and passivity are simply not options. The issue of politics, then, is not whether to get involved or not but rather how to acquire a rightful and representative place in the political arena.

How can more workers and clients get involved? The first step is educational: We shall discuss later in this chapter how administrators can foster empowering education in staff development and training. It goes without saying that educational messages, training, and development without structures of practice are likely to fail; like theory without action, a praxis is needed. Imbued with new consciousness about their political abilities, workers can present workers' and clients' needs to funders and politicians whose decisions will affect all greatly. Workers and clients form a base from which they garner active support to strengthen agencies and communities. The price of empowerment is action and hard work—no one else can do it for them.

ADMINISTRATIVE ISSUES AND INTERVENTION STRATEGIES

Empowerment-oriented administrators, agency directors, and managers who want to apply their philosophy may take heart in the fact that, historically, many such administrators have sought to serve as client advocates and to create and sustain empowering programs in their agencies. Many of the strategies discussed in this section have emerged and reemerged in this century. The recent focus of academicians on empowerment work has resulted in a few preliminary research studies that explore such work from the perspective of administrators attempting to support it. The barriers to developing and sustaining empowerment practice identified by administrators in one study includes the following:

- Funding issues, particularly the resistance of funding sources concerned about the longer times required for documentable results in empowerment-oriented approaches
- A social environment that involves political and philosophical differences with other agencies and agency competition
- Intrapersonal issues, especially those characteristics of clients or workers that seem to interfere with empowerment practice
- Interpersonal issues related to the client/worker relationship (Gutiérrez, GlenMaye, & DeLois, 1995)

Though these concerns regarding the integration of an empowerment philosophy focus mostly on work in programs, they also relate to service delivery systems as a whole.

Social work administrators work primarily in one of two approaches to implementing empowerment: (1) modifying patterns of service delivery in traditional organizations or (2) developing and operating alternative agencies and organizations. Many of the strategies we shall suggest apply to either of these approaches.

This section is organized around key points that have emerged from our discussions with empowerment-oriented program administrators, from related studies, and from our own experience. Many of these strategies relate to one or more of the barriers to practice we have identified.

Leadership

Understanding the meaning of leadership as it flows from an empowerment-oriented philosophy is critical to such practice. Common characteristics of individuals identified as effective leaders of empowerment-oriented programs or agencies include:

- The ability to articulate a clear vision of the values and goals of empowerment
- Demonstration of a strong commitment to these values and goals
- Willingness to take risks to assure program success
- A high level of creativity in problem solving
- The ability to form strong egalitarian collaborative networks (and in some cases, a social action movement) among workers, clients, community action groups, decision makers, and themselves
- The ability to reflect empowerment-oriented values in all aspects of program development and implementation

Like others involved in empowerment practice, such administrators find themselves simultaneously involved in the personal, interpersonal, and political aspects of effective leadership and development.

In the following discussion, activities such as fundraising, networking, legislative activities, board work, public education, and research will comprise externally focused activities. Staff development, supervision, and support, as well as client-centered activities, will be discussed as internally focused activities.

External Strategies

External strategies include resource development, working with boards, developing agency support, networking, legislative work, public education, and research development and dissemination. Empowerment-oriented administrators often focus on tasks related to organizational survival. Central to all agencies, the development and maintenance of a funding base often poses a special challenge to empowerment-oriented programs. Gutiérrez et al. (1995) suggest that some empowerment-oriented administrators have found funders reluctant to support these programs because they tend to require a relatively long time to demonstrate success. Historically, programs that successfully engage clients in empowerment-oriented activities have also faced conflict among funding, agency maintenance, and social action goals. As groups become more assertive, they often make demands on decision-making power structures that jeopardize program support.

Several empowerment-oriented directors interviewed by the Denver University Institute of Gerontology staff (1995) have also mentioned that many funding sources do not support nonhierarchical staffing models. As one administrator states, "We are often called to task for creative egalitarian staffing strategies. Many potential funders want to see a traditional staffing pattern." In a study by Cox and Lazarri (1982), and from interviews of administrators of 15 empowerment programs (Institute of Gerontology, 1995), empowerment proponents suggested the following funding strategies:

- Maintain a broad-based, multisource funding base when possible, such as government grants, private foundations, churches, civil groups, donations from individuals including clients, fees for service when affordable and appropriate, and income from profit-generating projects. Such a base usually enhances creativity and freedom in programming.
- Set aside funds to conduct pilot or demonstration projects of empowerment interventions or, in the case of large organizations, designate special ongoing units as empowerment sites using these funds.
- Subcontract resources to allow other alternative agencies/programs to provide empowerment interventions for the agencies' clients (a few administrators note that they took primary roles in creating these alternative agencies).
- Educate funding sources about the importance of empowerment interventions/programs, and keep them involved in all phases of operations, including outcome evaluations.
- Involve staff, clients, and other supporting networks in fund raising.
- Actively support the development of funding for the empowerment approach. For example, one can try to influence policy that guides program sources.

Overall, administrators state that getting and maintaining funds to support empowerment interventions require constant commitment and attention to new ways of developing funding sources. Critical to the development of empowerment program resources, public education activities require particular attention from administrators.

PUBLIC EDUCATION AS EMPOWERMENT ACTIVITY   Advocates of empowerment philosophy and programs need to take on public education as a key to their efforts. Once again, they require a multistrategy, multitargeted approach. Administrators report the need to develop educational strategies tailored to the educational needs of (1) political decision makers, (2) decision makers of foundations, (3) other potential private funding sources, (4) the public at large, (5) client-supported action groups, and (6) ongoing staff and client education. (Staff and client consciousness-raising strategies will be elaborated as part of the discussion of internal agency/program strategies.)

Many empowerment-oriented administrators conceptualize their problem-solving efforts as part of a sociopolitical movement. For example, the director of one disability program states that "no agency can be truly empowerment-oriented if it does not see its task as connecting the personal aspects of problems of its clients to the political aspects of these problems. To do so, you have to find ways to create a movement involving self-help and social action." Other such administrators have often mentioned the implications of this personal-is-political perspective for the educational role of administrators (Institute of Gerontology, 1995).

Commonly identified in the literature and by empowerment-oriented administrators are the following goals of public education:

1. To educate the general public about the issues and oppression experienced by the client population and to promote consciousness raising with respect to the way this issue relates to the needs and concerns of all members of society.

2. To raise the consciousness of decision makers regarding the important contribution of empowerment-oriented interventions to the physical and mental well-being of clients and their communities and also as a means to the solution of specific immediate problems.

These goals require long-term, ongoing communication and education. The involvement of clients, staff, and volunteers in these strategies is central to this process. Empowerment-oriented administrators frequently note the power of clients who speak for themselves, directly describing their circumstances to the press, in legislative hearings, at public meetings, and to service providers, client networks, and/or self-help groups. Other strategies commonly used by empowerment-oriented administrators include these:

- Persistence, or continuing to present issues even after negative outcomes.
- Focusing educational presentations when possible on "common needs" or common goals with the audience. For example, most empowerment-oriented programs have a preventive component that makes them in the long run cost effective.
- Using every opportunity to make communication contacts, formal or informal. For example, one can make presentations at the churches of targeted decision makers.
- Learning to use the media effectively, including developing strong support among members of the media.
- A thoughtfully planned, ongoing public education effort, closely related to the "networking" task of administrators.

NETWORKING AS EMPOWERMENT ACTIVITY Though networking includes educational strategies, it goes beyond education and consciousness raising to developing egalitarian, ongoing, mutual support and collective action among a number of often competitive entities. Networking efforts include working with staff, clients, and other program advocates to identify potential organizations for collaborative effort. Network cohorts frequently include client advocacy groups, other human service agencies and programs, members of key decision-making organizations including elected officials, family members of clients, advocacy groups, client groups with similar goals/issues, and groups with similar values such as churches and civic organizations.

Networking activity often includes mutual action to achieve common goals. One seeks to identify common needs and goals among one's own clients and those of other agencies, programs, or organized groups. This identification both solidifies network activities and contributes to consciousness raising. It also offers the opportunity to identify common sources of oppression in client groups and address them effectively. Further, this process leads to multiagency support of social transformation goals.

Empowerment-oriented administrators must develop ways to involve clients in these activities. Networks that lack the strong involvement of clients not only risk becoming paternalistic but also frequently lack vital information about client needs, client strengths, and the impact of programs on these. Worst of all, they miss optimum opportunities for client empowerment.

RESEARCH AS EMPOWERMENT ACTIVITY Models of research that incorporate client participation and focus on client strengths as well as inabilities are powerful tools for empowerment-oriented administration (Chapin, 1995). The participation of clients in research also provides an excellent opportunity to increase their involvement in agency operations as well as the external program support activities just discussed. Rapp, Shera, and Kisthardt (1993) note that the context of research for empowerment-oriented practitioners must be the contexts of their clients lives.

Some consciousness-raising efforts focus on increasing the public's understanding of clients and their situation as "all in the same boat" as themselves. Participatory research processes that describe clients' strengths and struggles will be greatly enhanced by such efforts. Because empowerment work seeks to identify strengths and engage individuals by building on personal, interpersonal, political, cultural, and spiritual knowledge and skills, research that primarily targets deficits or sees needs as problems tends to counteract this overall effort. Client involvement in research often helps administrators to document and articulate needs, situations, and positions, as well as the efforts of clients to struggle with their issues.

The victim-blaming strategies of decision makers who control resources often lose force when faced with a strengths assessment from a participatory research effort. Brown (1993) states that "participatory research is an empowering experience for participants, a process that validates their realities, and their rights as people to be heard, respected, and recorded as a part of history" (p. 4). In sum, participatory research offers an extremely effective strategy in empowerment-oriented administration.

POLITICAL ACTION AS EMPOWERMENT ACTIVITY Empowerment work at the administrative level involves active participation in federal, state, and local government policy. Research by the University of Denver Institute of Gerontology (1995) suggests a variety of strategies for this process, including the following:

- Actively participating in public education concerning issues; testifying at hearings; working to establish coalitions
- Developing educational materials, fact sheets, etc., concerning the issues of client constituencies
- Sharing information and organizing knowledge with consumer advocates
- Personal networking with decision makers; developing and maintaining ongoing positive relationships with sympathetic legislators

While these activities resemble those of most administrators, empowerment-oriented administrators must also seek to involve their staff and client constituencies heavily in as many aspects of their political efforts as possible.

To be sure, administrators also frequently discuss organizational barriers to political participation. Regulations or boards can prohibit such activities, as can assumptions that they violate Internal Revenue Service rules (propagated during the Reagan administration) that limit such participation by nonprofit agencies. Some programs have developed separate corporations—one for political action, the other for provision of services (for examples, see Pearlmutter, 1988).

In other cases, constrained administrators have developed ways to help others accomplish mutual legislative goals. For example, they can provide critical information to clients' rights groups, who *can* act. Empowerment interventions often successfully generate client involvement in political activity. An important challenge for administrators is how to form a partnership with clients that can sustain the frequent protest of people in power who attempt to restrict the politicization of social service efforts. Overall participation is integral to empowerment-oriented administrative leadership.

Internal Issues

Issues related to program development and implementation inside agencies include these:

- Program design strategies
- Administrator-staff-client relationships
- Staff development and training issues

PROGRAM DESIGN Empowerment-oriented administrators have the responsibility to initiate programs compatible with the empowerment philosophy.

TABLE 10.2
CHARACTERISTICS OF
EMPOWERMENT-ORIENTED PROGRAMS

Transfer of knowledge and skills useful in self-care to clients, their families, and communities.

Transfer of expertise to clients that will increase their competence in gaining needed resources from, or changes in, their environment (for example, training in how to be an advocate or a mediator, information on social and political systems, and training in methods of effective political participation).

Use of intervention strategies that help clients understand their personal problems in a broader perspective as public issues (thinking and acting in terms of the personal as political alleviates self-blame and helps individuals understand the internalized aspects of powerlessness).

Provision of training and motivation for clients to critically analyze their life situation and encouragement of consciousness-raising exercises and experiences.

Emphasis on cooperative and interdependent activities for accomplishment of mutual goals.

Provision of respected societal roles for elders.

Establishment of worker/client relationships that essentially represent partnerships, or are egalitarian in nature.

Enabling clients to develop or maintain personal support networks.

Enabling groups to take more active roles in decision making that affects their environment (place of residence, organizations that affect their lives, neighborhoods, communities, and country).

Evaluation of service provision in terms of its contribution to the realization of the goals of empowerment-oriented practice.

From *Empowerment-oriented Social Work Practice with the Elderly* (p. 94), by E. O. Cox and R. J. Parsons, 1994, Pacific Grove, CA: Brooks/Cole.

As our discussion of the current state of social services indicates, they must often face this task in a hostile environment. Any success on their part also obviously enhances their power to increase an empowerment focus in agency programs. Cox and Parsons (1994) suggest characteristics for empowerment programs that empowerment-oriented administrators value. Table 10.2 outlines these characteristics.

Administrators must emphasize client involvement in all program design, administration, and implementation. Often, one can introduce self-help or consciousness-raising opportunities into existing programs without additional costs. The following section elaborates the role of staff development in the promotion of empowerment-oriented programming.

ADMINISTRATOR-STAFF-CLIENT RELATIONSHIPS Client and staff involvement in all aspects of a program is critical to empowerment outcomes (Cox & Parsons, 1994; Gutiérrez et al., 1995; Lee, 1994; Shera, 1995). Besides working for this, administrators must develop egalitarian relationships among staff, workers, and clients. The constraints of most traditional organizations make this especially difficult. A third common goal with respect to administrator-client-worker relationships is to value each individual. Managers can explore the ways all members of the organization, including clients, appear from a philosophy that values human life and, consequently, each person (Shera, 1995). This translates into allowing as much individual freedom as possible to choose one's work at one's pace and with one's preferred methods.

Most administrators who have struggled to create egalitarian relationships within human service agencies discuss it actively as an ongoing process. As one administrator for a Denver empowerment-oriented organization states, "We are often going against many deeply ingrained ideas about staff/administrator roles and staff/client roles. Along with the freedom or partnership we are developing comes a lot of work and responsibility for everyone involved." Another administrator states that "in order for there to be real commitment there must be a collaborative effort—or staff and client ownership of programs—this can only happen in egalitarian structures!" (Institute of Gerontology, 1995).

With regard to approaches for promoting egalitarian environments, the following strategies have been identified:

- Using teams to accomplish program goals (teams composed of clients, staff, and administrators)
- Using revolving leadership on teams based on expertise or special knowledge related to specific tasks
- Constantly identifying and developing strengths of all individuals involved, which facilitates mutual respect

Many administrators have discussed the need to persist in providing leadership in the development of egalitarian relationships. As one advocate of egalitarian staff relations states, "We are often going against deep rooted socialization related to authority and ideas about what 'professionalism' means" (Institute of Gerontology, 1995). Several have noted a special challenge related to current trends in licensure that focus on "dual relationships" and "clinical relationships" based on expertise and authoritarian relationships.

Team building helps clients, workers, and administrators demonstrate their knowledge and skills and learn from each other. Shera (1995) stresses using the conflict inherent in team efforts in a constructive way to develop mutually supportive egalitarian relationships.

STAFF DEVELOPMENT, TRAINING, AND SUPERVISION   Based on the idea that a clientele educated by a democratic profession is essential to the well-being of organizations, empowerment practice may be the hope of social work. How does one ensure the participation of workers and clients, such as women or people of color? How do they come to provide education to constituent groups?

Current supervisory models err on the side of creating dependency on the "expert" supervisor; in other cases, workers must tend to their own needs. "Each alternative has the potential to engender powerlessness in a worker and in her practice" (Barouch & Hessmiller-Trego, 1994, p. 17). Peer group supervision offers a method for transforming power relations in practice. Though limited, the literature on such supervision shows some promising developments. Out of the work of Friere and the popular education movement, as well as the egalitarian elements in group work and community organization methods, conscientization and the dynamics of learning circles have arisen. Barouch and Hessmiller-Trego (1994) describe the elements of a model for peer supervision based on Freire (1970, 1978), which they claim are particularly useful in educating workers to:

- Identify the conditions they face
- Understand their root causes
- Formulate action strategies (and act on them)
- Facilitate collective reflection on these strategies

This model, they report, encourages participants to see their proactivity in its sociopolitical context.

Approaches that educate workers, clients, and administrators to be both teachers and learners embody the vision of education and supervision that inspires empowerment practice. Administrators may want to focus workers' efforts on helping clients become educators and organizers—people who can evaluate the human needs in their communities, work in groups to shape programs and curriculum, and acquire the teaching skills and leadership gradually, over several years. Administrators would seek every opportunity to help people practice a variety of methods by presenting oral reports, summarizing activities, and leading discussions in groups with several workers, each with their own approach to the dynamics of empowerment practice. One hopes these would include former clients and people of different classes, races, and genders. Staff development of this kind is demanding, requiring time for workers and clients to practice.

A staff development program could be designed to focus on the following:

1. Programming. One could develop an overview of empowerment education—its goals and constituents, as well as a comparative review of agency structures (in-house power relations). Objectives would include assessing the needs of units in order to plan appropriate short courses and conferences and designing evaluations to measure results. Once this internal work was completed—from a strong, nurturing home base—an external assessment of the local agencies and community would begin.

2. Teaching methods and approaches. In identifying those teaching methods best suited to empowerment, administrators might focus on how people learn, how to conduct stimulating group discussions, how to listen, and the uses of role play as a learning tool. They might also explore the use of case studies, media, visual aids, buzz groups, and brainstorming. In particular, evoking conflicts, and controversial thinking to teach creative approaches to the handling and resolution of conflict would prove helpful. Though not particularly new, these approaches would work in a new way given the values and attitudes of empowerment.

3. Developing and administering a staff development program. Administrators would develop an advisory/decision-making group of staff and clients who would direct educational programs, work on selecting practitioners and recruiting clients, set up a resource file, and participate in public relations and time management. The success of this sort of program demands administrators, coordinators, and directors with foresight, organizational abilities, and a deep commitment to empowerment.

Programming could include the following:

- Workers and clients would research an issue critical to the organization and community, select materials and design education/action plans, preview films and videos, prepare discussion questions, and gain teaching practice in groups in order to test development. Directors could also provide inspirational opportunities as equals to discuss shared problems.
- Retreats and summer institutes for workers and clients would broaden teams' experience and networks and develop deeper relationships.
- People would keep detailed logs that would become the basis for new materials and curricula.
- Saturday morning breakfast seminars on topics of personal interest to members would offer a place to renew relationship building and protected time to resolve differences and conflicts. Stress management, time management, interpersonal relationships, health, nutrition, family: Members would research materials, select topics, and help lead discussions.
- Apprenticeship within units/programs in organizations, as well as assigned tasks in other organizations, would enhance program delivery. Such "field work" would give workers and clients a chance to observe and contribute to ongoing programs. For example, they

could develop information applicable to the needs of a particular group, plan agendas, and lead seminars.

- Personal portfolios of their work, accomplishments, development and training, experience, and recognition/honors would be used as affirmation and documentation toward future education and advancement.

Education departments would emphasize the ways that agencies can teach self-care to clients, families, and communities. This transfer of expertise increases clients' competence in gathering resources from or making changes in their environment; that is, they become effective political participants. Empowerment education would foster the use of intervention strategies that help clients understand their personal problems as public issues, encourage thinking and acting in terms of the personal as political, alleviate self-blame, and help individuals understand the internalized aspects of powerlessness.

Empowerment-oriented training and motivation for workers and clients emphasize cooperative and interdependent activities for the accomplishment of mutual goals. As such, they could result in creative partnerships that may withstand the withering effects of current conditions and find wellsprings of strength only seen briefly in history but never really lost in the work for social transformation.

SUMMARY

This chapter provides an overview of challenges to empowerment practice at the service delivery level and suggests strategies or interventions of interest to agency directors, program administrators, service delivery planners, managers, supervisors, and other indirect service providers who wish to promote empowerment through their programs. We have stressed the importance of leadership visualizing and maintaining a focus on how their programs will serve the goals of larger social movements.

We have also suggested the challenges to the incorporation of empowerment philosophy and strategies into agencies under siege with respect to diminished resources and status. Ironically, as such challenges arise—program resources are cut; caseloads rise; client, worker and agency status deteriorates; and monitoring approaches become more cumbersome—knowledge and understanding of empowerment-oriented strategies has increased. Empowerment approaches require a holistic approach that allows long-term and versatile client-worker contact, often including the participation of families, friends, and communities. In addition, egalitarian relationships among agency leadership, staff, and clients, as well as egalitarian interagency networks, critically affect empowerment processes. The establishment of egalitarian relationships in hierarchical, bureaucratic organizations presents special challenges. In any case, integrating empowerment philosophy, values, and intervention strategies into all aspects of administration—fund-raising, networking, legislative work, public education, research development, staff development, and program design—will help make empowerment practice effective and enduring.

REFERENCES

Abromivitz, M. (1986). The privatization of the welfare state. *Social Work, 31*(4), 257–262.

Barnet, R., & Cavanagh, J. (1994). *Global dreams: Imperial corporations and the new world.* New York: Simon & Schuster.

Barouch, R., & Hessmiller-Trego, J. (1994, June). *Transforming power relations in practice.* Unpublished paper presented at the Bertha Reynolds National Conference, Seattle, WA.

Blau, J. (1992). *The visible poor: Homelessness in the United States.* New York: Oxford University Press.

Brown, P. A. (1993, October 7–8). *Participatory research: A new paradigm for social work.* Unpublished paper presented at the Education and Research for Empowerment Conference at the University of Washington, Seattle.

Chapin, R. (1995). Social policy development: The strengths perspective. *Social Work, 40*(4), 433–576.

Children's Defense Fund. (1996). *The state of America's children yearbook 1996.* Washington, DC: Author.

Colorado Association of Gerontological Social Workers (CAGS). (1995, March 17). Unpublished meeting notes. Institute of Gerontology, Denver, CO.

Cox, E. O., & Lazarri, M. (1982, March 17). *Administrative tasks for the social advocate in the 1980's.* Unpublished paper presented at the Council of Social Work Education (CSWE), New York.

Cox, E. O., & Parsons, R. J. (1994). *Empowerment-oriented social work practice with the elderly.* Pacific Grove, CA: Brooks/Cole.

Erickson, K., & Vallas, S. P. (1990). *The nature of work.* New Haven, CT: Yale University Press.

Fabricant, M. B., & Burghardt, S. (1992). *The welfare state crisis and the transformation of social service work.* New York: Sharp.

Freire, P. (1970). *A pedagogy of the oppressed.* New York: Seabury Press [This was Freire's most important work, the first to be translated into English. Its orientation is philosophical/theoretical.]

Freire, P. (1978). *Education for critical consciousness.* New York: Seabury Press. [This contains an important essay called "Education as the Practice of Freedom," which explains Freire's work in concrete terms.]

Freire, P. (1992) *Pedagogy of hope.* New York: Continuum.

Gutiérrez, L. (1990). Working with women of color: An empowerment perspective. *Social Work 35*(2), 149–154.

Gutiérrez, L., GlenMaye, L., & DeLois, K. (1995). The organizational context of empowerment practice: Implications for social work administration. *Social Work* 40(2), 249–258.

Holmes, G. E., & Saleebey, D. (1993). *Empowerment: The medical model and the politics of clienthood*. Paper presented at the Conference on Education and Research for Empowerment Practice, University of Washington School of Social Work, Seattle.

Institute of Gerontology. (1995). *Empowerment strategies in administration: A report of interviews with administrators*. Unpublished interviews from the University of Denver Institute of Gerontology.

Kamerman, S. B., & Kahn, A. J. (Eds.). (1989). *Privatization and the welfare state*. Princeton, NJ: Princeton University Press.

Karger, H. J., & Stoesz, D. (1994). *American social welfare policy: A pluralist approach*, 2nd ed., pp. 158–189). New York: Longman.

Lee, J. A. B. (1994). *The empowerment approach to social work practice*. New York: Columbia University Press.

Mirvis, P. (Ed.). (1993). *Building the competitive workforce*. New York: Wiley.

Parsons, R. J. (1995). *Empowerment based social work practice: A study of process and outcome*. Paper presented at the Council of Social Work Education, Annual Program Meeting, San Diego, CA.

Pearlmutter, F. D. (Ed.). (1988). *Alternative social agencies: Administrative strategies*. New York: Haworth.

Rapp, C. A., Shera, W., & Kisthardt, W. (1993). Research strategies for consumer empowerment of people with severe mental illness. *Social Work* 38(6), 727–735.

Shera, W. (1993, October 7–8). *Empowerment for organizations*. Unpublished paper presented at the Education and Research for Empowerment Conference, Seattle, WA.

Shera, W. (1995). Empowerment for organizations. *Administration in Social Work*, 19(4), 1–15.

Simon, B. L. (1994). *The empowerment tradition in American social work*. New York: Columbia University Press.

Staples, L. (1991). Powerful ideas about empowerment. *Administration in Social work*, 35(2), 149–154.

Zimmerman, M. A., Israel, B. A., Schulz, A., & Chekoway, B. (1992). Further explorations in empowerment theory: An empirical analysis of psychology empowerment. *American Journal of Community Psychology, 20*, 707–727.

Chapter 11

RESEARCH AS AN
EMPOWERMENT STRATEGY

Sung Sil Lee Sohng, Ph.D.
University of Washington, Seattle

INTRODUCTION

Research helps define the practice of the social work profession. Researchers offer judgments about the quality and relevance of findings to their colleagues, practitioners, and clients. In particular, they search for findings that clients can use to create a more just and sustainable world. As participants in community development, researchers serve as both users and creators of knowledge; as such, they need to reflect critically on the kinds of knowledge they produce and consume. When selecting a research topic or problem, they should ask how that research can potentially reduce oppression, injustice, brutality, and environmental destruction, and what information they need to create this impact. Such an approach must be partisan; that is, it should work for the emancipation of the excluded, rather than legitimate itself by reference to some "objective" social science that privileges professional discourse and elite domination. Producing knowledge does *not* demand a neutral, detached, "hands off" stance of "doing no harm." Rather, it requires a strong commitment by participating researchers and practitioners to share their expertise with the people, while recognizing that the communities directly involved must ultimately determine the direction and goals of change.

   In this chapter, I shall explore empowering research methodologies that will help to advance the production of knowledge for social transformation in postmodern society. To commit to empowerment's social agenda consistently, one must identify, facilitate, or create contexts in which historically silent and isolated people can understand and influence decisions that affect their lives. This commitment implies a conceptual reconfiguration.

Instead of presenting research as the detached discovery and empirical verification of *what is,* I pose an alternative vision that defines social work research in terms of its *transformative capacity.* This definition requires a bold shift in evaluating theory building from "Does this theory correspond with the observable facts?" to "How does this theory present new possibilities for social action?" and "Does it stimulate normative dialogue about how people can and should organize themselves?" At the core of this perspective lies a new framework to promote diversity and, simultaneously, to find the common ground needed in the struggle for transformative power and social change.

This chapter examines ways to develop knowledge that will lead to social action and transformation. The discussion mainly addresses the relationships among knowledge, power, and social movements. To contextualize the development of transformative knowledge within a contemporary sociocultural condition, the discussion begins with the politics of social research and postmodern critiques as a way of situating empowering research epistemologically and substantively. These critiques are linked to a critical agenda for the production of knowledge. Drawing heavily from participatory research and feminist research traditions, I bring forth a conceptualization of empowering research methodologies by presenting four basic tenets for transformative research and discussing their implications for researchers.

POWER, KNOWLEDGE, AND SOCIAL MOVEMENTS

Enlightenment values have long dominated Western culture. Modernism involved a rejection of tradition and medieval superstition, a positivist/empiricist belief in the lawful nature of the universe, and a desire to explain and control nature. As part of this project, social science has developed a worldview of progress through scientific rationality, objective knowledge, ethical neutrality, and the planned creation of social structures. It emphasizes the search for "grand theories" aimed to establish the generality, predictability, and verification of social laws characterized as "scientific." Scientific knowledge has served as a means of emancipation and a potential basis for further human freedom on a global scale. In the 20th century, social welfare has been regarded as a crucial part of this emancipatory project—enhancing human capacities, advancing human rights, and managing those disorganizations and dislocations that were the inevitable side effects of the social changes that accompanied modernization. This characterization of science and social science has provided an elaborate rationale and legitimation for the preeminence of science and its role in generating control over the distribution of resources, benefits, rights, privileges, and sanctions (Foucault, 1973; Westwood, 1991; Young, 1990).

Postmodern Critiques

Postmodernism challenges this account of Enlightenment progress by arguing that such universalistic claims mask modernity's Western, Eurocentric domination and control—its crimes against humanity in the relentless pursuit of order and progress (Foucault, 1973, 1977). The term *postmodern* is itself one attempt to name the disjuncture between the modernist view and the contemporary world, which is one of rapid change, not only in technology, social life, and politics, but also in ways of knowing and understanding.

Postmodernists' central argument is the crisis of the "grand narratives," the overarching explanatory theories, including capitalism, Marxism, and feminism, which have guided politics and organized social movements in the modern period (Lyotard, 1984). They maintain that its grand theories of individual and social development legitimated elite dominance and professional discourse, such as those of social welfare, which are concerned with the homogenization, surveillance, and control of subordinate populations (Foucault, 1991).

Questioning the modernists' emphasis on the "objective similarity" of social reality, postmodernists formulated *difference* and *diversity* as central constructs. To understand differences in social reality as experienced by subordinates in a Western-dominated world order—women, nonwhites, the poor, third world populations—requires a decentering of social thought that eliminates reliance on a singular, universal "truth" as an explanatory theory. The Western "grand narratives," which mask how they oppress those who are excluded and subordinated, must be *deconstructed,* whereupon their Eurocentric conceptions of the world make way for other expressions of human diversity (Leonard, 1995).

The postmodern critical perspective on Western culture is closely linked to the changing political economy of postmodern society. A world economy that has escaped the confines of national regulation and control characterizes postmodern society (Touraine, 1981). The decentering impact of global capital yields a more fragmented political and cultural terrain (Fisher & Kling, 1994). Modernist thought has long assumed that the forces of economic, political, and cultural centralization would eventually lead to the disappearance of particularistic outlooks and identities and to their replacement by generalized, bureaucratic, and class-oriented ones (Fisher & Kling, 1994). In contrast to this idea, the postmodern society is rapidly losing political and cultural centrality and control. As Young (1990) states, "Postmodernism can best be defined as European culture's awareness that it is no longer the unquestioned and dominant center of the world" (p. 19). That is, in the new global configuration, the margin or periphery has become the center, leaving the metropolitan core with the task of renegotiating its position. This is part of what Foucault (1977) calls the deconstruction of the sovereign self of the West with its totalizing, universalizing gaze and dominance—politically, economically and culturally. Post-modernism involves an approach open to reclaiming fragmented, subordinated, and local knowledge.

Power and Knowledge

Tied to the new global configuration is the way in which Foucault has conceived power relations. His model offers these elements: (1) Not a possession, power exists in its exertion; (2) Power is not primarily repressive but productive; and (3) Power comes from the bottom up. Here Foucault rejects the prevailing assumptions in the modernist claim that power flows from a centralized source from top to bottom and that power is primarily a negative force operating via a series of prohibitions and restrictions (Foucault, 1977). He argues that such theories do not address those forms of power that make centralized, repressive forms of power possible—namely, the myriad power relations at the microlevel of society (Sawicki, 1991). Foucault sees power operating in a multitude of forms in daily social relations. Crucial to the construction of reality, language, meanings, and rituals of truth, power functions in all knowledge and in every definition. Power is knowledge, and knowledge creates truth and therefore power (Foucault, 1980).

Nowhere is this more apparent than in relation to research paradigms based on the scientific model, which generates knowledge allied with professional power. Foucault's work is, therefore, crucial to the debate on social movements and the production of knowledge. First, his view of power involves multiple and fluid structures of ruling rather than fixed and binary opposites, suggesting that resistance is carried out in local struggles in daily social relations. This analysis of power helps explain why identity, community, and culture in the postmodern society become the contexts in which people come to construct and understand political life. Second, power in the postindustrial society is increasingly bound up with knowledge that normalizes elite domination. Third, by making the "grand theories" problematic, postmodernists have liberated space for a great diversity of narratives, including those concerned with social work research.

This understanding offers a different way of constructing transformative research. The debate no longer centers on quantitative research versus qualitative research, because both are modes of power and knowledge. Rather, researchers need to establish what conditions make the exercise of power possible. That is, any mode of analyzing and generating knowledge should focus on sites of struggle and conflicts in which the outcomes depend on the mobilization of forces for and against the issues at hand. Further, this approach must strive to emancipate the excluded rather than legitimate itself by reference to some objective social science that privileges the knowledge produced by Western academics and professionals (Leonard, 1995). Participatory and feminist research paradigms illustrate this point.

Participatory Research and Popular Movements

Originally designed to resist the intellectual colonialism of Western social research regarding third world development, participatory research has developed a methodology for involving oppressed people in analyzing and solving social problems. Participatory research has emerged in response to the crises of both the left and the right—that is, a degeneration of political democracy to (at best) periodic balloting to choose people from among the privileged to rule over the underprivileged, thus perpetuating elite domination. Such is the case in most countries labeled democratic, advanced, or developed. But some have observed similar signs in socialist countries where elites have failed to deliver sustained improvement to the material and cultural lives of the people, not to mention the failure of the socialist promise that working class people would be empowered to create their own history (Fals-Borda, 1991; Rahman,1991). A key weapon the elites have used to maintain their domination is the monopoly of "formal knowledge."

Such historical experience calls for rethinking the meaning of social transformation for people's liberation. The dominant view of social transformation has focused on the need for changing oppressive economic structures. However—and this is the distinctive viewpoint of participatory research—domination by elites is manifested in the control of not only material production but also the means of producing knowledge, including the determination of what legitimate knowledge is (Rahman, 1991). The one reinforces the other in augmenting and perpetuating this domination. Hence, the emancipation of oppressed populations cannot be guaranteed by "truth" or scientific progress; rather, people must continuously struggle for it in diverse ways. The critique of modernity suggests that, rather than the authority and power of intellectual elites and vanguard parties, dialogue with the oppressed offers the most likely means of emancipation. As Freire (1970) has emphasized, people can only be empowered by their own consciousness and knowledge. Consequently, people must develop their own ways to raise consciousness and generate knowledge.

Participatory research attempts to decentralize knowledge, as well as the power it confers, through the participation of ordinary people in gaining knowledge (Freire, 1970, 1974; Gaventa, 1988; Gaventa & Horton, 1981; Hall, 1981; Park, Brydon-Miller, Hall, & Jackson, 1993; Tandon, 1981). Because the creation of a people's knowledge prevents those in power from exclusively determining the interests of others, it in effect transfers power to those groups engaged in the production of popular knowledge. Participatory theorists maintain that "expert" knowledge has been essentially used for surveillance and control of subordinate populations predominantly seen and acted on as "targets of intervention." As a privileged holder of knowledge, the "expert" plays the role of adjudicator in defining problems, categorizing populations, distributing resources, and evaluating results. This role effectively reduces people's diverse desires and aspirations to the objectifying structures of professionally defined "needs."

Disenfranchised people can confront this monopoly of knowledge by gaining or creating their own knowledge, challenging what has been normally considered the province of experts. As Gaventa (1988) explains, this empowering experience produces much more than information. First, the process of confronting the experts and understanding their tools may demystify expertise. People may learn that the "scientific" foundation of policies and programs is not solid, but rather subject to conflicting viewpoints, misinterpretations, and fallibility. Second, people may come to appreciate their own experience and knowledge, which the dominant science has devalued. Third, those who participate in the unmasking of dominant knowledge *own* the knowledge they have gained. Fourth, in seeing that they can define their own reality, they may become inspired to change it. In short, the participatory process becomes a resource for gaining a greater consciousness; this new knowledge may in turn lead to action.

Participatory research tries to uncover how "oppressed" clients and communities can become acting subjects of their own emancipatory forms of social welfare provision, rather than acted-on objects of intervention. While one might argue that "empowered" communities depend on profound transformations of the present social order, moving toward such transformation depends in part on developing dialogical relations at every opportunity (Freire, 1970, 1974). Participatory research provides a framework for engaging in such relations whereby people pursue new and diverse forms of knowledge about social welfare, critique dominant ideologies, and challenge professional and bureaucratic power.

Developing such a dialogical relationship requires a strong commitment by participating social scientists to share their expertise with people, while recognizing that communities must ultimately and directly determine the course of their own change. Though researchers may play a catalytic and supportive role in this process, they must not dominate. Such a partnership is not easy to establish with people who have been victims of a dominating structure; traditional attitudes and negative self-images reinforce subordination to outside researchers. Further, the researcher may find relinquishing the role of expert difficult, hence imposing her or his ideas consciously or unconsciously. To counter such tendencies, the people must control the research—the people's independent inquiry—in which the professional consults and participates as an equal.

Participatory researchers' analysis of power relations to knowledge is consistent with Foucault's knowledge/power thesis concerning the political functions of dominant discourses and their rules of exclusion (Foucault, 1991; Shor & Freire, 1987). These elements of participatory research and postmodern critiques serve an emancipatory perspective and support the pursuit of diverse theories, strategies, and priorities in the struggle for transformative social change whereby people become acting subjects.

With participatory research, social movements in the postmodern society are no longer dominated by patriarchal white male leaders on behalf of the working class. Now, lesbians and gays, feminists, African Americans, and those working with the disabled and the homeless do so with their own constituencies, in their own communities, on their own behalf (Boyte & Riessman, 1986; Dalton & Kuechler, 1990; Gartner & Riessman, 1984; Katz & Bender, 1985; Weil, 1986; Yeich & Levine, 1992). Fostering indigenous leaders and new arenas and constituencies never before included to such a degree, they build community power (Gutiérrez, GlenMaye, & DeLois, 1992).

A Silenced Feminist Standpoint and the Women's Movement

In challenging male-centered models of reality and the denial of autonomous female identity, the women's movement laid the ground for feminist research. Feminist researchers argue that the experiences of women are often distorted or rendered invisible through male-dominated Western science and its connection to power (Ardener, 1975; Callaway, 1981; Hardings, 1986; Keller, 1978; Millett, 1970; Rich, 1976; Smith, 1974, 1987). One must remedy the lack of knowledge about women's lives, past and present, through a new approach that recognizes the firsthand experiences of women. In making the invisible visible, feminist scholars and activists assert that knowledge building should reflect female-centered thinking, action, and experience (Cook, 1988; Eichler, 1987; Maguire, 1987; Miles & Finn, 1989; Roberts, 1981).

In its attempt to uncover women's lives within a male world, and thus to critique male knowledge, the modernist approach to feminism constructed an essentialist approach—the notion that the oppression of women has some singular form discernible in the hegemonic structure of patriarchy. Because this basis for feminism is so universal, assumed to exist cross-culturally, women of color, third world women, and lesbians have challenged it for oversimplifying the complexity of women's lives and thereby marginalizing their political issues (Almquist, 1989; Beale, 1970; Chow, 1987; Collins, 1990, 1991; Higginbotham, 1983; hooks, 1984, 1989; Jorge, 1983; Lorde, 1984; Mohanty, Russo, & Torres, 1991; Zinn & Dill, 1994). As black feminists have proposed, a gender-focused feminist scholarship is less a strategy for political unity than an appropriation to promote white middle-class women's interests and privileges (Davis, 1981; Dill, 1983; hooks, 1984).

These challenges resonate with the postmodern critiques discussed earlier. If feminism is to grasp the nettle of postmodernism, the universalistic category *woman* must be deconstructed so that the multiple and *different* oppressions of women throughout the world are seen for what they are—the consequence of gender, race, and class oppression. Rather than focus on gender as invariably paramount—the privileged theoretical and political construct—Collins (1991) conceptualizes women's oppression as necessarily involving race, gender, and class. In women's oppression, the differences between women always receive attention in terms of their specific geographical location, class position, race, and ethnicity.

POSTMODERNISM AND THE POLITICS OF DIVERSITY

In putting pressure on inherent weaknesses in the essentialist (modernist) discourse of social movements, postmodern scholarship has moved away from the overarching explanatory theories, such as the assumed universality of women's oppression or the working class, toward an exploration of multiple voices and expression of multiple realities. As Albert et al. (1986) point out, the modernist means of stratifying society merely on the basis of class, gender, or race without examining the diversity within these groups have proved to be historically reductive, deficient, and ineffectual in designing strategies to combat oppression. Postmodern scholarship has emphasized the increasing importance and value of a polyvocal discourse—the voices of groups, such as women, people of color, gays and lesbians, and the disabled, whose life worlds have been denied recognition by modernist hegemony (Rivera & Erlich, 1992; Rosenau, 1992).

Increasingly, the postmodern social movements in the 1980s and 1990s have become fluid, ridden with contradiction, and dialectically complex (Fisher & Kling, 1994; Reeser & Epstein, 1991). This produces the diversity of resistance while fragmenting it. On the one hand, the postmodernist polyvocal discourse has opened up new forms of communication that come from challenging the silence experienced by many historically disenfranchised groups. On the other hand, this framework has exacerbated competition among discourses organized around new identities and primarily concerned with social and cultural issues disembodied from an analysis of political economy (Andersen & Collins, 1995; Touraine, 1981). In allowing an analysis of all tropes of these times under the cover of acknowledging diversity, cultural politics seem to have granted legitimacy to fragmented, polemic reassertions of "difference." Berman (1988) writes, "It shatters into a multitude of fragments, speaking incommensurable private languages; the idea of modernity, conceived in numerous fragmentary ways, loses much of its vividness, resonance, and depth, and loses its capacity to organize and give meaning to people's lives" (pp. 16–17).

In challenging the "difference politics" in postmodern social movements, feminist researchers call for urgent attention to the complex *relationality* that shapes people's social and political lives and defines the world in relational terms. Different oppressions not only inform one another, but they also connect through relations of power and ruling (Almquist, 1989; Collins, 1991; Davis, 1981; hooks, 1984). A world understood in terms of destructive divisions of gender, color, class, sexuality, and nation, it is also a world with many stories of resistance engaged by individuals and collectives in daily life. Here, Smith (1987) identifies the multiple sites of power in social institutions, as well as individual consciousness and experience, and emphasizes the "process of ruling," not the frozen embodiment of it, as a focus for inquiry and feminist strategies. These and other important contributions to transformative research theory and practice address the nature of the contemporary context for researchers—the appropriate locus of activism, ideology, strategies, and tactics.

A Transformative Agenda for Social Work Theory and Research

The themes I have presented can be brought together into a framework for transformative, empowering research. The challenge is how, in a postmodern context, to promote diversity—the central feature of contemporary resistance—but simultaneously find the commonalities necessary to fight for power and social change. Participatory and feminist researchers suggest that research needs to address the multiple forms oppression takes when power lies in diverse locations. They maintain that such an approach stimulates a discourse on situational theories, strategies, and priorities in the struggle for transformative social change; that is, local conditions frame this discourse. However, a transformative social research agenda cannot be narrowly postmodern in that issues of poverty, racial discrimination, violence, sexism, hunger, disease, unemployment, and others should not disappear into local agendas. What it does mean is that these issues are not constructed within a totalizing, universalizing discourse that has lionized monolithic, Eurocentric, and patriarchal structures and practice. For the participatory researcher, feminist, antiracist, etc., pursuing diverse, nonuniversalistic and cross-cultural expressions of human diversity and knowledge is crucial to constructing countervailing power. Knowledge gives and reinforces power. Thus, to a great extent, transformative research empowers when it enables people to create the kind of knowledge that yields power. Based on this, I offer four tenets for assessing whether research is transformative through its process (means) and through its use (ends) with respect to positive personal and social transformation.

Antidiscrimination as Ethical

Truman and Humphries (1994) offer important insights about ethical issues in conducting research. Most research textbooks suggest that research should be informed by moral principles including being truthful, respectful, and fair and avoiding acts that inflict harm. Such discussions, though, fail to examine issues of inequality inherent in the research process. The context of research—the social characteristics of all involved, methods, strategies, and conclusions—may all vest exclusive power and control of the research in the researcher. To counter this, Truman and Humphries (1994) and others propose "antidiscrimination" as a criterion for assessing how research is conceived and carried out: "By this we mean not a neutral, detached, 'hands off' concern with 'doing no harm.' We mean rather an active involvement in challenging assumptions based on unequal social relations, through reflexive, explicitly committed participation in the process of social change" (p. 14). This antidiscriminatory principle is consistent with both participatory research and feminist research.

All researchers are ethically obliged to assess their own values, motives, and research efforts: "What values drive our selection of research focus?" "Who will benefit from the research?" "How will the research findings be used?" "Will the research process be conducted safely and humanely?"

Research as Emancipatory

Transformative research is emancipatory when it reveals and unravels political repression, economic exploitation, cultural domination, and social manipulation. Examples of this type of research include documentation of homelessness and its relationships to economic and political decisions; documentation of the plight of refugees in relation to international and governmental policies; survey research on pervasive poverty; and documentation of poor health and housing conditions, violence, or discrimination. Such research contributes to transformation by making the workings of oppressive systems explicit (Deshler & Selender, 1991).

Even so, research that merely uncovers exploitation is not emancipatory. It must make the link to action explicit. This link is strongest when those who conduct the research take action themselves within their organizations or communities. Findings generated by one group can also be used by other groups and policy makers; strategic dissemination of findings to the media or to those who can take action is necessary. For example, in the case of the black lung movement in West Virginia, several researchers revealed to the miners that their breathing problems really came from the mines, not from inherent asthma as doctors had claimed (Derickson, 1983).

The lack of access to critical information, documentation, and evidence about how power works places people at a disadvantage in their efforts to change their circumstances. Generating this type of knowledge is central to liberatory social movements. All disenfranchised people need such knowledge; otherwise, they cannot fully participate in decisions that affect their lives. For example, Westwood (1991) shows how African Americans' lives and protests have been "psychiatrized" through the normal discourse of scientific research. The diagnosis offers a mystifying label of mental illness that has not helped African Americans understand the often frightening and painful experiences that constitute their lives. Through the collection of "narratives of sickness," participatory research has reconstructed their biographies, experience of mental illness, and treatment by psychiatry. The research does not end with the narratives generated through the extended interviews, however; it also includes statistical data indicating the overrepresentation of African Americans diagnosed as schizophrenic. As such, the research project illuminates how symptoms and diagnosis at the microlevel relate to policy design and implementation at the macrolevel. Such analysis links the overrepresentation of African Americans in the mental health system to the politics of racism.

Research as Empowering

Research that exposes and reduces the power of oppression, though essential, does not sufficiently cause sustainable change, because such change usually depends on the empowerment of people. Research activity should serve the emergence of marginalized and disadvantaged groups. Examples include participatory evaluation of community action, action research on the part of teachers in schools to improve their own practice, and the documentation of species extinction by Greenpeace. The Conrad study group (Conti, Counter, & Paul, 1991) describes how participation in community-action research projects affected the participants' personal growth. The people of Conrad, Montana, have been involved in long-term transformative research. The project began by providing community members a place to develop new friendships, share ideas with an expanding network of peers, and learn new skills. For example, meetings at the farmers' union opened with singing and cultural sharing. These bonding functions were followed and strengthened by learning activities that reinforced the members' sense of accomplishment. Learning critical-questioning skills was considered fundamental to personal development and for accomplishing community goals. The project provided members with the skills and knowledge gained through activism and the process of praxis, the circular relationship between action and reflection. Further, the project has engendered community action and provided people a means to employ skills by organizing a farmers' union and managing the community projects. Personal growth and empowerment came from experiencing the power of working together through caretaking, learning for fun, and tackling new problems.

Research as Political Action

Guided by praxis rather than by the canons of traditional research, transformative researchers engage in a continuous process of reflection and activity related to the knowledge people create locally and to the actions taken to solve pressing social problems. The appropriateness of a participant group's views and decisions can only be tested in action. Only in action can one determine whether their goals have been recognized and acted on, and whether obstacles remain. Ben-Tovim, Gabriel, Law, and Stredder (1986) elaborate this point in their action research project on policies related to race relations: "We came to understand the policies through our active involvement in local anti-racist struggles. In this way our knowledge of central and local policies was linked to the research process through action" (p. 4).

The researchers regarded their direct involvement in local organizations not just a fortuitous means of gaining information. On the contrary, they regarded the "action" aspect of their research essential. The actions they engaged in include attending meetings to discuss strategies and objectives, writing policy papers and using them for discussion and lobbying, doing local research for the use of organizations, and attending and organizing conferences.

Ben-Tovim et al. (1986) argue that policy analysis must address the political means by which a problem is reinforced or created, then politically challenge it. That is, the implementation and use of the research is built into the analysis from the outset. This is not a detached analysis but the basis for a constant reformulation, elaboration, and development of research problems and analysis with the goal of eliminating inequalities. When the power to name the conditions of injustice joins the power to act, research and political action become fully integrated.

IMPLICATIONS FOR
EMPOWERMENT-ORIENTED
RESEARCHERS

The researcher's role is far more significant than it may at first appear. Research helps define the practice of the profession. Those who frame the questions to be asked define the scope of inquiry and set the parameters for the answers. The research enterprise may thus provide the lens through which professionals and others view particular realities. Moreover, the methodology or the construct by which people observe a problem sets the boundaries for their subsequent observations. If a given methodology cannot address certain questions, the methodology limits one's understanding of reality (Karger, 1983). What one chooses to study and how one conducts research is, therefore, an issue not simply technical but inherently political. The focus of research, its methods, and its outcomes can all be part of a process that challenges existing structural sources of social problems and points to actions to solve them.

Taken together, the four tenets I have presented can form the basis for setting research priorities, designing research, and assessing whether research is transformative. The question inevitably arises as to which methodology best serves transformative research. Though conventional social sciences have been used to legitimize the status of dominant elites, they do not necessarily serve those ends inherently. I share the view expressed by Fals-Borda (1979) and Harvey (1990), who do not reject empirical research techniques that are positivistic; rather, they advocate adapting those techniques for emancipation and empowerment. A transformative approach is not defined by the techniques used. It can employ the whole gamut of research tools and analytic techniques, such as historical reconstruction, action research, multivariate analysis, and structuralist deconstruction. What matters most is that researchers, as socially and environmentally responsible people, make ethical choices in using their tools.

Researchers offer judgments about the quality and relevance of research findings. They search for findings that clients can use to create a better world. With their colleagues, researchers must debate ethical choices regarding priorities and the use of resources for research. As participants in community development, they are both users and creators of knowledge; as such, they need to be critically reflective about their research. They need to define and describe more clearly that empowering knowledge most useful for personal and social transformation. Neither the sponsors of research nor the methodological paradigm determine whether research will be transformative. The ultimate test is whether the research benefits the public good and reduces oppression, injustice, brutality, and environmental destruction.

The researcher's social responsibility lies not only in the selection of the research focus and in its conduct, but also in its consequences—who bene-fits from the use of knowledge.

REFERENCES

Albert, M., Cagan, L., Chomsky, N., Hahnel, B., King, M., Sargent, L., & Sklar, H. (1986). *Liberating theory.* Boston: South End Press.

Almquist, E. (1989). The experiences of minority women in the United States: Intersections of race, gender, and class. In J. Freeman (Ed.), *Women: A feminist perspective* (pp. 414–445). Mountain View, CA: Mayfield.

Andersen, M., & Collins, P. (1995). *Race, class, and gender: An anthology.* Belmont, CA: Wadsworth.

Ardener, E. (1975). *Perceiving women.* London: Dent.

Beale, F. (1970). Double jeopardy: To be black and female. In T. Cade (Ed.), *The black women* (pp. 90–110). New York: Signet.

Ben-Tovim, G., Gabriel, J., Law, I., & Stredder, J. (1986). *The local politics of race.* London: Macmillan.

Berman, M. (1988). *All that is solid melts into air: The experience of modernity.* New York: Penguin.

Boyte, H., & Riessman, F. (1986). *The new populism.* Philadelphia: Temple University Press.

Callaway, H. (1981). Women's perspectives: Research as re-vision. In P. Reason and J. Rowan (Eds.), *Human inquiry: A source book of new paradigm research* (pp. 457–471). New York: Wiley.

Chow, E. Ngan-Ling. (1987). The development of feminist consciousness among Asian American women. *Gender and Society, 1*(3). 284–299.

Collins, P. H. (1990). *Black feminist thought: Knowledge, consciousness, and the politics of empowerment.* New York: Routledge.

Collins, P. H. (1991). Learning from the outsider within: The sociological signifi-cance of black feminist thought. In M. Fonow and J. Cook (Eds.), *Beyond methodology,* (pp. 35–59). Bloomington, IN: Indiana University Press.

Conti, G., Counter, J., & Paul, L. (1991). Transforming a community through research. *Convergence, 24*(3), 31–40.

Cook, J. (1988). Integrating feminist epistemology and qualitative family research. *Qualitative Family Research Network Newsletter, 2,* 3–5.

Dalton, R., & Kuechler, M. (Eds.). (1990). *Challenging the political order: New social and political movements in Western democracies.* New York: Oxford University Press.

Davis, A. (1981). *Women, race and class.* New York: Random House.

Derickson, A. (1983, March). Down solid: The origins and development of black lung insurgency. *Journal of Public Health Policy,* pp. 25–44.

Deshler, J., & Seledner, D. (1991). Transformative research: In search of a defini-tion. *Convergence, 24*(3), 9–23.

Dill, B. (1983). Race, class, and gender: Prospects for an all-inclusive sisterhood. *Feminist Studies, 9,* 131–150.

Eichler, M. (1987). The relationship between sexist, non-sexist, and woman-centered and feminist research in the social sciences. In G. Nemiroff (Ed.), *Women and men: Interdisciplinary readings on gender* (pp. 21–53). Montreal, Canada: Fitzhenry & Whitside.

Fals-Borda, O. (1979). Investigating reality in order to transform it: The Colombia experience. *Dialectical Anthropology, 4,* 33–55.

Fals-Borda, O. (1991). Some basic ingredients. In O. Fals-Borda and M. Rahman (Eds.), *Action and knowledge: Breaking the monopoly with participatory action-research* (pp. 3–18). New York: Apex Press.

Fisher, R., & Kling, J. (1994). Community organization and new social movement theory. *Journal of Progressive Human Services, 5*(2), 5–23.

Foucault, M. (1973). *The order of things: An archaeology of the human sciences.* New York: Vintage Books.

Foucault, M. (1977). *The archaeology of knowledge.* London: Tavistock.

Foucault, M. (1980). *Power/knowledge: Selected interviews and other writings.* New York: Pantheon.

Foucault, M. (1991). Orders of discourse. In S. Lash (Ed.), *Post-structuralist and post-modernist sociology* (pp. 134–157). Aldershot, England: Edward Elgar.

Freire, P. (1970). *Pedagogy of the oppressed.* New York: Seabury Press.

Freire, P. (1974). *Education for critical consciousness.* New York: Seabury Press.

Gartner, A., & Riessman, F. (Eds.). (1984). *The self-help revolution.* New York: Human Sciences Press.

Gaventa, J. (1988). Participatory research in North America. *Convergence, 21*(2–3), 19–28.

Gaventa, J., & Horton, B. (1981). A citizens' research project in Appalachia, USA. *Convergence, 14*(3), 30–42.

Gutiérrez, L., GlenMaye, L., & DeLois, K. (1992, July 19). *Improving the human condition through empowerment practice.* Presentation to NASW/IFSW World Assembly, Washington, DC.

Hall, B. (1981). Participatory research, popular knowledge and power: A personal reflection. *Convergence, 3*(14), 6–19.

Hardings, S. (1986). *The science question in feminism.* Ithaca, NY: Cornell University Press.

Harvey, L. (1990). *Critical social research.* London: Unwin Hyman.

Higginbotham, E. (1983). Laid bare by the system: Work and survival for black and Hispanic women. In J. Kritzman (Ed.), *Class, race, and sex: The dynamics of control* (pp. 200–215). Boston: G. K. Hall.

hooks, b. (1984). *From margin to center.* Boston: South End Press.

hooks, b. (1989). *Talking back: Thinking feminist, thinking black.* London: Sheba Feminist Publishers.

Jorge, A. (1983). Issues of race and class in women's studies: A Puerto Rican woman's thoughts. In J. Kritzman (Ed.), *Class, race, and sex: The dynamics of control* (pp. 216–220). Boston: G. K. Hall.

Karger, H. J. (1983, May–June). Science, research, and social work: Who controls the profession? *Social Work, 28,* 200–205.

Katz, A., & Bender, E. (1985). Self help groups as a crucible for people empowerment in the context of social development. *Social Development Issues, 9*(2), 4–13.

Keller, E. (1978). Gender and science. *Psychoanalysis and Contemporary Thought, 1,* 409–433.

Leonard, P. (1995). Postmodernism, socialism and social welfare. *Journal of Progressive Human Services, 6*(2), 3–19.

Lorde, A. (1984). *Sister outsider.* Trumansburg, NY: Crossing Press.

Lyotard, J. (1984). *The postmodern condition: A report on knowledge.* Minneapolis: University of Minnesota Press.

Maguire, P. (1987). *Doing participatory research: A feminist approach.* Amherst: University of Massachusetts.

Millett, K. (1970). *Sexual politics.* Garden City, NJ: Doubleday.

Mies, M. (1983). Toward a methodology of feminist research. In G. Bowles and R. Klein (Eds.), *Theories of women's studies* (pp. 117–139). London: Routledge & Kegan Paul.

Miles, A., & Finn, G. (1989). *Feminism: From pressure to politics.* Montreal, Canada: Black Rose Books.

Mohanty, C., Russo, A., & Torres, L. (Eds.). (1991). *Third world women and the politics of feminism.* Bloomington, IN: Indiana University Press.

Park, P., Brydon-Miller, M., Hall, B., & Jackson, T. (1993). *Voices of change: Participatory research in the United States and Canada.* Westport, CN: Bergin & Garvey.

Rahman, M. (1991). The theoretical standpoint of PAR. In O. Fals-Borda and M. Rahman (Eds.), *Action and knowledge: Breaking the monopoly with participatory action-research* (pp. 13–23). New York: Apex Press.

Reeser, L., & Epstein, I. (1991). *Professionalization and activism in social work: The sixties, the eighties and the future.* New York: Columbia University Press.

Rich, A. (1976). *Of woman born.* New York: Norton.

Rivera, F., & Erlich, J. (Eds.). (1992). *Community organizing in a diverse society.* Boston: Allyn and Bacon.

Roberts, H. (Ed.). (1981). *Doing feminist research.* London: Routledge & Kegan Paul.

Rosenau, P. (1992). *Post-modernism and the social sciences: Insights, inroads, and intrusions.* Princeton University Press.

Sawicki, J. (1991). *Disciplining Foucault.* New York: Routledge.

Shor, I., & Freire, P. (1987). *A pedagogy for liberation.* New York: Bergin & Garvey.

Smith, D. (1974). A women's perspective as a radical critique of sociology. *Sociological Inquiry, 44,* 7–13.

Smith, D. (1987). *The everyday world as problematic: A feminist sociology.* Boston: Northeastern University Press.

Tandon, R. (1981). Participatory research in the empowerment of people. *Convergence, 24*(3), 20–29.

Touraine, A. (1981). *The voice and the eye: An analysis of social movements.* New York: Cambridge University Press.

Truman, C., & Humphries, B. (1994). Rethinking social research: Research in an unequal world. In B. Humphries and C. Truman (Eds.), *Re-thinking social research: Anti-discriminatory approaches in research methodology* (pp. 1–17). Aldershot, England: Avebury.

Weil, M. (1986). Women, community, and organizing. In N. V. DenBergh and L. Cooper (Eds.), *Feminist visions for social work* (pp. 187–210). Silver Spring, MD: National Association of Social Workers.

Westwood, S. (1991). *Power/knowledge: The politics of transformative research.* Convergence, 14(3), 79–85.

Yeich, S., & Levine, R. (1992). Participatory research's contribution to a conceptualization of empowerment. *Journal of Applied Social Psychology, 22*(24), 1894–1908.

Young, R. (1990). *White mythologies: Writing history and the West.* London: Routledge.

Zinn, M., & Dill, B. (1994). *Women of color in U.S. society.* Philadelphia, PA: Temple University Press.

Chapter 12

EVALUATION OF
EMPOWERMENT PRACTICE

Ruth J. Parsons, Ph.D.
University of Denver, Denver, Colorado

INTRODUCTION

Evaluation is a major focus in social work practice. Assessment of the effectiveness and efficiency of social work intervention is critical for funders, administrators, agency boards, practitioners, and clients. Social agencies are increasingly called on to explicate the results of their interventions. Though both costly and cumbersome, this task allows workers to articulate the intentions and results of social work intervention. In this chapter, I shall examine the issues concerning empowerment practice.

Perceptions of empowerment in social work vary among practitioners, researchers, and academics. Viewed as a value, a philosophy, a general paradigm, and a framework for practice, empowerment may be the most overly used but undefined concept currently found in social work literature. The array of intervention approaches presented in this book suggests the enormous complexity of the empowerment concept as it guides practice. As such, social workers who want to practice from an empowerment base may need specifically to address evaluation issues in order to overcome skepticism among agency administrators and funders regarding their capacity to make empowerment practice work. Because empowerment is an elusive concept, one may have a hard time showing how to operationalize it. Demonstrating the principles of intervention and identifying expected outcomes of an intervention may therefore demand special attention. Current approaches to program evaluation in social work suggest models and choices one may use in this task. However, the methods used in the inquiry must incorporate the philosophical premises and values embedded in empowerment. This means that the inquiry must include and amplify the voice of the consumer.

This chapter will examine empowerment principles and approaches as applied to practice evaluation methods—specifically, issues of power. Furthermore, the chapter will provide examples of evaluation studies in empowerment practice and discuss issues and barriers in carrying out such evaluations.

EVALUATION AND SOCIAL WORK PRACTICE

In evaluation, workers systematically monitor progress toward outcomes during all phases of social work practice and assess the overall efficiency and effectiveness of intervention outcomes. Evaluation involves judging by applying rules and/or standards to a given activity or set of activities. In short, evaluation lets one know how one is doing. As a gauge of intervention outcome, evaluation can serve the client as much as the worker and agency. Indeed, in empowerment practice, workers must design evaluations that benefit the client.

Why Evaluate?

Workers engage in evaluation for a variety of reasons: to determine whether an intervention was worth the effort, whether agency and clients were satisfied, whether the results were expected, and perhaps what was learned from the intervention (Parsons, Jorgensen, & Hernández, 1994). Workers also evaluate to build a knowledge base from their interventions. Enhancing agency staff's belief systems about the work they do is an important goal of evaluation. Many practitioners value empowerment but find it difficult to articulate its efficacy to funders and potential program managers. Ultimately, practitioners evaluate as a way to maintain accountability in practice—that is, which interventions work and why, specifically (Parsons, Hernández, & Jorgensen, 1994).

Program evaluation serves agencies and organizations by describing the program, linking it to the literature, explicating practice principles, and thinking through rationale and goals (Smith, 1992). One can view such evaluation as a mode of research in which one evaluates the need for the program and monitors its progress and outcomes. Or, one can view program evaluation as political action in terms of competitions for funds and an attempt to influence political decisions regarding interventions in human services (Smith, 1992).

Types of Evaluation

Types of practice evaluations have traditionally been categorized as *outcome* (or goal attainment), *process*, and *impact*. See Table 12.1 for a synthesis of these types and parameters for evaluating empowerment.

OUTCOME EVALUATION Outcome evaluation addresses the intended goals of the program. As discussed in this book, empowerment outcomes come from concepts of empowerment in the literature, as well as research studies of empowerment practice. Often referred to as *summative* evaluations, outcome evaluations determine to what extent an intervention has realized its goals and objectives. Quantitative outcome measures exist for various components of empowerment (see Chapter 1 for a discussion of these measures). These include such constructs as sociopolitical participatory behavior, perceived autonomy, power, control, self-efficacy, personal empowerment, perceived sociopolitical control, and many other constructs that represent expected outcomes in empowerment. One may use both qualitative and quantitative approaches to determine and assess outcomes.

PROCESS EVALUATION Often referred to as formative evaluation, process evaluation assesses the activities, methods, or means (program processes) employed to achieve the desired outcome. Process evaluation determines what actually takes place in a program and compares it with the original plans to see if activities need to be modified. Recent studies have provided information on resources for conducting such program evaluations. Such studies regarding the essential elements of empowerment practice may provide guides for process evaluation. Because empowerment is both a process and an outcome, assessing how clients change helps one evaluate empowerment. Because change may vary greatly among different populations and among individuals, qualitative methods may be the best choice for assessing it (see Kieffer, 1984).

IMPACT EVALUATION Impact evaluation involves assessing the impact an intervention has made on an identified problem. The problem may be specific, such as how an individual will overcome a disability, or general, such as racial or gender discrimination, poverty, or unemployment. An impact evaluation approach asks what difference a program has made in the severity, incidence, degree, or presence of oppressive effects of a targeted condition. For example, an empowerment approach may try to help certain people manage their severe and persistent mental illness. An impact evaluation would indicate the extent of change on given mental illness management indicators, usually chosen by the funders. If an empowerment approach were used in regard to policy changes in a particular program, an impact evaluation would examine to what extent the program had changed policies. Impact evaluation asks the question, "Was the social condition of the identified population improved as a result of the intervention?" One may employ all three types of evaluation—outcome, process, and impact—separately or in combination. Funders and administrators may guide choices about which type of evaluation to employ.

TABLE 12.1
TYPES OF EVALUATION

PROGRAM PROCESSES	OUTCOME OR GOAL	IMPACT
Methods	Results	Social condition
Strategies	Effects	Effects
Design	Products	Social problem
Implementation	Client states	

ISSUES OF POWER IN EVALUATION OF PRACTICE

Occupied with helping activities, social work practitioners do not often emphasize the evaluation of practice. Often, the impetus to evaluate comes from the administration or funding body rather than the practitioner. Therefore, the questions formulated for evaluation practice interventions and strategies often do not reflect the concerns of clients and practitioners. Clients in particular are too often disregarded, though they offer valid and reliable information about the efficacy of social work practice. To express the values of empowerment through assessment and evaluation, one must examine critically the assumptions, goals, and methods of evaluation. Few would suggest that such assessment is simple. Often viewed as a developmental process, different for different populations, empowerment assessment requires that social workers reconsider how they usually think about and implement practice evaluations.

Practice from an empowerment perspective indicates several fundamental shifts or transformations in the professional role (see Chapter 1). For example, one must go from viewing clients in terms of a deficit, blame, and pathology to focusing on their strengths, goodness, and aspirations. Also, professionals tend to see themselves as experts who know more than clients and who must therefore choose for them. Social workers must instead see their knowledge as merely different from that of clients; they must use clients' expertise, norms, and goals about themselves and their problems; and they must help clients choose and assume power over themselves. With the framework of "power with" rather than "power over," a social worker becomes an enabler, teacher, helper, or leader, serving as midwife to individuals in the process of self-empowerment. Practice necessarily becomes shaped and directed by the context of given problems, including the sociopolitical and cultural context of the client's population. Empowerment may involve different issues and challenges, depending on the socioeconomic status, culture, age, and gender of those involved. Therefore, assessment of empowerment must take place in the appropriate context and must support rather than undermine the empowerment of the participants. Moreover, this assessment must amplify the expertise of the client regarding his or her own problem situation in its context.

Rappaport (1990) has suggested that empowerment means identifying, facilitating, and creating contexts in which heretofore silent and isolated people gain understanding, voice, and influence over decisions that affect their lives. Further, the evaluator or researcher of empowerment must study it in the context of, and with the participation of, clients in a way that benefits them. Finally, Rappaport suggests that though empowerment research is not methodologically specific, how one conducts the research is critical. That is, the research should take place in the context of the people concerned and should benefit them; it should be collaborative and focus on strengths, not deficits.

In consideration of Rappaport's issues, Rapp, Shera, and Kisthardt (1993) have developed strategies in which research content and method empowers the population being studied, amplifies these people's voices, and represents their point of view. These authors suggest that the consumer's voice be amplified in context, vantage point, selection of outcomes and measures, data collection and analysis, and dissemination. Further, Whitmore (1991) makes a strong case that the evaluation of empowerment be constructed in a way that gives voice and political power to the participants in the program being evaluated. She suggests that since people have long recognized that research and evaluation are political processes, the question is no longer, "Is it science?" but instead, "What is the nature of the inquiry?" or "Who benefits from the process and who loses?" So, if evaluation amplifies some voice in the professional helping scene, it may as well be that of the clients. In keeping with empowerment philosophy, the client's voice must be amplified.

PRINCIPLES AND METHODS FOR EMPOWERMENT IN EVALUATION

Participatory evaluation and participatory research literature provide a conceptual basis for considering empowerment in practice evaluation. (See Chapter 11.) Whitmore (1991) suggests that from the outset, participatory research and evaluation strives to empower those with little or no power to control their lives. Empowerment is facilitated through participatory behavior (Kieffer, 1984); the key to this process is the extent to which participants can exercise power in decision making (Whitmore, 1991, p. 2). Brown (1994) suggests that the positivist tradition in research and in social work tends to be grounded not in people's reality, but in theories chosen by the researcher. Defining and naming by others reduces people's sense of agency and diminishes personal voice. She quotes Park, who describes participatory research as "an emerging self-conscious way of empowering people so that they can take effective action toward betterment of their life conditions" (p. 294). She suggests that participatory research empowers participants by validating their realities and their rights as people to be heard, respected, and recorded as a part of history. In this way, research assumes the aim of educating respondents, who are no longer subjects but participants. By revealing reality from the "world view of participants," participatory research gives a personal voice to those whose voices are not usually heard (p. 297).

Parsons, East, and Boesen (1994) utilize a feminist action research perspective in order to establish a closer relationship between scholarship and community empowerment. Similar to participatory research, *action research* is "a methodology for involving oppressed people in the analysis of and solutions to social problems" (Yeich & Levine, 1992, p. 1894). They suggest three ways in which action/participatory research supports an empowerment perspective: (1) The research process is about not only the discovery or verification of theoretical concepts, but also the development of people. Use of such strategies as oral history and examination of experience lead to such aspects of empowerment as validation of experience and critical thinking. (2) Action/participatory research uses the experience of the participants to validate and expand their own expertise. This growing knowledge, which comes from within rather than an external authority, leads to information that leads to power. (3) Given a reciprocity between researchers and participants, research can create social spaces in which members can contribute significantly to their own well-being. Chapter 11 has brought together the themes of postmodernism, participatory research, feminist research, and the politics of diversity to suggest a transformation agenda for empowerment research based on antidiscrimination emancipation, research as empowerment, and research as political. In a similar discussion, Holmes (1992) has summarized the major assumptions and goals of empowerment research. The following principles for evaluating empowerment-based programs and interventions have been drawn from these works.

- Methods and designs used to gather data should never subvert the empowerment of people and, where possible, should promote the empowerment of clients involved.
- The problems, solutions, needs, and aspirations that evaluation attempts to understand should be framed in terms defined by the group under study.

- The traditional values of social work and the empowerment agenda should guide the design and methods of evaluation.
- Evaluators have a greater obligation to client empowerment than to traditional social science values.
- The population under study should be collaborators and stockholders in the evaluation process.
- Design should encourage those under study to participate in knowledge building.
- Evaluation designs should recognize that those under study have authority over their own lives and possess abilities to express that authority in some way.
- Evaluation should elicit an understanding of how client groups have surmounted difficulties and coped.
- Evaluation design should accept social phenomena as they are, not try to simplify them.
- Research design should not create artificial encounters and environments from which to gather data.

Quantitative and Qualitative Methods

The emphasis on amplifying the consumer voice has raised an issue regarding quantitative versus qualitative methods. While funders emphasize quantification and statistical power as evidence of programmatic articulation, empowerment outcomes and processes by definition vary by differences in populations such as culture, gender, ethnicity or race, and by political views. Qualitative research designs provide an excellent starting point for understanding and defining empowerment; that is, capturing process and states in specific contexts of diverse populations. Focus groups, in-depth interviews, and participant observation all reflect the reality as defined by the individuals under study. In his analysis of research on empowerment, Zimmerman (1991) concludes that *too much* emphasis on quantitative documentation will probably distort one's understanding of important processes. As such, he claims, future research should include qualitative methods that attend to the developmental issues of individuals in particular contexts, have participants speak in their own voice, and involve them in the study design. He also advocates research strategies such as focus groups, in-depth individual studies, investigative reporting, and participant observation in order to complement existing quantitative measures. Such procedures must consider the developmental nature of empowerment and recognize that one's mastery of one's environment will likely vary according to culture, age, gender, ethnicity, race, and different domains of life.

In short, evaluating empowerment does not presume one method or another; rather, it follows the client voice as a guide in the selection of research questions and methods, whether quantitative or qualitative. Though methods for evaluating empowerment include the same quantitative methods used in traditional evaluation designs, it uses them not as singular preemptive approaches but along with qualitative methods for a holistic approach. The remainder of this chapter will describe evaluation methodologies that employ the principles of empowerment to evaluate practice.

EXAMPLES OF FACILITATING EMPOWERMENT THROUGH EVALUATION

I shall examine the following examples of evaluation of empowerment practice regarding how they use empowerment principles in the evaluation process; what type of evaluation each is, based on the previous discussion (see Table 12.1); and how the findings contribute to knowledge regarding empowerment practice.

Prenatal Program of the Canadian Department of Health and Welfare

Whitmore (1991) reports a participatory design for evaluation of an empowerment project involving single expectant mothers in a low-income area. The prenatal program sought to increase the participation of single expectant mothers in prenatal education programs by responding to their specific needs. Consistent with the program, the evaluation was based on a participatory design. Using the program participants and professionals as evaluators, Whitmore built a community-based team approach and studied both the *outcomes* of the program as reflected by the participants and the *change process* itself. Program participants who served on the evaluation team interviewed other program participants, a hard-to-reach population who did not tend to cooperate with outsiders. The evaluation team members, who were also program participants, knew the community's culture and thus intuitively how to approach their peers. Whitmore suggests that empowerment of participants in evaluation may occur through various participatory activities:

- Participation of technical evaluation tasks, such as questionnaire design and data analysis
- Group interaction on the evaluation team, which may expand people's support networks as they pursue specific actions toward program or organizational change
- Close work with an evaluation team, a subcommittee of an advisory committee

- Being assigned concrete tasks recognized as important by administrators and funders
- A written contract, including payment for those actually doing the work
- A carefully structured sequence of tasks that breaks down the evaluation process so that participants can understand exactly what to do and how to do it
- Attention to group process
- Publicity after the report has been issued

Participants in the evaluation process experienced outcome results similar to clients or consumers of empowerment programs in general. That is, evaluation participants identified three dimensions of empowerment outcomes in themselves: individual, group, and environmental. *Individual* outcomes included self-confidence, knowledge/skills, and fun/enthusiasm. *Group* outcomes included speaking to outside groups, challenging the social service system, and employment opportunities. Whitmore emphasizes that the evaluators had to be trained in the following skills related to facilitating communication among people:

- Listening
- Building trust
- Group dynamics
- Facilitating cooperation among different constituencies
- Power and power structures (how communities are organized)
- Who makes decisions and how power is manifested
- Issues of class, race, and gender
- Analysis of their own value system, experience, and interpretations of society

Using qualitative methods for both *process* and *outcome* evaluation, the study followed the principles discussed earlier in this chapter, including giving clients a voice, knowledge-building, and an opportunity to frame the problems to be studied. Findings suggest that the program had positive effects on clients' support systems and information base for making decisions, two of the outcome components previously identified. One impact of the program was the improved health of clients.

Evaluation of an AFDC Coalition

Parsons, East, and Bosen (1994) have used group members and the group process to evaluate the outcomes and processes of a community coalition called All Families Deserve a Chance (AFDC). The coalition was formed to give voice in the decision-making process of welfare reform to recipients. The staff used a community organizing intervention to promote recipients' empowerment. The concept of *praxis* from feminist action research was employed to assess the effectiveness of the coalition. Using group-interview techniques, researchers tape-recorded a discussion by the members regarding the outcome and process of the coalition's work. In addition, four members were interviewed for fuller descriptions of the process they had experienced as members. From transcriptions of the taped interviews, an account of the data was written that identified individual, group, and community change toward empowerment. This account was taken back to the members to consider, counter, amplify, and confirm. Based on this input, researchers revised the report. They also gathered information from the department of social services regarding the impact of the coalition's work and from the coalition staff member regarding the process of the group. Confirmed by members of the coalition, the final report was disseminated by the researchers and members, who together presented the project at two National Conferences.

Praxis—action-reflection-action—provided coalition members with "ways and words to think about this" that they hadn't used before. Presenting the findings led at least one member of the coalition to participate in an international women's conference, and ultimately to full-time employment. This research design gave clients a voice and tools to become stakeholders in the evaluation and participants in knowledge building for themselves, for the program, and for empowerment theory.

FINDINGS   This study provided *outcome* findings (see Table 12.1). The outcomes were identified as *individual development*, such as self-efficacy and self-esteem; *group processes*, such as commonality, group consciousness, reduction of self-blame, and education; and *community changes*, including means of participation, communication processes, management of change, and accountability (Parsons, East, & Boesen, 1994). These findings confirm the construct of personal, interpersonal, and community empowerment outcomes (Cox & Parsons, 1994).

A Study of Process and Outcomes in Five Empowerment-based Programs

In one study (Parsons, 1994), I used group interviews and individual qualitative interviews to identify program processes, client change processes, and client outcomes in five empowerment-based programs. These qualitative interviews gave voice to clients and staff as to their understandings of empowerment, their interactive experiences in these programs, descriptions of how change occurs in clients involved in these experiences, and perceived outcomes in clients. I combined qualitative data from clients and staff to form a profile of practice activities in the programs, as well as

TABLE 12.2
COMPONENTS AND DIMENSIONS OF
EMPOWERMENT DEVELOPMENT (OUTCOMES)

PERSONAL (Self-Perception)	INTERPERSONAL (Knowledge/Skills)	COMMUNITY/POLITICAL PARTICIPATION (Action)
Self-awareness	Assertiveness	Giving back
Self-acceptance	Setting limits on giving	Taking control in other
Belief in self	Asking for help	domains
Feeling that you	Problem solving	Making a contribution
have rights	Critical thinking	
Self-esteem	Accessing resources	

change process and outcomes in clients (see Table 12.2). I categorized these outcomes into dimensions from existing literature (Cox & Parsons, 1994; Zimmerman, 1991). In the *personal* dimension of empowerment, clients and staff identified increased self-awareness, self-acceptance, belief in self, and self-esteem, as well as a feeling of having rights.

In the *interpersonal* dimension, they identified assertiveness, setting limits on giving, asking for help from others when needed, learning new or better problem-solving strategies, and the acquisition of critical thinking. In the broader dimension of *community and political participation*, clients and staff identified such outcomes as giving back to others and affecting the general problem areas they were experiencing. For example, some people might volunteer at the women's shelter after they no longer need the service. Some might educate others about certain shared problems, taking a proactive stance regarding such problems and generalizing this proactive behavior to many domains of their lives. I took written results back to clients and staff for feedback and further input. This "praxis" approach embodies *reflection on the action*, for the written reports let clients reflect on their experiences.

The Colorado Mental Health and Consumer and Family Development Project

Manning (1994) directed an evaluation of the Colorado Mental Health Consumer and Family Development Project through a research team composed of mental health consumers, family members, and professionals. The project aimed at facilitating the empowerment of consumers and family members. The evaluation design triangulated qualitative and quantitative methods to determine the nature of the intervention and its effects. By actively engaging consumers and family members as researchers in the study of their own social conditions, Manning used a participatory research methodology. Training of consumers and family members took place in an intensive retreat-type setting followed by the formation of diads with professionals until they became comfortable with conducting interviews on their own. In monthly meetings, they made sampling, design, and analysis decisions. The research team attended one professional conference on qualitative research. It also conducted focus-group interviews with consumer and family support groups in five rural towns in Colorado, as well as two suburban settings. Individual interviews were conducted with 17 informants consisting of leaders and providers of services as well as family members who participated in the project services.

FINDINGS Findings from this study identified consumers' and family members' perceptions of barriers to empowerment, what empowerment means to them, their experiences of the project services, and the perceived outcomes of these services. Table 12.3 summarizes the first three of these. Descriptions, in the families' own words, of what empowerment means confirm existing literature regarding the dimensions and components of empowerment.

Consumers and family members who participated in the research team identified these positive experiences: developing teamwork skills, finding

TABLE 12.3
CONSUMERS' AND FAMILY MEMBERS' PERCEPTIONS OF EMPOWERMENT

BARRIERS TO EMPOWERMENT	MEANING OF EMPOWERMENT	EXPERIENCE IN EMPOWERMENT-BASED SERVICES
Poverty	Self-determination/ choice	Needs are heard
Stigma of mental illness (external and internal)	Information and education	Connections feel like friendship
Iatrogenic effects of institutionalization	Respect from others	Development of history of a group
Lack of power in relationship with professionals and others	Distribution of power in decision making	Exchange of information and sharing
	Self-respect	Feelings of belonging and sharing
	Ongoing involvement	Acceptance without stigma
	Contribution to others	Support
		Going public or "coming out" with mental illness

commonalties, getting involved, discovering and understanding many perspectives, and learning how to cooperate. These experiences led to changes in their perceptions of each other, to power through unity, and to the development of a common purpose. Using empowerment principles in the evaluation included giving not only a voice to the consumers of the program, but also training and opportunities to experience new knowledge and skills as well as the role of researcher. Besides creating opportunities for these consumers to engage in an additional empowering process, the studies have augmented the profession's knowledge of expected outcomes and processes of empowerment-based intervention. Participatory and praxis models of evaluation have empowering qualities in themselves, as well—both Whitmore and Manning have reported the benefits of participation in the evaluation, beyond client consumer benefits. However, these models also provide opportunities to amplify the voices of consumers. The final section of this chapter will focus on the findings of these studies and other literature regarding the practice elements and program processes found in empowerment-based interventions.

PRACTICE STRATEGIES OF EMPOWERMENT PRACTICE

The literature and the studies just cited offer an emerging picture of the practice strategies that clients and workers have identified as useful for promoting empowerment. Researchers have tapped client voices to determine those experiences most meaningful to them that have helped facilitate change. Qualitative approaches allow one to hear the client's unique experience of a given program. Through either systematic research or practice wisdom, several authors have developed elements of empowerment practice, or program *process* elements. Chapter 1 contained a discussion of these. Table 12.4, a synthesis of these practice elements (Cox, 1988; Cox & Parsons, 1994; Gutiérrez, 1989; Gutiérrez, DeLois, & GlenMaye, 1995; Manning, 1994; Parsons, 1994; Saleebey, 1992; Simon, 1994; Solomon, 1976), provides guidelines for evaluating the program process in empowerment practice, that is, those elements that should be present in a programmatic intervention when empowerment is the desired outcome.

Table 12.4 suggests that the environment plays a critical role in facilitating empowerment. One study (Parsons, 1994) found that in each program both clients and staff suggested the importance of an environmental ambiance and a culture that facilitate empowerment. Manning's study (1994) confirms this for consumers and families of services for the mentally ill. One needs to establish a cohesive collective work to create safety and opportunities to interact and to set up relationships, to tell personal stories

TABLE 12.4
PRACTICE ELEMENTS OF EMPOWERMENT

COHESIVE COLLECTIVE	COLLABORATIVE RELATIONSHIP WITH PEERS AND PROFESSIONALS
Safety	Experiencing power
Interaction	Clients' perceptions honored
Relationship/trust	
Being heard and validated	Clients' voices amplified
Mutual aid	Clients as teachers/helpers
Interdependence	
Creation of hope	
Collaborative action-taking	

STRENGTHS-BASED ASSESSMENT	EDUCATIONAL FOCUS
Shared learning	Belief in client
Coping capacities and motivation	Trying out new skills
	Consciousness raising
Focus on individual and environment	Conflict management
	Resource access
Fostering client belief in self	
Challenge and confrontation	

and be heard, to make mutual decisions regarding problems to work on, to access resources, and to take action. Interdependence, hope, and collective action require trust and support.

Relationships among all those involved must be collaborative, their power shared. Clients' perceptions of problems and choices—their voices—must be amplified in the decision-making process. Social workers should expect clients to contribute as well as receive. Strengths-based, collaborative assessment emphasizes clients' views of problems and coping. Workers should expect clients to take risks and should challenge and confront them to believe in themselves. Further, practitioners need to focus on both clients and their environment.

An educational focus provides a place for learning and trying out new skills. This focus includes information regarding the sociopolitical context of common problems and increases the consciousness of participants. New skills such as advocacy, brokerage, and conflict management help clients access resources.

Practitioners can use Table 12.4 as a checklist for creating empowerment program strategies. These attributes of empowerment interventions provide parameters for process evaluations.

CONCLUSION

Empowerment is complex because it means different things to different populations. Both a process and an outcome, it has many dimensions and components. Practitioners who implement or evaluate empowerment programs must understand this complexity. Including program participants in the evaluation process not only empowers them through the act of participating, it also amplifies their voices in impact, outcome, or process evaluations. No matter what kind of questions one wants to answer in evaluation, one must amplify the voice of clients in their perceptions of empowerment, their experiences as participants, and their perceptions of outcomes in themselves and others.

REFERENCES

Brown, P. A. (1994). Participatory research: A new paradigm for social work. In L. Gutiérrez & P. Nurius (Eds.), *Education and research for empowerment practice* (pp. 291–302). Seattle: Center for Social Policy and Practice, School of Social Work, University of Washington.

Cox, E. O. (1988). Empowerment of the low income elderly through group work. *Social Work with Groups, 11*(3/4), 111–125.

Cox, E. O., & Parsons, R. J. (1994). *Empowerment-oriented social work practice with the elderly.* Pacific Grove, CA: Brooks/Cole.

Gutiérrez, L. (1989). *Empowerment in social work practice: Considerations for practice and education.* Paper presented to the Council on Social Work Education, Annual Program Meeting, Chicago.

Gutiérrez, L. (1990). Working with women of color: An empowerment perspective. *Social Work, 35*(2). 5–8.

Gutiérrez, L., DeLois, K. A., & GlenMaye, L. (1995). Understanding empowerment practice: Building on practitioner based knowledge. *Families in Society, 76*(9), 534–544.

Holmes, G. (1992). Social work research and the empowerment paradigm. In D. Saleebey (Ed.), *The strengths perspective in social work practice* (pp. 151–164). New York: Longman Publishers.

Kieffer, C. (1984, Winter/Spring). Citizen empowerment: A developmental perspective. *Prevention in Human Services, 3,* 9–36.

Manning, S. (1994). Colorado Mental Health Consumer and Family Development Project: Program Evaluation Report. Denver, CO: Colorado Division of Mental Health.

Parsons, R. J. (1994, March) *Empowerment based social work practice: A study of process and outcomes.* Paper presented to the 41st Annual Program Meeting, Council on Social Work Education, San Diego, CA.

Parsons, R. J., East, J. F., & Boesen, M. B. (1994). Empowerment: A case study with AFDC women. In L. Gutiérrez & P. Nurius (Eds.), *Education and research for empowerment practice* (pp. 259–272). Seattle: Center for Social Policy and Practice, School of Social Work, University of Washington, Seattle.

Parsons, R. J., Jorgensen, J., & Hernández, S. H. (1994). *The integration of social work practice*. Pacific Grove, CA: Brooks/Cole.

Rapp, C. A., Shera, W., & Kisthardt, W. (1993). Research strategies for consumer empowerment of people with severe mental illness. *Social Work, 38*(6), 727–735.

Rappaport, J. (1990). Research methods and the empowerment social agenda. In P. Tolan (Ed.), *Researching community psychology* (pp. 51–63). Washington, DC: American Psychological Association.

Saleebey, D. (1992). *The strengths perspective in social work*. New York: Longman.

Simon, B. (1994). *The empowerment tradition in American social work*. New York: Columbia University Press.

Smith, M. J. (1992). *Program evaluation in the human services*. New York: Springer.

Solomon, B. (1976). *Black empowerment: Social work with oppressed populations*. New York: Columbia University Press.

Whitmore, E. (1991). Evaluation and empowerment: It's the process that counts. *Networking Bulletin, 2*(2), 1–7.

Yeich, S., & Levine, R. (1992). Participatory research's contribution to conceptualization of empowerment. *Journal of Applied Social Psychology, 22*, 1894–1908.

Zimmerman, M. (1990). Taking aim on empowerment research: On the distinction between individual and psychological concepts. *American Journal of Community Psychology, 18*, 169–177.

Zimmerman, M. (1991). *The measurement of psychological empowerment: Issues and strategies*. Unpublished manuscript.

Chapter 13

CREATING OPPORTUNITIES FOR EMPOWERMENT-ORIENTED PROGRAMS

Lorraine M. Gutiérrez, Ph.D.
University of Michigan, Ann Arbor

Ruth J. Parsons, Ph.D.
University of Denver, Denver, Colorado

Enid Opal Cox, D.S.W.
University of Denver, Denver, Colorado

PRINCIPLES OF EMPOWERMENT

In this book we have tried to refine our definition and understanding of empowerment practice. Toward this end, we have presented the methods and challenges involved in empowerment practice with different populations, fields of practice, and levels and types of intervention. By presenting the depth and breadth of empowerment in the field, we hope that individual practitioners will gain a clearer understanding of how to conduct this work in a range of settings. Let us summarize what the book has suggested about empowerment practice.

A heterogeneous group of authors contributed to this book. Practitioners, academics, or both, they represent expertise in a variety of social work practice settings. They have described their understanding and conceptualizations of empowerment as well as related practice programs. From these descriptions, they have exemplified in their chapters what they each perceive to be the most important principles.

Specific Principles

These principles are combined and analyzed here to generate the central themes of empowerment practice identified by the authors.

THE ENVIRONMENT/CULTURE The environment in which clients and workers work together needs first and foremost to feel like a safe and supportive place, physically and psychologically. Trust is critical in this environment, which must foster a sense of community.

UNDERSTANDING THE WHOLE PERSON IN CONTEXT Structural inequalities and oppression play major roles in powerlessness. One needs to see the whole person in order to focus on both personal and environmental factors, on strengths instead of deficits, and on the person rather than on a diagnosis or presenting problem. Respect for the client's unique qualities, values, and experiences enables the practitioner to accept the client's definition of his or her problem. The client's personal and cultural background is important data for understanding the problem situation. At the same time, the practitioner engages with clients in expanding their view of problems to the environmental context.

THE HELPING PROCESS Empowerment is facilitated through a helping process that fosters self-confidence, gives clients a voice, and promotes self-respect and self-control in the relationship. The helping process provides opportunities for clients to experience capability, dignity and worth, and strength—to take risks, make their own decisions, gain knowledge and skills, learn critical thinking, participate in new roles, educate staff and other clients, participate in mutual aid and support groups, participate in collective action toward social change, and work with others on personal change and political change. This process also fosters clients' awareness of being an expert on their own problems, their understanding of rights and self-determination, and a change in how they see themselves—from passive beneficiary of services to active consumer of services.

THE RELATIONSHIP Given time, a partnership model of "power with," not "power over," develops. Eventually, all involved share power and leadership through collaborative planning and work.

MULTIPLE ROLES In empowerment practice, workers take on multiple roles—educator, supporter, broker, and especially advocate and negotiator, in which the worker models advocacy skills and teaches them to the client. The worker promotes clients' involvement in organizational development and seeks to amplify the clients' voice in the organization. Essential to any good social work practice, meeting basic needs plays a particularly important part in empowerment practice. The worker needs to recognize that empowment works in phases and thus must choose actions to suit whichever phase the client or client group is in.

These principles confirm the framework presented in the first chapter. However, a reading of the preceding chapters presents a challenge to social workers and to their profession: To fulfill its potential as a mechanism for change, empowerment practice requires conceptualizations of practice that differ from traditional medical and expert-oriented models. Effectively practicing empowerment means changing professional education and the very structure of the profession. In this chapter, we explore the barriers and contradictions involved in empowerment practice and propose ways that human service workers can become empowered to bring this work to its fullest potential.

CHALLENGES TO EMPOWERMENT

Empowerment has been a traditional theme within the social work profession (Simon, 1994). Over a century ago, this profession was founded in reaction to the problems associated with capitalist development (Dressel, 1994; Simon, 1994; Wenocur & Reisch, 1989). Conditions such as the concentration of wealth, large-scale immigration, and an economic recession led to a crisis in the welfare state. One response to these conditions was the development of social reforms and the creation of the social sciences (Simon, 1994; Wenocur & Reisch, 1989).

Today, the social work profession faces similar conditions of economic dislocation. Over the past decade, income differentials have become more pronounced, and the proportion of the population considered middle class has shrunk (Dressel, 1994). Of particular concern, three sectors of the U.S. population that have traditionally possessed little power or few social resources have increased: people of color, older people, and people with disabilities. Within the next 50 years, immigration and fertility patterns will lead to an increasingly multiracial, multicultural, and multiethnic society (Gutiérrez, 1992a). At the same time, conditions of economic inequality and economic stratification by gender and race have not abated (Dressel, 1994; Simon, 1994). Because both women and people of color continue to experience economic and social disadvantages, these demographic projections have led to concerns that the United States could become a nation of poor children, youth of color, and elderly European Americans, none of them capable of producing the economic resources necessary for supporting existing social services or other social goods (Ozawa, 1986; Sarri, 1986; Williams, 1990).

As practitioners, activists, and scholars concerned with social justice, we believe that our profession stands at a critical juncture. Many of these changes will occur regardless of how our profession responds. Professionals can nonetheless choose to work for social justice and equality in an increasingly diverse world or work to reinforce current calls for social control. Taken to what we hope is an extreme, will this role focus on the development of new programs or more "scientific" methods to allocate shrinking resources, or will professionals work to create more opportunity for all? The path they take will be affected by their professional mission as well as their ability to view themselves and their own work from an empowerment perspective.

The empowerment perspective proposes that only through changes in the distribution of power can these trends be reversed. In identifying methods for empowerment practice, this book and others (Lee, 1994; McWhirter, 1994; Miley, O'Melia, & DuBois, 1994; Pinderhughes, 1989; Rees, 1991; Simon, 1994; Solomon, 1976) have presented a vision for ways that social work policy and practice can facilitate positive social change. This literature has emphasized three methods for transformative practice: critical *education* and consciousness raising, the *democratization* of the helping relationship, and a *focus on client and community strengths* rather than problems (Gutiérrez, DeLois, & GlenMaye, 1995; Parsons, 1994). In this book we have tried to demonstrate how one can carry out these methods with different populations, fields of services, and forms of practice.

Given the potential of empowerment practice for addressing the conditions of social inequality, what has limited its wide-scale implementation? One barrier has been fragmentation within the field as to the meaning of empowerment as a practice method. Although most agree on the importance of "empowerment" to the field, fewer agree on what it implies for practice and policy. This lack of clarity has contributed to the confusion regarding empowerment and its implications for our profession. Other barriers to the implementation of empowerment practice include the concerns discussed in the following sections.

Current Scholarship

Table 13.1 presents a review of the 45 articles published in social work journals in the United States from 1976 to 1991, identifying trends in the definitions of empowerment and its theoretical foundation (Gutiérrez, 1992b). Most articles focus on microlevel methods. Often, they refer to ways that changes in individual consciousness and functioning can contribute to

TABLE 13.1
FOCUS OF 45 EMPOWERMENT ARTICLES
ON DIFFERENT LEVELS OF CHANGE

LEVEL OF CHANGE	NUMBER OF ARTICLES	PERCENT OF 45 ARTICLES
Individual	26	58%
Family	14	31%
Group	14	31%
Social network	1	2%
Organization	10	22%
Community	16	35%

From *Macro Practice for the 21st Century: An Empowerment Perspective*, by L. Gutiérrez, October 1994 (Paper presented at the First Annual Conference on the Integration of Social Work and Social Science, School of Social Work, University of Michigan, Ann Arbor).

social change, with little articulation of how this might occur. Basing a strategy of social change on individual development is a slow process at best; some have even suggested that without efforts on the institutional level, it will be ineffective (Albee, 1986; Bailey & Brake, 1975; Khinduka, 1987; Serrano-Garcia, 1984). Although this gradual process may appeal to the majority of social workers who practice with individuals, its effects on the social and political environment will not be seen for many years. This suggests that the development of knowledge and practice methods on the macrolevel is lacking and needs further development.

TABLE 13.2
THEORETICAL BASES OF
EMPOWERMENT LITERATURE

THEORETICAL BASE	NUMBER OF ARTICLES	PERCENT OF 45 ARTICLES
Psychology	20	44%
Sociology	14	31%
Political science	2	4%
None	13	29%

From *Macro Practice for the 21st Century: An Empowerment Perspective*, by L. Gutiérrez, October 1994 (Paper presented at the First Annual Conference on the Integration of Social Work and Social Science, School of Social Work, University of Michigan, Ann Arbor).

THE THEORETICAL BASE Consistent with this focus on individual change, most of the literature referring to a theoretical base has centered on psychology (see Table 13.2). Within psychology, the most influential theories have addressed self-efficacy and locus of control, women's development, consciousness raising, and community psychology. Within sociology, the primary work cited has been power dependence theory or Marxist theories of change. Thirteen of the articles made no reference to theory at all. If the profession is to develop an approach to empowerment focused on larger system change, theories of social, political, and economic power must be incorporated into the knowledge base. Professionals need to look at the research on social movements, social organizations, political economy, and political power to understand how to translate empowerment from individual to collective levels.

The Focus of Professional Education

As currently structured, most professional education focuses on direct practice, specialization, and work with small systems (Sarri, 1986). This suggests that changes will need to occur for empowerment practice to flourish. Although accreditation standards call for a focus on social justice and human diversity (Council on Social Work Education, 1994), efforts to teach this content are uneven and at times unfocused. Only a handful of schools teach practice from a social justice framework.

Work from an empowerment perspective calls for learning different methods of practice. Group work, organizational change, and administrative practice call for a different set of skills than specialized individual work requires: an awareness of group processes, interpersonal interaction, organizational theory, and power dynamics. As a form of intervention, empowerment also requires a sharing of information, control, and resources that does not usually occur in individual work (Garvin, 1985; Gutiérrez et al., 1995; Hirayama & Hirayama, 1985; Longres & McLeod, 1980). Education for empowerment practice requires a background in the skills necessary to work effectively with groups, organizations, and communities. The educational process must also focus on developing within students a commitment to the principles of democracy, equality, and noncompetitive and nonviolent forms of power. By working in partnership with community members, social workers will develop a new form of "expert knowledge" (Adams & Krauth, 1994).

Social Control

The social work profession has considerable socially sanctioned coercive power over specific populations, such as applicants for public assistance or parents under investigation for child neglect. Interventions developed to help individuals cope with, rather than change, difficult situations have also been identified as another way social workers carry out this role (Bailey & Brake, 1975). Some scholars have proposed that social workers should recognize and accept this role, but reframed in a positive sense: that the profession can "control dependency" through the provision of services or through social reform (Popple, 1985). Most individual practitioners, however, ignore the political dimension of social work and how it affects the ways society, including client populations, perceives social workers. Because this perception can create conditions of social distance, mistrust, and poor communication between workers and clients, it interferes with their ability to work toward empowerment.

To contribute to the empowerment of disenfranchised groups, professionals need to recognize their role within society and engage in a process of political education of themselves and others (Frumkin & O'Conner, 1985; Resich & Wenocur, 1986). Through this exploration, they can identify ways to work more effectively as allies to the people and communities they serve.

Investment in Professional Status

The desire for professional status reinforces social distance between social workers and client systems. Based on expert power, this professional status makes effectively implementing empowerment methods based in mutuality, affirmation of strengths, and democratic processes difficult (Frumkin & O'Conner, 1985; Resich & Wenocur, 1986).

Ironically, social workers may embrace present models of practice based on the expert role in an attempt to counteract the feelings of powerlessness they may experience in their work (Sherman & Wenocur, 1983). By seeing themselves as experts, and the client as deficient and ineffectual, social workers can experience personal control and power (Pernell, 1985; Pinderhughes, 1989; Weick & Vandiver, 1982). Empowerment practice, which requires a sharing of power and control between worker and client, can only occur when social workers will *not* be threatened by the collaborative role and are assisted and supported by managers and educators in restructuring power and control.

The Management of Human Service Organizations

The mission of an organization regarding social change significantly affects its ability to support empowerment practice. As described by Garvin (1985), one can best practice empowerment in a setting that "takes a social view of the problems of oppressed people" (p. 463) and that sees clients as capable of solving their own problems. Besides this perspective regarding clients' needs and capacity, an organization that supports empowerment practice would also allow flexibility in workers' roles, such as involvement in advocacy as well as treatment (Bock, 1980; Longres & McLeod, 1980; Pernell, 1985; Shapiro, 1984). From an administrative perspective, this support requires funding sources that do not mandate a specific form of practice and would not circumscribe the organization's involvement in community or political activities (O'Connell, 1978). That is, to themselves practice in empowering ways, the organization and funders must not limit these efforts (Frumkin & O'Conner, 1985; Resich & Wenocur, 1986).

To carry out empowerment practice, programs must develop a similar process in their own administrations. Research on organizational empowerment suggests that the structure of social service organizations can affect individual and community empowerment. The ability of individual workers to share their power with clients and engage in the range of interventions required for empowerment practice can depend on the support they receive for this type of work and their own feelings of personal power.

STRATEGIES FOR SUPPORTING EMPOWERMENT PRACTICE

The preceding discussion has focused on the daunting challenges to empowerment practice, which have effectively interfered with the profession's ability to work for social justice. However, the tradition of society's reinforcing these conditions should not continue to function as a barrier. As educators, staff, or administrators, individual workers can do many things to challenge current conditions and work for positive change.

Within the context of existing programs not all program participants may be able to engage in social action. Nonetheless, all social workers *can* think about political empowerment and how to empower themselves to create a more equitable world. An organization or program can be empowering, and it can be empowered—that is, gain the resources and power to meet its goals. Such an organization works at full capacity to gain the resources it needs to do the job well. It can wield influence in the larger political world. Organized as a vehicle for the empowerment of staff, clients, and the community, it maximizes the power of its workers and constituents to participate fully in the governance of the organization (Gerschick, Israel, & Checkoway, 1989; Zimmerman, in press).

From an empowerment perspective, a successful program is one that works itself out of a job—for example a battered women's shelter that is so effective on the community level that violence against women ends, or a displaced homemakers' program that eliminates age and gender discrimination in education and jobs. Social workers must never strive to perpetuate their own status but must look toward improving that of the individual and communities with which they work. Only by applying the empowerment model to themselves in their own position can social workers begin to gain the means to change these larger systems.

Personal Power

A critical first step for social workers is developing their own power on the personal level. This requires *recognizing the power they already have*. As individuals working in organizations, they need to analyze their power in the workplace. Then, they could strategize how to use the power they have to gain more power to mobilize for change. A third move involves identifying their allies in the organization or community and identifying how they can work together with those allies to meet common goals of community and social change.

For example, in a project that concerned low-income families in a multicultural urban community, each case manager spent hours every week advocating for clients with massive and intractable bureaucracies. Supervisors and top administrators within the organization were more concerned with fulfilling client statistics and billing for "patient hours" than in affecting the community. Through dialogue with each other and with their clients, the direct service workers and team leader recognized that case advocacy was making a limited impact on the overall problem. They then invited parents involved in parenting education groups to participate in a class action against one of the large bureaucracies. This case eventually resulted in expanded resources for poor families (Gutiérrez, 1991).

In this situation, the workers recognized the power they had as links between their clients and the larger community. They had also learned that as long as client statistics were completed, the larger bureaucracy was relatively unconcerned about their daily work. What they might have seen as a lack of support became an opportunity to expand their role with the community. Dialogue with their clients and individuals at similar organizations led to the involvement of attorneys. Involvement of legal assistance removed some of the risk from the individual workers and cemented alliances between the two organizations.

Social Power

A second step social workers can take to implement empowerment is to *increase their ability to influence others through social power*. Social power derives from such things as one's social position (such as supervisor), one's role (such as parent), one's interpersonal skills (such as conversational ability), one's credibility (appearing knowledgeable), or one's attractiveness (either physical or personal) (Feld, 1987; French & Raven, 1968). Some of these bases of power are ascriptive—based on race, gender, or class—but others can be achieved as one develops social skills or attains new social positions. To increase social power, one can focus on enhancing one's social position. One can also develop interpersonal skills or a social network.

The founding of Abused Women's Aid in Crisis provides an example of interpersonal and political empowerment (Roy, 1977). Roy worked as a social worker in a Head Start center in a low-income, ethnically diverse community in the Lower East Side of Manhattan. In her first year at the center, she became increasingly aware of the problems faced by abused women—at that time there were no specific shelters or programs. She felt frustrated in her efforts to help individual battered women get the legal and social supports they needed. However, she began to develop her own network of other professionals concerned with the issue. On the basis of these contacts, she worked with others to organize a community conference on wife abuse. By providing a forum for education, advocacy, and coalition building, this initial conference contributed to the development of battered women's services in New York City.

This situation exemplifies interpersonal empowerment because Roy built her power base through developing skills and interacting with others. She, and the other human service workers, had to learn quite a bit about laws, regulations, and policies before they could become effective advocates. Once they acquired this knowledge, they could identify gaps in existing programs and organize for further changes in policy. The community conference provided an effective forum for connecting with others.

Political Power

A third step involves working with others *to influence the political and economic system. Political empowerment* is the ability to influence the allocation of resources in an organization or community through formal or informal means (Parenti, 1978). Most commonly gained through collective action and collaboration with others, political empowerment is necessary for social workers to truly influence societal conditions.

Empowerment on the political level involves the other types of empowerment we have described. For example, it requires keeping up with legislative and local political developments and their implications and attempting to influence the process through advocacy. It may mean filing a complaint with the U.S. Civil Rights Commission or other administrative boards. It may mean working more closely with local businesses and community groups so they can learn about what one is doing and how it benefits them. It may also mean working through other organizations to use this influence if direct political advocacy is not possible through one's job. The most important piece of political empowerment is coalition building—working with others in one's state, regional, and national networks to advocate for change.

The two examples we have just looked at involve elements of political empowerment. In the first, individual workers organized to involve clients in class advocacy efforts. In the second, the individual workers organized a community conference to network and reach the eyes and ears of local decision makers (Roy, 1977). You can find many more such examples throughout this book, particularly in the chapters that discuss work with specific populations. To engage in political empowerment, one must look beyond one's specific "job description" and think of ways to work for positive change.

CONCLUSION

Creating opportunities for empowerment practice requires using one's own knowledge, power, and skills to make effective change. It also requires an optimism regarding human and social potential. As stated by Simon (1994), "Only practitioners who have believed deeply that people can change and that environments can be transformed have been able to work from an empowerment perspective in a sustained fashion" (p. 3). While some current demographic trends engender feelings of doom, they can also inspire one to create a more equitable society. This chapter highlights ways in which everyone can play an important role in making that vision a reality.

By working in partnership with communities, the profession can play a positive social role in the coming years. Social workers must maintain a positive focus not only on the strengths and possibilities out in the world, but also on the strengths and possibilities of their profession. The order of change we propose here requires both transformational leadership and optimism regarding this endeavor. Although empowerment can enhance current practice and help solve many of the problems facing society, without concurrent changes in the structure of social work and the education of practitioners, the profession cannot help effectively. As the social work profession enters the 21st century, its members must take a hard look at their roles and mission and find ways to work together for a more equitable society.

REFERENCES

Adams, P., & Krauth, K. (1994). Empowering workers for empowerment based practice. In L. Gutiérrez & P. Nurius (Eds.), *Education and research for empowerment practice* (pp. 183–194). Seattle: Center for Social Policy and Practice, School of Social Work, University of Washington.

Albee, G. (1986, August). *Powerlessness, politics, and prevention.* Paper presented at the meeting of the American Psychological Association, Washington, DC.

Bailey, R., & Brake, M. (1975). *Radical social work.* New York: Pantheon Books.

Bock, S. (1980). Conscientization: Paolo Friere and class-based practice. *Catalyst, 2,* 5–25.

Council on Social Work Education. 1994. CSWE Curriculum Policy Statement. Alexandria, VA: Author.

Dressel, P. L. (1994). And we keep on building prisons: Racism, poverty and challenges to the welfare state. *Journal of Sociology and Social Welfare, 21*(3), 7–30.

Feld, A. (1987). Self-perceptions of power: Do social work and business students differ? *Social Work, 32,* 225–230.

Freire, P. (1972). *The pedagogy of the oppressed.* New York: Seabury Press.

French, J., & Raven, B. (1968). The bases of social power. In D. Cartwright & A. Zander (Eds.), Group Dynamics (3rd ed., pp. 259–269). New York: Basic Books.

Frumkin, M., & O'Conner, G. (1985). Where has the profession gone? Where is it going? Social work's search for identity. *The Urban and Social Change Review, 18*(1), 12–19.

Garvin, C. (1985). Work with disadvantaged and oppressed groups. In M. Sundel, P. Glasser, R. Sarri, & R. Vinter, (Eds.), Individual change through small groups (2nd ed., pp. 461–472). New York: Free Press.

Gershick, T., Israel, B., & Checkoway, B. (1989). *Means of empowerment in individuals, organizations, and communities: Report from a retrieval conference.* Ann Arbor: Center for Research on Social Organizations, University of Michigan.

Gutiérrez, L. (1991). Empowering women of color: A feminist approach. In N. Hooyman & M. Bricker-Jenkins (Eds.), *Feminist social work practice in clinical settings* (pp. 199–214). Beverly Hills, CA: Sage.

Gutiérrez, L. (1992a). Empowering clients in the twenty-first century: The role of human service organizations. In Y. Hasenfeld (Ed.), *Human service organizations as complex organizations* (pp. 320–338). Newbury Park, CA: Sage.

Gutiérrez, L. (1992b, October). Macropractice for the 21st century: An *empowerment perspective.* Paper presented at the First Annual Conference on the Integration of Social Work and Social Science, School of Social Work, University of Michigan, Ann Arbor.

Gutiérrez, L., DeLois, K., & GlenMaye, L. (1995). Understanding empowerment practice: Building on practitioner based knowledge. *Families in Society, 76*(9), 534–544.

Hirayama, H., & Hirayama, K. (1985). Empowerment through group participation: Process and goal. In M. Parenes (Ed.), *Innovations in social group work: Feedback from practice to theory* (pp. 119–131). New York: Haworth.

Khinduka, S. (1987). Community development. In F. Cox, J. Erlich, J. Rothman, & J. Tropman (Eds), *Strategies of community organization* (4th ed., pp. 353–362). Itasca, IL: Peacock Press.

Lee, J. (1994). *The empowerment approach to social work practice.* New York: Columbia University Press.

Longres, J., & McLeod, E. (1980). Consciousness raising and social work practice. *Social Casework, 61, 267–277.*

McWhirter, E. (1994). *Counseling for empowerment.* Alexandria, VA : American Counseling Association.

Miley, K., O'Melia, M., & DuBois, B. (1994). *Generalist Social Work Practice.* Boston: Allyn and Bacon.

O'Connell, B. (1978). From service delivery to advocacy to empowerment. *Social Casework, 59*(4), 195–202.

Ozawa, M. (1986). Nonwhites and the demographic imperative in social welfare spending. *Social Work, 31,* 440–445.

Parsons, R. (1994, March). *Empowerment based social work practice.* Paper presented at the Annual Program Meeting of the Council on Social Work Education, San Diego, CA.

Pernell, R. (1985). Empowerment and social group work. In M. Parenes (Ed.), *Innovations in social group work: Feedback from practice to theory* (pp. 107–117. New York: Haworth.

Pinderhughes, E. (1989). *Understanding race, ethnicity, and power: The key to efficacy in clinical practice.* New York: Free Press.

Popple, P. (1985). The social work profession: A reconceptualization. *Social Service Review, 59*(4), 560–577.

Rees, S., (1991). *Achieving power: Practice and policy in social welfare.* North Sydney, Australia: Allen & Unwin.

Resich, M., & Wenocur, S. (1986). The future of community organization in social work: Social activism and the politics of profession building. *Social Service Review, 60,* 70–93.

Roy, M. (1977). *Battered women: A psychosociological study of domestic violence.* New York: Van Nostrand Reinhold.

Sarri, R. (1986). Organizational and policy practice in social work: Challenges for the future. *Urban and Social Change Review, 19,* 14–19.

Serrano-Garcia, I. (1984). The illusion of empowerment: Community development within a colonial context. In J. Rappaport, C. Swift, & R. Hess (Eds.), *Studies in empowerment: Toward understanding and action* (pp. 173–199). New York: Haworth.

Shapiro, J. (1984). Commitment to disenfranchised clients. In A. Rosenblatt & D. Waldfogel (Eds.), *Handbook of clinical social work* (pp. 888–903). San Francisco: Jossey-Bass.

Sherman, W., & Wenocur, S. (1983). Empowering public welfare workers through mutual support. *Social Work, 28*(5), 275–279.

Simon, B. L. (1994). *The empowerment tradition in American social work.* New York: Columbia University Press.

Solomon, B. (1976). *Black empowerment.* New York: Columbia University Press.

Weick, A., & Vandiver, S. (Eds.). (1982). *Women, power, and change*. Silver Spring, MD: National Association of Social Workers.

Wenocur, S., & Reisch, M. (1989). *From charity to enterprise: The development of American social work in a market economy*. Chicago: University of Illinois Press.

Williams, L. (1990). The challenge of education to social work: The case of minority children. *Social Work, 35*, 236–242.

Zimmerman, M. (in press). Empowerment: Forging new perspectives in mental health. In J. Rappaport & E. Seidman (Eds.), *Handbook of community psychology*. New York: Plenum.

INDEX

Child welfare system, 153
Chronic homelessness, 111
Church of Mary Magdalene, 46–47
Class, 9, 11, 52
Classism, 9, 48
Client-worker relationship, 9–11, 117–118, 172–173
Collaborative relationships, 149–150
Colorado Mental Health Consumer and Family Development Project, 214–216
Communities of color, 26, 52–64
Community-based empowerment practice, 147–148
Community Voice Mail (CVM), 122, 124
Competition, 103–104
Compulsory heterosexuality, 66–67
"Conflictive" relationships, 103–104
Conscientization, 36
Consciousness
  barriers to, 38–39
  defined, 36
Consciousness raising, 11, 18–19, 21, 36–39, 42, 69, 81, 86, 119, 128, 178, 223
  of disabled people, 81
  of gays, 69
  of homeless people, 119, 128
  of lesbians, 69
  personal, 37
  political, 37
  of women, 36–39, 42, 54
Consumer perceptions of empowerment, 215
Consumer perspectives of empowerment, 95–97
Contract with America, 45
Co-optation, 104
Council on Social Work Education, 68
Crack cocaine, 53
Critical thinking, 5
Cultural domination, 32
Current scholarship, 223–225
CVM, 122, 124

Denver University Institute of Gerontology, 175
Diagnosing, 90
Dialogue, 140–141
Dimensions of empowerment, 1, 117–121, 134
Disabled people, 73–84
Disempowerment, institutional, 94
Diversity
  politics of, 194–195
  respect for, 11
Domestic violence, 43–45
Double-bind situation of women, 33
Dropouts, school, 155–156

Eastside Domestic Violence Program (EDVP), 44–45
Education
  critical, 223
  mutual, 138–139
  professional, 225
  public, 176–177
Effects, iatrogenic, 91
Empowerment
  assumptions of, 142–143
  through capacity building, 150
  challenges to, 222–227
  through collaborative relationships, 149–150
  of communities of color, 52–64
  community-based, 147–148
  consumer perceptions of, 215
  consumer perspectives of, 95–97
  defined, 1, 35, 148
  dimensions of, 1, 117–121, 134
  of disabled people, 27, 73–84
  through extended family networks, 150–151
  of families, 146–162
  family member perceptions of, 215
  of gays, 65–72
  general goal for, 13
  of homeless families, 110–129
  of homeless people, 110–129
  human factors and, 104–105

TO THE OWNER OF THIS BOOK:

We hope that you have found *Empowerment in Social Work Practice: A Sourcebook,* useful. So that this book can be improved in a future edition, would you take the time to complete this sheet and return it? Thank you.

School and address: ————————————————————————————

Department: ————————————————————————————

Instructor's name: ————————————————————————————

1. What I like most about this book is: ————————————————

————————————————————————————

————————————————————————————

2. What I like least about this book is: ————————————————

————————————————————————————

————————————————————————————

3. My general reaction to this book is: ————————————————

————————————————————————————

4. The name of the course in which I used this book is: ————————

————————————————————————————

5. Were all of the chapters of the book assigned for you to read? ————

    If not, which ones weren't? ————————————————————

6. In the space below, or on a separate sheet of paper, please write specific suggestions for improving this book and anything else you'd care to share about your experience in using the book.

————————————————————————————

————————————————————————————

————————————————————————————

————————————————————————————

————————————————————————————

Optional:

Your name: _____ Date: _____

May Brooks/Cole quote you, either in promotion for *Empowerment in Social Work Practice: A Sourcebook,* or in future publishing ventures?

Yes: _____ No: _____

Sincerely,

Lorraine M. Gutiérrez
Ruth J. Parsons
Enid Opal Cox

FOLD HERE

NO POSTAGE
NECESSARY
IF MAILED
IN THE
UNITED STATES

BUSINESS REPLY MAIL

FIRST CLASS   PERMIT NO. 358   PACIFIC GROVE, CA

POSTAGE WILL BE PAID BY ADDRESSEE

ATT: *Lorraine M. Gutiérrez, Ruth J. Parsons, Enid Opal Cox*

Brooks/Cole Publishing Company
511 Forest Lodge Road
Pacific Grove, California 93950-9968

FOLD HERE